LAW WITHOUT ENFORCEMENT

INTEGRATING MENTAL HEALTH AND JUSTICE

i

D0316431

Law Without Enforcement

Integrating Mental Health and Justice

Edited by

NIGEL EASTMAN
St George's Hospital Medical School

and

JILL PEAY
London School of Economics

·HART·
PUBLISHING

OXFORD and PORTLAND, OREGON
1999

Hart Publishing
Oxford
UK

Published in the United States by
Hart Publishing c/o
International Specialised Book Services
5804 N.E. Hassalo St, Portland
Oregon 97213–3644 USA

Distributed in Australia and New Zealand by
Federation Press Pty Ltd
PO Box 45, Annandale
NSW 2038, Australia

Distributed in the Netherlands, Belgium and Luxembourg by
Intersentia, Churchillaan 108
B2900 Schoten, Antwerpen
Belgium

Hart Publishing is a specialist legal publisher based in Oxford, England.
To order further copies of this book or to request a list of other
publications please write to:

Hart Publishing, 19 Whitehouse Road, Oxford, OX1 4PA
Telephone: +44 (0)1865 434459 or Fax: +44 (0)1865 794882
e-mail: hartpub@janep.demon.co.uk

British Library Cataloguing in Publication Data
Data Available
ISBN 1 901362–75–2 (paperback)

Typeset in 10pt Sabon
by Hope Services (Abingdon) Ltd.
Printed in Great Britain on acid-free paper
by Biddles Ltd, Guildford and King's Lynn.

Dedicated to

LYDIA SYNCLAIR
1945–1998

Preface

Is current mental health law effective? This question, posed to us by Department of Health officials, constituted the starting point of a process which has culminated in *Law Without Enforcement*. Our waspish response to the question, "It depends on what you mean by 'effective', and who is defining it", began immediately to chart some of the complexities of an otherwise superficially straightforward question. At its simplest, the question could seem to place law alongside any other therapeutic intervention aimed at improving national mental health. Indeed, the recent argument, represented by the 'therapeutic jurisprudence' movement, that all law should be designed towards therapeutic advantage, clearly implies that mental health law should be seen as equivalent to a clinical tool. The obvious counter view, characteristically represented by lawyers rather than clinicians, is that, although English and Welsh mental health law does indeed have a therapeutic purpose, much of it is properly concerned with the protection of patients' civil rights against unjustified therapy or deprivation of their civil liberty.

The juxtaposition of these two approaches to mental health law describes a core public policy tension in the field between the pursuit of paternalistic welfare and autonomy derived justice. It also explains our response to the Department's question, since the range of definitions of effectiveness is likely to be both more subtle and wider than is represented by the mere juxtaposing of paternalism and autonomy, and is probably as wide as the numbers of groups who effect and are affected by mental health law. At a governmental level, and reflecting public concern, the aspect of effectiveness which has come to dominate the debate has been neither national mental health *per se* nor patients' civil rights, but rather societal protection from a perceived threat of violence by the mentally disordered. This concern has become almost identified with the policy of community care itself; even though, whilst some inquiries after homicide have identified individual failures of community care, there is no substantial evidence either that the incidence of serious violence by the mentally disordered is increasing any more than it is in the general population or that much violence is generally attributable to a failure of community care.

This book, which is one end-point of a project we undertook for the Department, partly reflects a desire by them to have some considered answers to these complex questions. It recognises that, underpinning any attempt to describe the operation of current law and any national discussion of possible detailed mental health law reform, there must be wider consideration of the inherent conflict (and sometimes congruence) between the varying social purposes of mental health law. So, in undertaking a project which addressed the 'effectiveness' debate, we recognised that there would be different definitions of effectiveness predominating in different 'stakeholders'; indeed, we took a wide view of the academic, practitioner and user disciplines and methodologies which might be able to offer relevant perspectives on the field. Our approach, therefore, was wide-ranging and collaborative, and went beyond consulting 'the great and good of mental health and law', namely those directly involved in, and knowledgeable about, the field. Rather, we also included contributors offering a number of generic methodological skills likely to be relevant to defining and maximising the effectiveness of mental health law. Amongst the disciplines represented in the book, therefore, are economics, history, social science (including social anthropology), organisations theory, decision-making theory and philosophy, alongside more predictable contributions from mental health and social work professionals, from users and from academic and practising lawyers. Such an amalgam was implied not only by the fact that all those skills are individually relevant to the questions at hand but because the role of law itself is intrinsically intertwined with issues of economics and service resourcing, social structure and functioning, and with individual and group decision-making; it is also influenced by philosophy, particularly by moral philosophy as it is perceived and applied by mental health actors. It follows therefore that law cannot be seen simply as 'effective' or not, but as offering only one contribution to the objective of improved national mental health. Hence, the economic theorist would pose the question, in a multi-agency and multidisciplinary system, in a different form, that is, "What is, or can be, the marginal contribution of law to mental health outcome?". This is not to imply that the contribution of law is, or can be, only minimal (taking the colloquial understanding of the word 'marginal'), although it *may* be so, but rather it is to ask what contribution to mental health, beyond that achievable through the service system itself, does or can law offer, either existing law or some putative new law?

The question posed by the Department of Health inherently implies a need for empirical data and research. Linked to the project reflected in this book, the Department has commissioned a major programme of research, both secondary research aimed at gathering together what empirical evidence already exists (including from other jurisdictions) and new empirical research, which is designed to expand on the low knowledge base (at least in this jurisdiction) about how law is used by practitioners and what are its various therapeutic and civil rights effects. However, the role of our project, and one role of this book, is to pose and attempt to answer a range of underpinning questions; that is, questions which both suggest a research agenda and a set of methodologies *and* suggest a conceptual framework within which to view the findings of empirical research. As Oppenheim indicates in Chapter 12, there can be no sensible research without clearly defined social policy questions; we would add "carefully thought out and justified from a variety of disciplinary and methodological perspectives". Additionally, the outcome of any empirical research must be set into an informed evaluative framework, informed both by the variety of relevant academic perspectives and by the variety of actors and agencies who apply or are affected by mental health law. So, whilst our book does touch on some of the research information already available, it strives mainly to set a social and ethical public policy context within which existing research, and that which will emerge, can be understood and interpreted. It therefore lays a foundation for the evaluation of existing law and for the designing of new law.

The project which has given rise to this book was pursued in two major stages. The first brought together 20 academics, practitioners, users and government officials in a 24-hour 'think tank', which we jointly chaired. We particularly wish to acknowledge this original group, since they were so influential in setting the context for the book; the participants were Andrew Ashworth, Peter Barham, William Bingley, Nicholas Bosanquet, Alec Buchanan, Fiona Caldicott, Tony Elson, Phil Fennell, Chris Heginbotham, Andrea Humphrey, Joe Jacob, Dilys Jones, Vivien Lindow, Eric Matthews, Geoffrey Pearson, Larry Phillips, Oliver Thorold and Sandra Walker. The agenda for the 'think tank' was entirely open beyond the title of the project itself and the method highly interactive, with each participant having only five minutes for a presentation of their main concerns and views, presentations which were scattered throughout the 24 hours according to the direction of travel of the discussion. The end point of this stage of the project set the agenda for a further meeting. This involved nearly all of the original 20 plus a further 40 participants who were chosen largely for their direct involvement in mental health care (or its receipt) and law. The 60 met for two days and, again, although the agenda was more tightly defined than for the first stage and there were longer (usually 15 minute) presentations, the method was still highly interactive. The presentations were mostly by members of the original 'think tank', supplemented by several others. The contributors to the book have, in turn, come almost entirely from the original group and the presenters at the second stage. The proceedings of this latter stage also resulted in the compilation for the Department of a shortlist of recommended 'practice points'.

The book reflects, we hope, the method of the project we have just described. Namely, it aims to have the character of a 'think book'. Many of the chapters are jointly authored by contributors from different backgrounds who have not previously written together. Indeed, one chapter is co-authored by a wife and husband team who, despite their common professional interests, have never before written together (and may never do so again). Moreover, the majority of the authors have had the benefit of exposure to the others, through the two meetings, and we hope a cross-fertilisation of ideas emerges in the book. Cross-fertilisation was also aided by our unusually interventionist level of editing. Whilst we endeavoured to maintain individual author autonomy (of course) we also strove to encourage pursuit of the related, inter-related and conflicting threads inherent to the field under study. So initially, and arising out of the agenda which was derived in the first stage of the project, we set unusually detailed content guidelines and then edited more heavily than is common in multi-authored collections. We hope that the result has the character of 'chapters around a table', reflecting the real table around which the original 'think tank' sat and discussed.

Our title, *Law Without Enforcement: Integrating Mental Health and Justice*, is reflected both in our exploration in chapter 1 of the use of legal coercion and its likely avoidance by mental health practitioners and in chapter 13, our Afterword, which attempts to set the book's emergent themes into a context of the need for law reform; the satisfaction of which need, we argue, should effectively finesse the twin objectives of mental health and justice. We recognise, of course, that it may be idealistic to strive for a solution which integrates citizens' civil liberties, their health needs and their 'just deserts', whether those be to resources or to punishment. Equally, there are likely to be highly problematic tensions between the aspirations of individuals, their families and associates, and of society. However, we suggest that one route forward would be to place the treatment of the mentally disordered much more on a par with that of the physically ill (something for which both the 1959 and 1983 Acts ostensibly did strive). Employing some form of test of capacity – applicable equally to physical and mental illness – rather than the current status test of having "a mental disorder of a nature or degree which makes it *appropriate* for [a patient] to receive medical treatment in hospital" may be one solution. Another, which is also explored in the book, might be to address the arguments in favour of doing without or doing away with distinctive and discriminatory legislation; in turn, this might serve to de-stigmatise images of the mentally disordered and enhance the probability of early preventive treatment.

The book also explores whether, in order to achieve desired outcomes, what we need is more law, or different law or merely more resources. In short, what can the law add to substantive outcomes – both mental health and justice, since each is enhanced by resources? Our argument is that the marginal contribution of law to mental health outcome is likely to be greater where there are fewer service resources, since those with disabling mental health problems may be more likely to be dealt with coercively, whether for their own benefit or the benefit of others, in a context of a deficiency of resources. The law's influence will then be greater both in the sense of its influence on aggregate outcomes and in respect of the allocation of resources between individuals. Moreover, greater coercion which is driven by lesser resources will, in turn, amount to one justification for more procedural law.

So, the book looks both at existing mental health law and beyond it. Beyond it in three senses. First, it addresses how decisions are taken in the shadow of the law. Secondly, it recognises that many decisions about the mentally ill derive from legislation which is not mental health law *per se*, properly reflecting the fact that mentally ill people have problems above and beyond their illness, albeit problems which may be aggravated by the presence of illness. And thirdly, the book considers how improved mental health decisions might be taken in future (whether by amending, abolishing or replacing the current Act or by altering the way in which it is currently employed). Given that it is published at a time when the government has set in train a substantial review of both mental health care services and related law, it is to be hoped that the book will offer a contribution to the debate about each, not only at the time that it is published but also as time and new thinking about services and law unfolds.

Our thanks go to all of those who have supported this book, both those we know about and all of those others who have contributed in their various ways to the completion of the chapters. We would, however, particularly like to acknowledge the efforts made by Rhian Whitehead, Kay Marshall and Christopher Snowdon and to thank Andrew Ashworth and Adrian Grounds. We are also grateful to the Department of Health for providing financial support and the impetus for the original project. The book is dedicated to Lydia Sinclair. Had she lived she would have co-authored one of the chapters; much more importantly, she would have continued her work as a life-long activist in the field.

NE   JP
St George's Hospital   London School
Medical School   of Economics

September 1998

Contents

The Contributors

PETER BARHAM is a psychologist and social historian of mental health. His books include: *Schizophrenia and Human Value* (1993); (with Robert Hayward) *Relocating Madness* (1995); and *Closing The Asylum* (1997). He is currently writing a book on the insane servicemen of the Great War. He is the founder, and former chairman, of the Hamlet Trust, which supports mental health reform in Eastern and Central Europe. He is a research associate at the Wellcome Institute, Associate Fellow of the British Psychological Society, and Hon. Research Fellow in the History of Medicine, University College London.

MARIAN BARNES has a longstanding interest in mental health and citizenship. She has researched the implementation of the 1983 Mental Health Act, been a member of the Mental Health Act Commission, and has studied mental health user groups and their role in enhancing the citizenship of people with mental health problems. She is currently Director of Social Research in the Department of Social Policy and Social Work at the University of Birmingham.

ANNIE BARTLETT is a Senior Lecturer and Consultant in Forensic Psychiatry at St George's Hospital Medical School and Springfield University Hospital. She is additionally qualified in Social Anthropology. Her research interests include social theory applied to the practice of psychiatry, the study of institutions and the evaluation of health services with particular reference to gender ethnicity and sexual orientation.

WILLIAM BINGLEY is a lawyer by training, and since 1990 has been the Chief Executive of the Mental Health Act Commission. He was Legal Director of MIND (National Association for Mental Health) from 1983 to 1989, when he was seconded to the Department of Health as Executive Secretary of the Working Group preparing the Mental Health Act Code of Practice. He was a member of the Secretary of State's Working Group on the Future of High Security Psychiatric Provision, and is on the Scoping Study Review Team, which is examining mental health legislation for the Department of Health.

NICK BOSANQUET is Professor of Health Policy at Imperial College, University of London. He is a health economist and formerly worked at the Centre for Health Economics at the University of York. He has served as special adviser to the House of Commons Select Committee on Health Services, 1988–90. His main interests are innovation and service development in pharmaceuticals and health care. He has worked as a consultant for the WHO, the World Bank and for the UK Department of Health, as well as for health agencies and pharmaceutical companies. He is carrying out research on economics and management in mental illness.

IAN BYNOE qualified as a solicitor in 1977. He has worked in private practice and in law centres, including one based in a psychiatric hospital. From 1988 until 1994 he worked at the mental health charity, MIND, first as its Legal Officer and, from 1990, as its Legal Director. Since 1994, Mr Bynoe has been a Research Fellow at the Institute for Public Policy Research and worked as a freelance trainer in health and social services law and practice. He has recently been appointed a full time member of the Police Complaints Authority.

FIONA CALDICOTT is Consultant Advisor to the High Security Commissioning Board for Psychiatric Care and Honorary Psychiatrist, South Birmingham Mental Health NHS Trust. She is the immediate past-president of the Royal College of Psychiatrists. She now works as Principal of Somerville College, Oxford, and is a member of the Broadcasting Standards Commission.

EDNA CONLAN MBE is a mental health service user, advocacy worker and trainer for Milton Keynes Mental Health Advocacy; she is also the founding chair and honorary president of the UK advocacy network of user-run advocacy projects and patients' councils. She is the former co-chair of European Network of Users and Survivors of Psychiatry. She is currently the Chair of Focus on Mental Health Association of Large Mental Health Organisations.

NIGEL EASTMAN is Senior Lecturer in Forensic Psychiatry at St George's Hospital Medical School, University of London, and a Consultant Forensic Psychiatrist in the NHS. He is doubly qualified as a psychiatrist and barrister. His academic work has focussed on law in relation to mental health. He is Chair of the Law Sub-Committee of the Royal College of Psychiatrists, also sitting on the Mental Health and Disability Committee of the Law Society.

TONY ELSON is the Chief Executive of Kirklees Metropolitan Council. He is also a member of the High Security Psychiatric Services Commissioning Board for the NHS Executive. His interests lie in the promotion of public policy in the field of mental health, whilst he has also taken a leading role in policy formation in respect of community safety, local health strategy and cross-service and cross-agency working in local communities.

CHRIS HEGINBOTHAM is the Chief Executive of East and North Hertfordshire Health Authority and a former National Director of MIND (National Association for Mental Health). His research has variously concerned health care ethics and resource allocation, community health and social care, and management development for clinicians. He is the co-author of *Mental Illness: Prejudice, Discrimination and the Law* (1991).

TONY HOLLAND is a University Lecturer in the Section of Developmental Psychiatry within the Department of Psychiatry at the University of Cambridge. He has been in his current post since 1992 and also holds an honorary contract with Lifespan Healthcare NHS Trust as a Consultant Psychiatrist.

ERIC MATTHEWS is a Professor in the Department of Philosophy, University of Aberdeen, with a longstanding interest and numerous publications in the philosophy and ethics of medicine, especially psychiatry. He is a member of the National Committee of the Royal College of Psychiatrists' Philosophy Group.

BRAM OPPENHEIM is an Emeritus Reader at the LSE, where he has taught the principles of social research methodology to some 25 generations of graduate students from many countries. He is also well-known for his research work in the mass media, in social medicine, in political socialisation in many nations, and for his contributions to peace research and conflict resolution. He has been a frequent consultant, e.g. to the World Health Organisation. His latest book is a contribution to Holocaust studies.

GEOFFREY PEARSON is Wates Professor of Social Work, Goldsmiths College, University of London. He is the Editor of the *British Journal of Criminology* and Vice-Chairman of the Institute for the Study of Drug Dependence. His published work includes *The Deviant Imagination* (1975); *Hooligan: A History of Respectable Fears* (1983); and *The New Heroin Users* (1987).

JILL PEAY is a Senior Lecturer in Law at the LSE, a barrister and an Associate Tenant at Doughty Street Chambers. She has a particular interest in offenders suffering from mental disorder. Amongst other publications, she is author of *Tribunals on Trial* (1989) and editor of *Inquiries after Homicide* (1996). She is a member of the Department of Health's Scoping Study Review Team, set up to review mental health legislation.

LAWRENCE PHILLIPS is a Visiting Professor of Operational Research at the LSE and a Director of Facilitations Limited. As an 'engaged' social scientist, he works with individuals and teams in organisations, helping them to use their different perspectives on an issue of concern to arrive at an agreed way forward.

GENEVRA RICHARDSON is Professor of Public Law and Dean of the Faculty of Law at Queen Mary and Westfield College, University of London. From 1987 to 1992 she was a member of the Mental Health Act Commission. In 1996–7 she chaired the Independent Inquiry into the Treatment and Care of Darren Carr. Her publications include *Law, Process and Custody: Prisoners and Patients* (1993). She is the chair of the Scoping Study Review Team established by the Department of Health to review mental health legislation.

OLIVER THOROLD is a barrister specialising in mental health law. Between 1978 and 1981 he worked in the legal department of MIND. He has been involved in several major inquiries, including the Ashworth Inquiries of 1992 and 1997–8, and in numerous cases involving both domestic and European law relating to mental health.

ANTHONY ZIGMOND is a Consultant Psychiatrist based in Leeds. He is a Mental Health Act Commissioner and a Second Opinion Appointed Doctor. He is the co-author of the *Hospital Anxiety and Depression Scale* and has served on a number of Royal College committees and homicide inquiries.

1

Law Without Enforcement: Theory and Practice

NIGEL EASTMAN and JILL PEAY

To obsessives and pedants the Mental Health Act 1983 is a misnomer. Indeed, rarely can the title of a statute have been so misleading about its content; misleading to the extent that its supposed subject does not reappear within the body of the Act.[1] For the Mental Health Act (and its associated Code of Practice[2]) is not about promoting or regulating psychiatric well-being; nor is it about patients' rights to treatment for their disorders (with the notable afterthought but practically limited section 117). Rather, it is an Act which deals for the most part with compulsory admission to and discharge from hospital (and guardianship); consent to treatment; provisions for patients involved in criminal proceedings; safeguards for patients (including the Mental Health Review Tribunal (MHRT) and the Mental Health Act Commission (MHAC)); the after-care of patients (in a very limited fashion) and various provisions concerning the management of the property and affairs of patients, and of the movement of patients within and outwith the UK. Even the supplementary Mental Health (Patients in the Community) Act 1995 is similarly limited, for this is a short Act concerned primarily with the supervision of (former detained hospital-based) patients in the community.[3]

Since the 1983 Act was a consolidation Act, its long title "An Act to consolidate the law relating to mentally disordered persons" is accordingly no more helpful about the objectives or the content of the Act. Looking now at the thrust of the 1983 Act it seems outmoded, principally because the primary focus and locus of care have changed dramatically since the early 1980s; namely, from a hospital base out into the community. Also, although both the 1983 Act and its precursor, the 1959 Act, had their roots in an approach to mental health which tried, as far as was then possible, to treat mental and physical illness alike (that

---

[1] With the exception of references to, e.g., the Mental Health (Scotland) Act 1960 or the Mental Health Review Tribunal.

[2] Department of Health and Welsh Office (1993).

[3] The 1995 Act serves to insert various provisions into the Mental Health Act 1983 and the Mental Health (Scotland) Act 1984 to provide a system of supervision of care in the community. In England and Wales the new provisions are known as 'after-care under supervision' (ACUS), known in the vernacular as 'supervised discharge', and in Scotland as 'Community Care Orders'.

is, on a voluntary basis with compulsory provisions for the mentally disordered being curtailed to those who were both seriously ill and who required treatment in the interests of their own health or who posed a danger to themselves or others), both Acts none the less reflected the emphasis of much earlier legislation designed to regulate separate institutions and systems of care for the insane.[4] The 1983 Act remained hospital-based, and *compulsory* treatment could and can only lawfully be given under the Act to patients detained in hospital. This emphasis on in-patient treatment arguably makes the 1983 Act incompatible with the needs of the majority of mentally disordered people, who are, and are most sensibly treated, in the community. From this perspective, the Act is not just misleading and outmoded; it may in practice also place barriers in the way of patients' access to treatment, whilst at one and the same time impeding their return to the community (partly through stigma) after a period of detention ends. Finally, the focus of resources still remains heavily hospital-based, whilst illness and need remain community-based.

This book is concerned variously with mental health law: its distinctive nature; its limitations as a species of law; the problematic nature of permissive law operated coercively by practitioners who have been trained in consensual treatment; the manner in which the resultant conflicts between pragmatism, policy and/or principle work themselves out in a multi-agency context where not all parties are striving to achieve the same objectives or have the same understanding of the law; and with the different manifestations and purposes of law in a mental health context. It is thus partly a description of where we are (and have been) in mental health law and partly a tentative prescription of where we might go. It also asks whether we could develop a legislative strategy for improving quality in the prevention of mental disorder and in the therapy, care and containment of those suffering from mental disorder? Should we even try to do so?

Stark as it may appear, we pose the latter question in response to Fiona Caldicott's assertion that an era dominated by psychiatric pessimism and heightened awareness of risk is *not* a good time for legislative reform, for it would set the wrong moral and clinical tone.[5] But is not the "risk society" in which we now live one which will be ever-present?[6] For, as Beck asserts, risk is not just a part of an essential calculus, an attempt to make the unforeseeable foreseeable, but also embodies "manufactured uncertainty"; the production of risk, and the need for its consequent management, emanates from scientific and political efforts to control and minimise risk.[7] As knowledge expands so does manufactured uncertainty. Hence, our attempt to understand why risks materialise contributes to, rather than deflates, our perception of risk.[8] Similarly, in a

---

[4] Jones (1993); Unsworth (1987); Gordon (1993a).

[5] Caldicott, Conlan and Zigmond (this vol.).

[6] Beck (1992); Giddens (1994).

[7] Beck (1998).

[8] In the mental health field, this is perhaps epitomised by the 'industry' surrounding inquiries into the circumstances surrounding homicides by those who have had contact with the mental health services. See Peay (1996).

political climate which has permitted both the abolition of the *doli incapax* rule and the introduction of curfew orders for children as young as 10[9] in response to the perceived 'threat' they pose, how much greater is the likelihood that we will be draconian in our dealings with the mentally disordered, the epitome not of innocence but of dread, danger, death and catastrophe?[10] Douglas's argument that the politicisation of risk revolves not around taking risks but exposing others to them, together with her assertion that European culture's focus on individuals "has ended by turning the word for 'risk' into a word for 'danger' ",[11] is peculiarly apt in relation to a negative conceptualisation of the mentally disordered. For, as we discuss below, the mentally disordered are perceived as posing an unquantifiable danger, and yet the responsibility for preventing this risk is transferred to those charged with caring for them. And when the professionals err, blame is ascribed. Again as Douglas notes, our system:

> "is almost ready to treat every death as chargeable to someone's account, every accident as caused by someone's criminal negligence, every sickness a threatened prosecution. Whose fault? Is the first question. Then, what action? Which means, what damages? What compensation? What restitution? And the preventive action is to improve the coding of risk in the domain which has turned out to be inadequately covered."[12]

The argument which we elaborate below is that this climate of fear and blame is underpinned both by the spectre of the absence of mental order and by an Act which is amorphous in its body and soul. In such a context, now is not only the right time to tackle these issues but it is urgent that we do so.

MENTAL HEALTH AND MENTAL HEALTH LAW

We began this chapter by making some preliminary remarks about the nature of mental health law and of the practice of mental health care. Although we expand briefly on this theme below, the chapter then goes on to pose a series of questions. First, we ask whether mental health law has features which distinguish it from law generally – and we answer yes; secondly, whether mental health practice is distinctive from conventional medical practice – and again we answer yes, but argue that the distinctions are not as acute as might be presupposed; thirdly, whether the presence of law (aside from other factors) distorts the practice of mental health care – again we answer yes; fourthly, whether the law is capable of being shaped by mental health sciences – to this, although we would intuitively wish to answer yes, we suggest that, in theory, the influence of other disciplines over law is likely to be limited and that, in practice, the law has tended generally to be unresponsive to mental health imperatives. Fifthly, we

---

[9] Crime and Disorder Act 1998.
[10] Douglas (1992).
[11] *Ibid.*, at 53.
[12] *Ibid.*, 15–16.

ask whether any effectiveness of the law in achieving its objectives can justify the distortion of mental health practice to which we have already adverted. Here we argue that the law is not, in fact, at all effective, but that this is attributable as much to the general ineffectiveness of law as to its particular ineffectiveness in the mental health field. Moreover, we argue that, in mental health care, its effective presence is an objective towards which we should especially strive. Finally, we conclude the chapter by tentatively outlining an argument for the abolition of mental health law in its current form, with a view to replacing it with legislation in respect of incapacity (which would relate to treatment of both physical and mental disorders) and in respect of those who pose a clear and current danger (which, again, would relate not just to those suffering from mental disorder, where the danger is most likely associated with danger to their own health). This is an argument to which we return in chapter 13, our "Afterword".

We have already adverted to the peculiar delicacy of sentiment as a feature of mental health law, and in particular of the Mental Health Act 1983, which makes the field distinctive. Yet, and in defence of the legal misnomer, it is curiously in keeping with common notions of mental health, which are defined by the absence of illness, disease and disorder rather than by the presence of something tangible. The 1983 Act tackles the problem by defining "mental disorder" in broad terms and by further providing definitions for three out of four forms of mental disorder; namely, "mental impairment", "severe mental impairment" and "psychopathic disorder" (states all arguably at the margins of mental health). The Act notably adds a catch-all phrase to the definition of mental disorder, so that it includes "any other disorder or disability of mind".[13] However, it fails to provide any definition of the key concept of mental illness, a potentially worrying omission since it is the most frequently used classification. This cannot be because constructing a definition would have been impossible; indeed, a closed definition of mental disorder (including a definition of mental illness) was proffered before the 1983 Act was introduced[14]; equally, a definition might have been imported by way of required linkage to one of the accepted international classificatory systems for mental diseases, currently ICD 10 or DSM IV.[15] But, as the Act stands, it is for clinicians to determine what constitutes mental illness, whether it is present in any given patient, and whether it is present to the requisite degree; in short, definitional power under the Act rests on clinical judgement. Indeed, it was in partial recognition of the temptation for clinicians to apply "mental illness" inappropriately widely that the 1983 Act did clarify one matter (but again a negative matter); that is, "promiscuity or other immoral conduct, sexual deviancy or dependence on alcohol or drugs" do not suffice alone to bring someone even within the broader classification of mental disorder.[16]

---

[13] Mental Health Act S.1(2), (MHA) 1983.
[14] Department of Health and Social Security (1976) at Appendix II.
[15] WHO (1992); American Psychiatric Association (1994).
[16] S.1(3) MHA 1983; Hoggett (1996) at 118; Jones (1996) at 23.

Deciding whether mental health has been re-established must accordingly be doubly problematic; for example, can a patient whose illness is in remission and who has no active symptomatology, but who has a recurrent pattern of breakdown on cessation of the medication, be said to be suffering from a mental disorder? A positive answer to this question seemed to be given in *The Falling Shadow*,[17] which argued that it was unnecessary to wait for a patient's psychosis to "ripen" in order for the patient to be detainable under the Act if she had previously demonstrated that, on cessation of medication, she had become psychotic and if she was again refusing medication. This emphasised the disjunctive character of the phrase "[mental illness] of a nature or degree", implying that no "degree" of current disorder was necessary for detainability if there was a relevant historical "nature". The counter-position is well argued in a Mental Health Act Commission Discussion Paper[18] which suggests that, whatever the historical nature of the illness in the patient, *some* degree of current symptomatology is required and that sectioning cannot be 'prospective' of this. It also suggests that there is an inverted sliding scale between nature and degree which determines varying combinations of the two as justifying liability to detention. Hence, the more serious is the historical nature of the person's disorder the less current degree of symptomatology is required, and vice versa.

This definitional morass contrasts, for example, with the WHO's definition of "health", which is pitched remarkably high; namely, "a state of complete physical, mental and social well-being and not merely the absence of disease". Yet, even this 'maximal concept', aspiring to the highest possible standard, leaves physical and mental well-being undefined.[19] It is, of course, intuitively attractive to define mental health in terms of 'an absence of' rather than 'the presence of' since it seemingly sets limits on our social obligations.[20] Positive mental health for all sounds like a recipe for defining unending need which is approachable, although not attainable, only by bottomless resource spending. However, this approach may be seductively and falsely reassuring, seriously underestimating the level of provision required merely to attain the negative; even achieving the absence of mental ill health is likely to be extremely resource costly. And, where the criterion is set at a minimum level, should this not generate an individual 'right' to health care, where a higher criterion could avoid such imposition? The latter raises a particularly contentious broader question; that is, whether the law can (and should) play a role in delivering substantive rights, rather than being directed merely towards protecting procedural rights (ensuring that the distribution of services is equitable and justifiable).[21] This is

---

[17] Blom-Cooper *et al.* (1995). The disjunctive interpretation of 'nature or degree' has been confirmed in *R v MHRT for S. Thames Region, ex parte Smith* (1998).

[18] Mental Health Act Commission (1998).

[19] Montgomery (1992).

[20] Negative definitions are not uncommon; responsibility in criminal law is often defined (explicitly or implicitly) in negative terms, e.g., where there is no suggestion of duress, drunkenness or insanity.

[21] Plant (1992).

a question which takes on even greater complexity when applied to mental health, where the use of compulsion may properly generate reciprocal rights.[22]

Another marked feature of mental health law arises from the ability of mental disorder to affect third parties, through fear of, and occasionally actual, attacks by the mentally disordered on others. This, together with the perception of professionals and policy-makers that the autonomy of the mentally disordered can be adversely affected in circumstances where they decide to harm themselves or their health, has determined unusual Parliamentary, governmental and judicial responses to mental disorder by comparison with other medical conditions. Mental health care is therefore provided within a more highly politicised context than applies to other clinical services, albeit the latter are, of course, subject to political forces in relation to their overall resourcing and organisation. Such political responses have been pursued through primary legislation, case law and administrative measures, the latter including direct government guidance to mental health care providers and purchasers which is sometimes potentially contradictory of law.[23] It is also of particular note that the recent politicisation of mental health care is clearly distinguishable from the nature of the political debate which preceded passage of the 1983 Act, which was largely associated with anti-psychiatry complaints of social control being pursued through (allegedly spurious) psychiatric diagnosis (or labelling) and treatment.[24]

Legal and administrative measures are applied to the mentally disordered across an extremely wide range of legal fields. However, measures directed specifically at care of the mentally disordered seem particularly likely to arise from (explicit or implicit) public-policy attitudes driven by special factors. As a result, they are often determined in relative isolation from other administrative or legal interventions which also relate to mental disorder; for example, where the objective is treatment of a physical disorder but where the person has a mental disorder which affects their capacity to choose their treatment. This lays the foundation for legal and/or ethical incoherence between different areas of public policy, and related law.

Responsibilities on clinicians going beyond, and even conflicting with, the interest of the individual patient are not unique to mental health care. There are infectious diseases which have long been legally notifiable and, increasingly, the right of a doctor to breach confidence to the Driver and Vehicle Licensing Agency (DVLA) about the behaviour of irresponsible epileptics is developing into a duty.[25] However, there is a clear distinction between responsibilities for public health which relate to the potential for harm to the public arising directly from disease *and* responsibility for controlling attacks by patients which are either not solely, or even directly, attributable to mental disease. Indeed,

---

[22] Eastman (1994); Richardson (1993).

[23] See Afterword (this vol.) concerning the conflict between the DoH Guidance on Discharge into the Community and s.72 of the Act.

[24] Szasz (1974); Szasz (1973); Gostin (1975), Foucault (1967); Sedgwick (1982).

[25] GMC (1995) at Appendix 11–12.

although the 1983 Act clearly allows doctors to recommend detention of the mentally disordered for the protection of others, this is reflected in only one of the tertiary criteria for detention; it is necessary first to determine that the person has a mental disorder of a nature or degree that makes it appropriate for them to be detained for medical treatment before public protection becomes a legal issue. Beyond these precise subtleties, however, it seems clear that public expectations and political rhetoric have moved in the 1990s to a new and much higher level as regards the required public-protective role of psychiatrists and other mental health care professionals. This is typified both by the focus on homicides by the mentally disordered in receipt of recent care and by provisions in the Criminal Justice Act 1991 and in the Crime (Sentences) Act 1997, which emphasise a public-protective function of psychiatrists in the criminal justice system itself. In a similar vein, the Crime and Disorder Act 1998 includes health authorities amongst those agencies who may participate in developing crime and disorder strategies. Aside from the importance to clinicians of this development of their role from 'health advisor' to 'public protector', such a change is likely substantially to alter the willingness of patients to consult them, including many patients who pose *no* risk to the public. Overall, therefore, a policy of moving clinicians from being responsible for public health to being responsible also for public protection (even if it is disguised under a spurious definition of 'public health') is likely to have far-reaching effects which must be addressed in terms of its total effect, not just its effect on the particular patients who drive the policy.

Reflecting this unusual and developing political backcloth, there has been increasing use in recent years by government of a variety of legal and administrative measures directed at the core of mental health care,[26] as well as imposition by the government of mandatory independent inquiries to be held after any homicide by a psychiatric patient.[27] There has also been growing activity in the civil courts concerning mental disorder, particularly relating to the definition of incapacity to consent to treatment[28] and to overriding competent consent through utilisation of the 1983 Act,[29] as well as through determining circumstances justifying breach of confidence in the interest of the safety of third parties.[30] In addition, there has been further judicial definition of 'nervous shock' as a legal form of psychiatric injury[31]; whilst the Law Commission has published major reports concerning both civil incapacity[32] and psychiatric injury.[33] Although these legal and administrative measures and reports are likely to exert

---

[26] Department of Health (1994); Department of Health (1993); Department of Health (1996); the Criminal Procedure (Insanity and Unfitness to Plead) Act 1991; the Criminal Justice Act 1991 (ss. 4 and 2(2)(b)); the Mental Health (Patients in the Community) Act 1995; the Crime (Sentences) Act 1997.

[27] Department of Health (1994a).

[28] *Re C* [1994]; *Re MB* [1997].

[29] *B* v. *Croydon Health Authority* [1995]; *Tameside and Glossop Acute Services* v. *CH* [1996].

[30] *W* v. *Egdell*, [1990].

[31] *Page* v. *Smith* [1996]; *Alcock and Others* v. *Chief Constable of South Yorkshire Police* [1992].

[32] The Law Commission (1995a).

[33] The Law Commission (1995b).

an impact on mentally disordered people, and upon clinical and related managerial staff and services, which varies according to the proximity of any particular measure to the person or service concerned, taken as a whole they represent an obvious general influence. In sum, such a profusion of measures both emphasises the increasing intervention of law into mental health *and* the degree of legal turmoil and confusion which has developed over the legal definitions and responses to mental disorder in a variety of legal contexts. Yet, there has been only limited analysis of the clinical, service and ethical implications of such provisions considered individually, and very little attempt to cross relate the various public policy stances to mental disorder which can be inferred from, or sometimes can be seen overtly and explicitly to lie behind, recent legal and administrative developments.

Mental health law – a distinctive presence?

The conjunction and embodiment of law and medicine in mental health are distinctive from the perspective of both disciplines. Looking first from the perspective of law, mental health law is non-paradigmatic, being law that has no effective means of enforcement, and no caucus to give its application momentum. 'Law' is not, of course, a unitary entity, although it can be theorised as such.[34] Rather, and for our purposes, it should be thought of as a jumble of historically contingent attempts to deal with various problems, conflicts and social issues. Clearly, how one conceptualises law is problematic. Here is not the place for a review of that literature, indeed we are not qualified as authors to conduct such a review; however, a taste of it might help to understand why we wish to argue that mental health law is distinctive, even if only as representing the extreme of a continuum of different types, forms and functions of law.[35] First, mental health law does not nest neatly within Austin's model of commands issued by a sovereign and backed by sanctions; despite the 1983 Act we would argue that there are no defined and binding rules with clear or limited sanctions external to the individual and imposed by the state. In Austin's model, derived primarily from criminal law and, thus, superficially most apt for a body of law dealing with the deprivation of liberty, mental health law would be something of a eunuch; for the rules are neither clear nor effectively enforced. Indeed, those potentially empowered by or subject to the Act are likely to be drawn towards doing their best to avoid resorting to it, given that to use the Act invites regulation of them. Nor does mental health law fit readily within Hart's model of "primary" rules of obligation and "secondary" power conferring, procedural, jurisdictional, remedial and generally facilitative rules; for the Act is imbued with clinical discretion (not duties) at its lowest level. Whilst there clearly are safeguards embodied in the Act, in practice, these barely satisfy the term reme-

---

[34] See, e.g., Kelsen, extracted in Freeman (1994).
[35] Freeman (1994).

dial, for they are patchy and institutionally highly limited. Foucault's notion that an understanding is more likely to be achieved by focussing on the way in which power is located at the extreme points of its exercise – where power becomes "capillary" – and where he asserts, "it is always less legal in character", has its attractions.[36] Indeed, the manifest forms and ways in which domination and subjugation are exercised within social relations probably best capture the realities of day-to-day mental health practice. However, whilst our analysis does descend to a level of detail which questions how power works between individuals – for example, between doctor and patient – we are also interested in how those parties will, on occasion, invoke more traditional forms of law to justify or challenge the relationship between them. Thus, in relation to mental health practice, there is unlikely to be one clear understanding of the nature of law; and even if there were, mental health law is not readily categorisable.

Even if we were to adopt a layperson's approach – namely that the law is what the law says on the face of the statute – clarity would still evade us. 'The law' is often not clear, and lack of clarity is likely to impede the attainment of the law's objectives. That is to assert nothing novel. However, to non-lawyers, the assertion that increasing the complexity of law (in an attempt to produce law that will be highly specific in its impact) can objectively increase rather than decrease the decision-maker's freedom may be somewhat more surprising.[37] Similarly, to assert that even seemingly mandatory rules are subject to discretionary application is commonplace; rules need discretion to be applied. Accordingly, it is not a matter of choice between rules and discretion, but of what mix to have; and acknowledgement that the tension between rules and discretion is such that giving discretion can both undermine the advantages of having rules (for example, in terms of the certainty of outcome) and facilitate the promotion of the objectives lying behind the rules (in terms of achieving justice and fairness in any given set of circumstances).[38] Once the central role of discretion in the application of law is acknowledged, legal decisions come to be recognised for what they are; not "simple discrete and unproblematic" but "complex, subtle, and part of, or the culmination of, a process, in which external constraints, such as organizational and occupational rules, norms, procedures and resources also operate".[39] Again, here is not the place for a detailed examination of the nature of legal decision-making and the interplay between rules and discretion, it has been done excellently elsewhere[40]; however, the general point is important to our argument.

Although we discuss further below the way in which the application of the law is "fundamentally an interpretative exercise",[41] at this stage one illustration may suffice of our theme that mental health law is peculiarly vulnerable to the

[36] Foucault (1980), reproduced in Freeman (1994) at 892; Hunt and Wickham (1994).
[37] Damaska (1975) at 528.
[38] Schneider (1992).
[39] Hawkins (1986) at 1187.
[40] Hawkins (1992).
[41] Galligan (1986) at 1.

vagaries of discretionary application. The statutory criteria which govern the decisions of MHRTs[42] are drawn in mandatory language – the tribunal *must* discharge the patient if it is satisfied of any of a number of criteria; at face value, mandatory language limits the decision-maker's options and enhances for patients the substantive value of the tribunal as a safeguard against unjustified detention. However, these criteria are cast in negative terms, for example under section 72(1)(b) the tribunal "shall" direct discharge where they are satisfied that the patient "is *not* then suffering from mental illness" etc. This reflects an approach which seeks to reconcile patients' rights with a perceived need for public protection; proving a negative is, in practice, sufficiently problematic, if not impossible.[43] However, the tribunal is also imbued with therapeutic values which nest uneasily with a perspective that seeks to promote individual rights. The consequence is that tribunals frequently reach decisions that reflect what they consider to be in the best (therapeutic) interests of the patient, rather than fulfilling their role as a (legal) safeguard against unnecessary detention. Thus, mental health law is, in some respects, the repository of extreme 'therapeutic jurisprudence',[44] serving to magnify what is already a deeply cautious stance built into the statutory language. It embodies discretionary standards which are applied on a discretionary basis. Superficially 'legal', such law crystallises an approach that encourages "the freedom to be influenced by factors other than the law".[45]

In addition to the unsatisfactory nature of the law *per se*, mental health law is peculiar in that it fails to have any application to the vast majority of those with mental health problems. At one level this is both understandable and laudable; the Percy Commission strove to achieve a system of mental health care in which the vast majority of patients were to receive care informally "without deprivation of liberty, to all who need it and are not unwilling to receive it",[46] hopefully thereby de-stigmatising their status. Although such patients (whether consenting and hence 'voluntary', or not objecting and hence 'informal') are admitted to hospital under the authority of section 131(1) of the 1983 Act, they are admitted without the formalities and procedures necessary for those who are *detained* under the Act. One obvious consequence is that these informal patients do not 'enjoy' any of the statutory safeguards embodied in the Act.

Testament to the fact that the Percy Commission's aspirations have been achieved in practice are the statistics on in-patients formally detained under the 1983 Act. In 1996–7, only about 9 per cent of all admissions were formal admissions[47] and, of those 24,191 patients, the overwhelming majority were patients

---

[42] See for further details, Richardson and Thorold (this vol.).
[43] Peay (1989).
[44] Wexler and Winick (1996).
[45] Hawkins (1992) at 44.
[46] Royal Commission (1957) at para. 291.
[47] DoH (1998).

admitted under Part II of the Act (i.e. civil admissions) and not those sent by the courts or prisons under Part III of the Act. Indeed, only 1,883 patients came via this latter route as a result of their involvement in criminal proceedings. Although the general admission figures represented something of an increase over those in 1986 (when formal admissions stood at around 6 per cent), the figures consistently reflect the fact that the vast bulk of admissions to hospital are achieved without resort to the formalities associated with detention. It is also noteworthy that the marginal increase in the use of compulsion since the early 1990s has been attributed mainly to greater awareness by doctors of their powers to detain[48]; it was the 1993 edition of the Act's "Code of Practice" which drew attention to the fact that patients could be detained in the interests of their own health and "not simply for their safety or the safety of others".

Aside from indicating that the Percy approach has been enshrined in practice, these admission statistics highlight the exceptional nature of those patients who are subject to compulsion, for they are a *selected* sample of those whose mental health problems bring them into contact with clinicians. As Grounds rightly reminds us, there is resort to the Act much less frequently than could be legally justified; the Act permits clinicians to section in many more cases than they actually do.[49] It is, thus, not *use* of the Act but *neglect* of it which is so striking. Its influence arises as much from being a brooding presence, encouraging clinicians and patients to organise their relationships in its shadow, as it does from its direct relevance to circumstances coming strictly within its ambit of regulation. Indeed our title, *Law Without Enforcement*, reflects this curious feature; mental health law is used as a method of last resort and not first choice.[50]

However, confining the law to this 'last resort' status conceals a multitude of relationships involving varying degrees of capacity (on the part of the patient) and coercion (by the clinician). As stressed above, the bulk of those with mental health problems are dealt with either voluntarily (where consent to admission or treatment is obtained) or informally (where patients, though lacking the capacity to consent, do not object to admission). But a third category exists; the '*de facto* detained'. These include patients who may assent to admission in the knowledge that coercion could be employed, where 'consent' is not forthcoming; alternatively, such patients may be unable to consent, and are admitted informally and thereafter remain physically in hospital because they lack the wherewithal to express their objection by leaving. The problems raised by this latter group have only recently been subject to debate following the House of Lords decision in the case of *R* v. *Bournewood Community NHS Trust, ex parte L*[51] (hereinafter referred to as *Bournewood*). As Lord Steyn observed, the unsatisfactory legal position of (compliant) incapacitous patients who are detained in

---

[48] *Ibid.*, para. 3.3.

[49] Grounds (1997), personal communication.

[50] This theme parallels work on the 'regulatory' inspectorates, where legal powers form a backdrop for extensive informal interventions; see Hutter (1997) and (1988).

[51] Judgment of 25 June 1998.

fact but not (seemingly) in law[52] exposed "an indefensible gap in our mental health law"[53]; for these patients are diagnostically indistinguishable from compulsorily detained patients and yet enjoy none of the requisite safeguards against unqualified control by the caring professions. Finally, it is also notable that only a technical matter of statutory interpretation prevented Lord Steyn from doing that which he clearly felt should be done; namely, filling this gap in the law by way of requiring detention. Had he been able so to do, the average number of patients detained on any one day would have increased almost three-fold, from 13,000 to 35,000. Thus have the vulnerabilities and deficiencies of current mental health legislation been laid bare.

Whilst the position of many civil patients demonstrates an unsatisfactory avoidance or circumvention of the Act, those with mental health problems who offend are equally rarely dealt with under the provisions of the Act (partially accounting for the large numbers of prisoners identified as having significant mental health problems[54]). Such offender-patients also suffer from the lack of an adequate range of mental health defences available at trial.[55] However, reform in this area has been devoted primarily to increasing the court's sentencing options and not to addressing issues of prior culpability.[56] Mentally disordered offenders may thus be doubly disadvantaged; hardly any gain benefit from their disorder by securing an acquittal on grounds of insufficient responsibility, whilst few of those who are convicted are treated solely as mentally disordered when they are sentenced. Of those few sent to hospital, many then attract mental disorder attributions about their future offending in subsequent consideration of their discharge, sometimes thereby unjustifiably extending their period in (therapeutic) detention.

Of course, the under-utilisation of the Act by doctors and other professionals may be partly attributable to the absence of any clearly defined enforcement measures. In short, no person or body is charged with enforcing the Act; there is no mental health police force. In practice, individual psychiatrists act to police the exercise of their own discretion, an arrangement endorsed by an Act which has clinical judgement as its cornerstone. Moreover, those judicial and regulatory bodies established under the Act, namely the MHRT and the MHAC, are an itinerant presence; with tribunals hearing cases largely in response to applications *by* patients[57] and the Commission being served by a mere 165 (part-

---

[52] The House of Lords were split 3–2 on whether the facts of L's case amounted *in law* to his being detained.

[53] *R* v. *Bournewood* [1998] at 305.

[54] Gunn *et al.* (1991b), Singleton *et al* (1998).

[55] Mackay (1995); Mackay and Kearns (1994).

[56] See the Criminal Procedure (Insanity and Unfitness to Plead) Act 1991. The introduction of the hospital and limitation direction under the Crime (Sentences) Act 1997 is a further manifestation of the phenomenon; whilst failing to address the substantive issue of whether the mentally disordered should be held criminally responsible, the order provides an additional sentencing option to 'resolve' the doubts that remain at disposal. See Eastman and Peay (1998).

[57] Although the 1983 Act introduced automatic hearings for patients who had not exercised their right to apply to the MHRT, this only comes into effect once during the initial period of detention

time) Commissioners. In this context, it is misconceived to think of the 1983 Act as being subject to a regulatory system akin, for example to the Health and Safety Executive.[58] Whilst Hutter admirably charts how that inspectorate's legal powers mainly form a backdrop for extensive informal interventions, with its powers being invoked only as a last resort, they are none the less an active presence seeking to sustain positive standards.[59] In contrast, both the MHRT and the MHAC serve merely to ensure that, when professionals justify the exercise of their discretion by exhorting the law, they do so within the explicit terms of the Act. For both bodies have a remit which requires them to establish whether mental health professionals are *staying within* their discretionary powers and not whether they are *using them per se*, in a positive sense. Thus arises the concept of negative enforcement. The impact on the behaviour of practitioners of regulation within the law is to encourage avoidance of the law. Practitioners can avoid criticism from the Commission and challenge from the MHRT by *not* using their powers under the Act. By contrast, where discretion is exercised outwith the Act, there are no special legal consequences and there is no redress.[60] In this context mental health law works as both a stick and a carrot, but where neither pain nor pleasure is realised.

Use of the Act is further distinguished from use of much other law in that, although a series of parties – amongst others doctors, approved social workers, nearest relatives and the patient – have designated roles to play, they may *all* have good reason for avoiding those roles. This contrasts markedly with most other areas of law, where at least one party will have an interest in driving the law along – whether it be as plaintiff, parent, prosecutor, potential divorcee, professional protestor or aggrieved citizen. Although sufferers, their carers and their relatives may have an interest in extracting services from the system, they rarely perceive the law as a proper or effective instrument for achieving their objectives. Moreover, where such lay parties acknowledge that their relationship with the patient is likely to continue after the current crisis has been managed, being cast in the role of the one who initiated or as one who participated in the sectioning process is unlikely to facilitate that relationship.[61] Thus, not only is mental health law avoided but, when there *is* resort to it, that resort is often reluctant, generating none of the momentum associated with other legal processes. This is an important theme, with much of its importance deriving from the fact that mental health law does permit the most extreme of intrusions – loss of liberty and the imposition of treatment – and should therefore properly be subject to law. It is a theme to which we return later in the chapter.

---

if the patient does not apply and once after renewal if a three year period elapses in which the patient has not had a tribunal review.

[58] See Hutter (1997) and (1988).

[59] *Ibid.*

[60] Of course, the law of negligence or breach of contract would apply where appropriate.

[61] The Code of Practice similarly acknowledges that the ASW rather than the nearest relative is usually the right applicant: para. 2.30.

Is mental health practice distinctive?

Looking now from the perspective of health care, is the practice of psychiatry and of other mental health professions out of keeping with the conventions and mores of the rest of health care practice? Here is not the place for a comprehensive review of the structure and delivery of medical care in England and Wales. Our concern is, in any event, primarily focussed on the interactive nature of the relationship between patient and clinician, which we suggest below may be neither classical nor participatory, but 'endured'. However, two preliminary organisational points bear emphasising. First, application to mental health of the model of primary, secondary and tertiary care does differ from its application to physical medicine, in that mental health care, certainly of the seriously mentally ill, is offered routinely by secondary level community mental health teams.[62] By contrast, on-going community care of chronic physical ill-health is usually offered by primary care teams. One effect of this unusual expression of the model in mental health care can be to cause confusion of responsibility for (especially) the less than severely mentally ill, albeit that co-operative and seamless primary and secondary mental health care does offer substantial benefits.

Secondly, the funding of care generally has implications for the nature of mental health care provided. The model of health care in the UK[63] may be conceived of crudely as one where the service is free at the point of delivery, with the patient (consumer) initiating the search for treatment and demanding it, and/or retaining the right to refuse but not to demand treatment; the doctor (agent) deciding on need[64]; and the government (principal) paying. This model is conducive to government perceived (feared) overprovision. During the 1980s–1990s a government keen to cap spending introduced various financial constraints, including the now partly abandoned purchaser/provider model, in an attempt to regulate doctors' (spending) choices. However, this model becomes skewed in mental health care where the patient may be less enthusiastic about treatment and the doctor/principal/'society' keener, either because of

---

[62] Primary care essentially equates with general practice care; secondary care is specialist care (usually hospital-based) to which primary care physicians refer; tertiary care is offered (again usually in hospital) by 'sub-specialists' who receive referrals from secondary level specialists. In mental health care, primary care deals with the vast bulk of morbidity; secondary care is represented by general mental health care teams, dealing with serious psychotic and neurotic illnesses; an example of tertiary level care is a specialist forensic psychiatric service (which can be solely hospital-based, in medium or high security, or which can also operate community services in parallel with secondary and/or primary care).

[63] Bevan *et al.* (1996).

[64] 'Need' is defined by the DoH in terms of a remediable problem (that is, there is, in terms of current technology an ability to benefit from health care intervention); 'demand' represents those perceived problems for which health care intervention is sought, either or both by the sufferer/practitioner, and which is made effective by adequate purchasing or commissioning power; 'supply' is health care that is available and/or consumed in relation to either need or demand. There can be profound mismatches between the three. See, in relation to mentally disordered offenders, Cohen and Eastman (1999).

a public interest in sustaining a mentally healthy community or, more likely, because of an interest based in social protection or hygiene. In the latter circumstance, it is less likely that spending will be constrained, or at the least not constrained in the same fashion or pattern. For dangerous patients this analysis certainly appears correct, since there *has* been a relative explosion in forensic psychiatric services, for example with the number of NHS medium secure beds increasing from 700 to 1,259 between 1992–8[65] (not matched in general services). Ironically, although such health purchasing should be led by 'need', which is strictly defined by (the patient's) ability to benefit, *and* although a further central tenet of modern health planning is user involvement, much purchasing of forensic psychiatric services occurs against the wishes of the patient and arguably mainly for the benefit of society.[66] Indeed, one aspect of this point, the role of the patient in defining/expressing his/her needs, is applicable even to civilly detained patients. In any event, in circumstances where mental health consumers are increasingly becoming active advocates *for* treatment, such that the debate shifts from conflict between rights and compulsory treatment to conflict between consumers of mental health resources and those of other resources, is it not likely that this will imply a further adjustment to the funding model, putting mental health care and practice more on a footing with physical care?

We turn now to the nature of the doctor–patient relationship. One seminal analysis of this is Jacob's *Doctors and Rules*. Yet, Jacob specifically excludes any consideration of the position of those who consult doctors with "mental disablement", on the ground that:

> "the focus of the book is on the mode and form, not the subject of medical practice. The focus is concerned with who does things and how they get done, not to whom they are done nor what is done nor really why"[67]

and for him mental health practice does not represent the central paradigm of medicine, since:

> "the mainstream of medical practice is concerned with the secondary care of acute illness".[68]

Whilst he recognises that his omission is based on some problematic assumptions, to wit "it assumes an objective reality to both physical and mental disability and also that they can be distinguished",[69] our own argument is rather that, although mental health practice is distinctive, it bears more similarities to conventional medical practice than might at first blush seem likely.[70] Moreover,

---

[65] H. Jones, DoH (personal communication). Including the private sector, the expansion is even more marked.

[66] Cohen and Eastman (1999).

[67] Jacob (1998) at 25. First published in 1988, this book was reissued in 1998 with a lengthy "Afterword".

[68] *Ibid.*, 25.

[69] *Ibid*, 25–6.

[70] Relatedly see Fulford (1998) for a detailed philosophical rebuttal of the anti-psychiatry literature which asserts that the disease model is inherently misapplied by psychiatry; Fulford emphasises the conceptual uniformity of physical and mental disorders in terms of "loss of function".

its points of distinction are crucial in highlighting some of the less explicit features of conventional practice. For example, in conventional medicine, Jacob questions the extent to which it is possible for the doctor–patient relationship to be genuinely consensual where "need on one side and expertise on the other is presupposed". Put in the economist's language, it is far from a perfect market since the supplier has vastly greater knowledge than the demander, albeit that negligence law, through the *Bolam* test, puts a requirement on the doctor to share some of that information with the patient. In non-consensual mental health practice the same presuppositions are made, except that it is the *doctor's* presupposition of the patient's need which is critical, together frequently with the patient's *suspicion* of the doctor's expertise. How does this rebalancing work itself out in practice, and does it shed any light upon the practical operation and relevance of law?

Reviewing three ways of conceiving medicine: scientific, participatory and classical, Jacob adopts the third, despite its being "anathema to democracy", because the first two are found wanting.[71] Whilst the participatory theory is closest to notions of informed consent, Jacob questions the reality of "equal interest" on which it rests:

> "The engaged practitioner does not have either the patient's pain nor can he or she share the same hope of cure, the one wants restoration and the other if no more a job done well. In a nutshell, medicine deals with patients, sick people. It does not deal with citizens."[72]

Hence, although "consent may be free it cannot be full. The asymmetry of the relationship prevents it".[73] Rather, his description of the classical theory of the doctor–patient relationship, where "the physician gives orders not advice",[74] explicitly recognises that the patient's moral agency is "suspended for the duration of the relationship".[75] As the clinician's role becomes paramount, the argument that the medical profession must protect the patient's moral agency when providing treatment gains force.[76] This shift from patient to doctor is emphasised at times of serious illness and in emergencies. However, and herein lies our interest, it is arguable that these arrangements are thrown into stark relief where the doctor–patient relationship falls under the Mental Health Act. For here, the loss of agency is both all too prominent (and has a formal system of safeguards to protect that loss) and based not solely on the seriousness of the patient's disorder at the point of treatment but upon their status as someone who has satis-

---

[71] Jacob (1998), 204–8.
[72] *Ibid.*, 206.
[73] *Ibid.*, 208.
[74] *Ibid.*
[75] *Ibid.*, 52
[76] E.g., following the *S* case, the BMA welcomed the CA ruling and said that the case showed an inappropriate use of the Mental Health Act. The fact that a woman has moral obligations to her foetus "does not mean the health professionals of the courts can compel her to fulfil them". See Dyer, C (1998).

fied the necessary criteria to bring them within the Act. This is true even though, in practice, medically perceived seriousness may often be correlated with perceived detainability. Thereafter, arising from this test of status, doctor and patient are bound together by law across time. This binding fundamentally affects the nature of the relationship for, unlike physical illness, where the patient can choose at any time to end the relationship (even in circumstances that are manifestly to their detriment), both doctor and patient understand (possibly to differing to degrees) that their relationship will continue on an explicitly coercive basis or against a background of coercion.

Such recognition is not without consequences. The imperatives of 'doing good and avoiding doing harm' (with the latter usually taking precedence over the former) are embodied in the Hippocratic Oath[77]:

> "I will prescribe regimen for the good of my patients according to my ability and my judgement and never do harm to anyone."

This is not to say that, in the weighing of costs and benefits action is never taken where harm may precede the doing of good. When a surgeon recommends an operation she does so knowing that her patient will suffer immediate but short-term harm for medium term benefit and can thereby gain the patient's consent to this strategy. But where the psychiatrist does the same (without necessarily the same 'guarantee' of benefit), consent may not be forthcoming from the patient, either because she does not believe the doctor (often attributed by the doctor to illness) or because the patient does not weigh the costs and benefits in the same way as the doctor, for example because the side effects of the treatment are intolerable to that patient. Yet the 1983 Act permits consent to be overridden, and not just for that treatment at that moment in time; rather, it provides for non-consensual treatment by detaining the patient for a specific period of time wherein consent may be overridden (and a *course* of treatment pursued; psychiatry is not, after all, similar to the excision of a tumour). The circumstances of detention thereby change both the context of treatment and its direction beyond detention; both place and time are prescribed.

Again, one illustration of the consequences of this pattern of 'endured and enduring' relationships may suffice. The recurring calls by some psychiatrists for some form of community treatment order ('CTO'), although recognising the reality of a shift in locus for the site of treatment from hospital to community, may fail to acknowledge a reality of 'care' in the community, namely, that only willing patients will volunteer themselves for treatment. 'Control' in the community is as amorphous a concept as 'mental health',[78] even though a threat of recall to hospital may encourage specifically the taking of medication. Moreover, the time frame for the benefit analysis is not this patient over the next

---

[77] See also the new (draft) Hippocratic Oath which includes the notion of a duty towards the public (Hurwitz and Richardson (1997)). This may make individual mental health care directed also at social protection less alien to psychiatrists.

[78] Eastman (1997).

six hours or six days, but this patient over the next six months (or much more). Resort to compulsory treatment now (the 'quick fix') may jeopardise a long-term therapeutic relationship which could otherwise have been to the patient's benefit.[79] Similarly, resort to compulsion of this patient may incur disbenefits in respect of other patients. In conventional medicine, such comparison of patients' benefits is usually thought of in negative terms – if I do this kidney transplant on patient A, patient B will have to stay on dialysis longer. The public health calculus is an arithmetical one. In mental health, the clinical process of self-reflection is, rather, if I resort to compulsion with patient A it may create an aura that will prevent patients B, C and D (to say nothing of E, F and G) coming for treatment; the sum total of benefit will be thereby reduced. There are thus clear public health arguments about the totality of mental health that do not so readily apply in the conventional arena. In turn, there may be legitimacy in thinking of mental and physical medicine as being distinct and in redefining and reforming the definition of public health medicine in relation to mental health. Indeed, interestingly there is little evidence of either the practice, or even the labelling, of the discipline of 'public health psychiatry', as distinct from 'community psychiatry', which is largely conceived of as the practice of psychiatry in the community.

Mental health law – a distorting presence?

One might approach the problem from the alternative starting point that it is the presence of the *law* rather than the nature of the relationship stemming from a different legal context which makes mental health practice distinctive. If physical medicine were subject to the same aura of compulsion would not stigma quickly arise, with all of the concomitant suspicion which can then intrude into the patient–doctor relationship? The risk that compulsory HIV testing, together with all of the potential ramifications of a positive result for other areas of people's lives, would drive sufferers away from the caring agencies has produced a health policy which is rightly cautious about its negative and counterproductive impact.[80] But this is caution in respect of a numerically limited health problem. To take a more commonplace example: if doctors acted in a coercive and not merely an advisory capacity with respect to infectious (but not wholly disabling) illnesses, which are not 'legally notifiable', such as the 'flu, how long would it be before patients avoided the GP's surgery and resorted to overdosing on "Lemsip Maxstrength" at work rather than reveal the nature of their problem? What if GPs had, not the positive role of providing sick notes, but the negative role of confining 'flu sufferers so as to minimise the risk of

---

[79] See Caldicott, Conlan and Zigmond (this vol.).

[80] Law, resources and discrimination bred out of fear intermingle; there is evidence that some GPs are removing HIV positive status patients from their lists—illustrating a theme, not of patients avoiding doctors because of their fears, but of doctors fearing resource and expertise costly patients.

infecting others? Would fewer of the potentially eligible present themselves for treatment? Indeed, where redundancy and unemployment remain a real risk, how *are* doctors to take account of the fact that patients may weigh less heavily the risk of their infecting their work-mates than the risk of losing their job?

Herein lies one of the central dilemmas for mental health practice which no amount of law adequately communicated is likely to redress; namely, the considerable stigma which it engenders in the minds of patients, potential patients, their families, friends, work-mates and their potential employers. Doctors and lawyers, all too familiar with the rules of confidentiality and the ethics of their respective professions, can argue that such stigma is misplaced because the distinction between physical and mental illness is outdated and irrelevant, and that, even if it were not, a patient's medical history is confidential. They may even argue that the law on employment protection would prevent an unjustifiable sacking on the basis of mere medical grounds (whether psychiatric or a susceptibility to colds and 'flu). Patients however, who live in a world of ambiguity and uncertainty, do not draw their conclusions on the basis of how the world should operate (law in the books) but from their lived experiences of how it does operate (law in action) or even (exaggerated) fears of how it might operate (as with the fear of crime). To illustrate: medical confidentiality is not like the confessional, guaranteeing that one's details will never be shared with others – indeed, not to share such information in a multi-disciplinary multi-handed system for the delivery of care would be negligent.[81] The sharing of information in such contexts is required and commonplace. However, in the spirit of 'idle talk costs lives' anyone who has had treatment in an NHS hospital (or even sometimes in a busy group practice) will be aware that confidentiality all too easily gets subsumed into anonymity. As the person in the next bed does not know who you are, it does not matter that your intimate details are discussed with only the flimsy auditory protection of a curtain. But what if you *do* know the person in the next bed, or the practice pharmacist lives in your street or is a peripheral member of your local social nexus? The informal networks which real people inhabit make their assessments of the practical limitations of confidentiality all too telling. And it is these which may constitute the real bar to seeking treatment, or revealing that one suffers from a disorder which others do not understand, may fear and will certainly use to re-evaluate (in your mind) their assessment of you. Stigma is deep-rooted, with tentacles that stretch, in the minds of the well and the unwell, way beyond the boundaries set by law or good clinical practice.

Returning to the impact of the presence of law, three questions might be asked. First, does the mere existence of an illness-specific law contribute to such

---

[81] *Coles* v. *Reading District Hospital Management Committee* [1963]. The NHS was developed on the basis that the patient would be transferred from one person to another and that responsibility for the patient would shift; any system that did not ensure the proper communication for safeguarding a patient's interests could be negligently wrong. The patient died from a failure to receive an anti-tetanus injection.

tendencies in a negative way? Secondly, does the mere association of mental illness with provisions for offenders in the same Act do more to create negative images of the mentally ill than to foster positive (compassionate) images of offenders blighted by disorder? And thirdly, does the presence of law shift doctor–patient relationships by encouraging the regulation of those relationships outside law? The effectiveness of the surgeon's scalpel is irrespective of the patient's fear of the knife, but works only when employed. The effectiveness of the psychiatrist's clinical tools (and the use of compulsion through law can be thought of as a clinical tool) may be greater in prospect (that is, the patient complies through fear of resort to compulsion) than in use (where compulsion may generate resentment and a reverse placebo effect,[82] *as well as* future non-compliance). Hence, where psychiatry is largely about the maintenance of relationships aimed at facilitating treatment other secondary and tertiary medical care is about the constraining (depersonalisation/objectification) of disease (albeit leavened with some holistic kindliness) with a view to termination of the relationship once treatment is effected. This distinction is exemplified by the notion of community mental health care as it is applied in the UK that is, an ongoing therapeutic, and sometimes attempted controlling, relationship with protective and clinical conditions requiring indefinite attention and care.

An alternative approach would be to argue that conventional medicine works to a large extent because the patient believes in the doctor (whether through status, trust or a continuing relationship); that disorders are best treated holistically (that is, with a recognition that one treats the person and not the illness/disorder); and that one's capacity to choose rationally may be (a) limited by knowledge and understanding and (b) affected directly by the illness (whether through desperation, exhaustion or whatever). In this context, there is much less to choose between mental and physical illness than might at first be thought. Equally, there may be less justification for a special legal framework; indeed, the legal framework may create as many clinical problems as it solves. Such an approach would be in keeping with the moves towards replacing specialist mental health legislation with respect to admission to hospital and consent to treatment with a general test of incapacity, applicable equally to the treatment of both physical and mental conditions.[83] Moreover, if it is the presence of law in the ambit of mental health that makes us 'dehumanise' those with mental health problems (despite vesting them with additional procedural rights and safeguards), is it not time we looked again at the justifications for such special law?

---

[82] For those advocates who believe that consent itself is therapeutic (see, e.g., Lidz *et al.* (1984)), there must be scope for arguing that imposed treatment is anti-therapeutic.

[83] See Grisso and Appelbaum (1998); Hoge *et al.* (1998); Lidz *et al.* (1995).

Is the law capable of being shaped by mental health sciences?

This question can be addressed in both theory and practice.

Leaving aside the comparative natures and practical relationships of law and mental health sciences *per se*, one approach to viewing law relating to mental disorder is to construct a mental sciences critique of it, looking at the inter-disciplinary frontier just from the psychiatric side of the border.[84] Such an approach can be applied to any legal mental construct or measure, although it has been developed mostly in relation to whether particular legal provisions are 'jurisprudentially therapeutic'.[85] It may also be differentiated from an analysis of mental disorder constructs and measures occuring in different legal and pub-lic-policy fields which is written purely in terms of a legal analysis *per se*. For example, 'disease of the mind' (a criminal legal construct) bears little relation to any reasonable medical equivalent, albeit it may be coherent within a legal dis-course. A mental sciences critique approach represents a pale shadow of an approach which assumes, as does one important legal theorist, Gunther Teubner, that the law is 'autopoietic', or 'self-referential', such that it *cannot* incorporate the concepts and 'thinking' of another discipline, including where it purports to utilise that other discipline as evidence within its own delibera-tions.[86] Hence, according to this analysis, because it is *impossible* for law to reflect scientific reality (including, for example, mental science concepts of wel-fare), any comparison erected, between different legal concepts which is written in terms of a mental sciences critique would appear to be meaningless. There is, of course, an established critique of this theory,[87] but, if the autopoietic argu-ment is at all valid, then we should observe not only inconsistencies between representations of mental disorder in different legal fields (because each field is itself individually self-referential) but also general variation of the law away from mental science concepts of mental disorder (because the law is unable fully and coherently to incorporate such mental science concepts).

There is one further distinction which is necessary to make and which also arises out of consideration of the alleged problem of legal autopoieises. To reit-erate, it is argued by Teubner that a discipline other than law *cannot* comment on legal provisions *because* any other discipline will necessarily use different constructs and ways of thinking from those of the law. Specifically, the law nec-essarily operates solely within a discourse of its own. To assume otherwise would be not just like asking a German to comment on the thinking of a Russian (there could, of course, be a reasonable translation from the one language into the other), or even asking a German to comment on the thinking of a Taiwanese (some attempt at a cultural and 'thinking' translation, as would be necessary, could be grafted onto any language translation). Rather, it would be like asking

---

[84] Eastman (1992).
[85] Wexler and Winick (1996).
[86] Teubner (1993).
[87] Blankenberg (1984).

a Martian to comment on the thinking of an Earth human. He/she (or would it be it?) would not even know where to start. However, *recognition and exploration* of this (alleged) profound autopoietic difficulty which the law perhaps poses to, for example, any author of a critique of it from a different discipline sits alongside an understandable wish to attempt an explanation of *why* the law thinks, or has been constructed by social and/or political forces, in particular ways in particular contexts. Clearly, this book does not refrain from such an attempt in some of its chapters. Hence, it sometimes does seek to explain the origins of legal discourse (that is, its specific language, communication methods, rituals and procedural rules, as well as its substantive principles) in terms of social, political or economic science. It also seeks to address what seem to be the public-policy objectives which are implied by the law, sometimes by reference to a political critique of the law. To emphasise the approach by way of a comparison, classic critiques of psychiatry itself, such as that of Foucault,[88] are, first, descriptive of the adverse 'empowering of psychiatry'. Secondly, and more illustratively, Foucault offers not only a critique of the discourse of psychiatry itself from a social and political perspective but also suggests reasons *why* psychiatry has been 'constructed' so as to achieve such psychiatric empowerment. In addressing law, this book similarly tries to elicit what *are* the relevant public policy objectives, as well as showing *how* such objectives are pursued by way of specific measures. It also goes further, suggesting what should be the objectives of policy which might be pursued by legal means and what, in broad terms, should be the nature of those means.

Alleged legal insularity, which has profound implications for the law's potential effectiveness as a tool of mental health policy, may be represented ultimately in the seemingly inherent tension within such law between welfare and justice. This is a conflict with multiple representations both in civil and in criminal law contexts. However, returning to the autopoietic theory of law, if the core debate is between Teubner and his 'co-operationist' critics[89] then, as King and Piper point out in relation to child care law (which may offer some analogies with mental heath law), "[there is] in a sense a move away from the welfare/justice conflict".[90] Hence, whereas 'integrationists', for example, Wexler[91] writing about therapeutic jurisprudence, would seek the closest possible coming together, in pursuit of the 'correct' (balanced) decision of the two principles of welfare and justice (although Wexler would deny the need for the subjugation of civil rights justice to principles of welfare), by contrast, those adopting the Teubner view would simply anticipate 'interference' between the law and mental sciences or child welfare sciences (as are dealt with by King and Piper). Again to quote the latter two authors:

---

[88] Foucault (1967).
[89] Blankenberg (1984).
[90] King and Piper (1995).
[91] Wexler and Winick (1996).

"All that results are simultaneous statements about the child [for which read, 'patient' or 'mentally disordered defendant'] and its problems, which, like parallel lines, never meet but continue along their own path. Instead of joint or co-operative decision therefore, information about the child [patient or defendant] is 'constituted anew' within the legal . . . discourse".[92]

The cogency of this argument, both generally, legally and specifically in relation to the analogy of child care law, suggests that a similar situation may exist in mental health law and related criminal law.

Against the analogy with child care law however, and clearly against adopting generally a Teubneurian view of mental health law, is the fact that such law is written, often with open ended or absent definitions (for example, of mental illness *per se*); this can be expected to give considerable influence to mental sciences. Yet, although the influence of the therapeutic model is evident in, for example, the workings of tribunals,[93] and although this clearly arises from the breadth of definitions within the Act itself, ultimately the insularity of the law from mental sciences may still also be evident; for example, in the decision of the Court of Appeal that it was not unlawful to detain for medical treatment a psychopath thought medically to be untreatable.[94] Somewhat similarly, highly restricted consideration on the part of the Court of Appeal of the safety of criminal convictions is described by Nobles *et al.*[95] as originating from "the construction . . . of what a miscarriage of justice amounts to . . . founded on a discourse involving an understanding of its constitutional position . . . that discourse . . . is distinct from the discourses of miscarriages of justice that operate in other settings". Nobles *et al.* convincingly illustrate the point by reference to one eventually freed appellant who observed "I don't think people in there have got the intelligence or the honesty to spell the word justice, never mind dispense it".

Taking the child care law analogy further, it is interesting to note that, perhaps of all branches of the law, that branch has been, and is increasingly, the most legally flexible in its adoption of child welfare sciences (King and Piper's term for all those fields of expertise which are applied in child welfare courts) at the expense of strict rules of due legal process, extreme flexibility of expert evidential rules and even the adversarial system itself. By analogy, what we know of the operation of MHRTs tends towards a conclusion, from one empirical study,[96] of demonstrated *lack* of the protection of justice which is usually and properly afforded by strict procedural legal rules in courts; this is discarded by tribunals, in the (presumed) pursuit of welfare (the patients' or others'). As regards whether the courts, in adjudicating the legal processes of tribunals, similarly 'accommodate' mental welfare sciences, another study[97] may give some

[92] King and Piper (1995) at 21–2.
[93] Peay (1989).
[94] *R. v. Cannons Park MHRT, ex parte A* [1994]. However, see now also *R(A Patient)* v. *Secretary of State for Scotland and Another* (1998).
[95] Nobles *et al.* (1993) at 19; see also Nobles and Schiff (1995) and Schiff and Nobles (1996).
[96] Peay (1989).
[97] See Richardson and Thorold (this vol.).

answers. However, in spite of the dominance of tribunals by the clinical model, increasingly doctors complain of 'adversarial' tribunal processes.

In summary, there is an inherently problematic relationship between law and mental health sciences and, in spite of the example of the pursuit of welfare at the expense of justice which tribunals afford, attempts at therapeutically advantageous law are bound to face the hurdle of a profound disparity of constructs and understanding between the two disciplines.

LAW'S POSITIVE PURPOSE – OVERRATED OR OUT OF REACH?

For law to be effective, certain attributes are generally held to be required;[98] namely:

- – clear objectives expressed through clear maxims;
- – maxims that are adequately communicated, adequately resourced and emanate from an authoritative source;
- – maxims that are compatible with society's prevailing *mores* and conventions;
- – clarity in respect of how the law may be complied with;
- – reward for compliance or punishment for breach;
- – a clear method of enforcement.

With the notable exception that mental health law does emanate from an authoritative source, it otherwise largely fails these tests. However, even if mental health law looks technically 'unsound', it *may* none the less be 'effective'[99] by substantially achieving its purpose in practice (despite its theoretical shortcomings). Whether mental health law is effective in conventional legal terms might be explored by thinking about the following questions:

1. The 'adherence' question – are the rules obeyed by the actors to whom they apply?
2. The 'effectiveness' question – if the rules are obeyed does this adherence to law achieve its stated objectives?
3. The 'consequences' question – what external impact does the presence of law and adherence to it have on other concurrent systems?

Adherence

'Flouting' of the law is not confined to mental health. Socio-legal scholars have long been interested in the gap between 'law in the books' and 'law in action'. However, what may be peculiar to mental health law is significant resistance of

---

[98] See, e.g., Cotterrell (1992).

[99] The definition of effectiveness is discussed below, particularly in relation to the often competing objectives of welfare (including protection) and justice.

practitioners to its usage *per se*. Although, for example, the police may have resented aspects of the Police and Criminal Evidence Act 1984 they quickly learnt to stay creatively within it. Indeed, McBarnet has argued that much of the law relating to the regulation of the police contains within it sufficient discretion to enable the police to use legislation to legitimate their own, less legitimate, practices, thereby managing the gap between rhetoric and reality in the legal system.[100] This practical management has been illustrated in studies of police practices.[101] The permissive nature of the law gives officers the opportunity to manage the rules in their pursuit of 'crime control'. Three categories emerged from the 1983 study; first, working rules which the authors argued were internalised, effectively acting as principles to guide everyday actions; secondly, inhibiting rules, which were external to the actors and primarily deterrent in their effect, being specific in character, these were likely to be enforced and refer to visible behaviour; finally, there were presentation rules, which served to impart an acceptable gloss to actions actually informed by the working rules. Moreover, since the rules failed to set out clearly the protections for suspects' civil liberties so as to give them practical effect, the police, in practice, enjoyed considerable leeway to shape their practices in accordance with situational exigencies.[102] Thus, where the relationship between rules and law is problematic, generating new rules may prove an irrelevance to practice, particularly where the organisational culture socialises new entrants into the use of the rules.[103] In contrast, in mental health, practitioners may seek to avoid use of the law (whether through fear or ignorance of it, *or* through a reluctance to become entangled with its safeguards and thereby to find themselves 'judged') and regulate their relationships with patients outside its ambit. This may be no bad thing, depending on the objectives still achievable and deleterious side-effects. But the ability of law somehow to act as a neutral regulator of behaviour is, if acknowledged at all, much overrated. People use law; law does not use people. Law is not an actor, only an instrument of the human actors whose interests it represents. As a result, the key question is not how the law *thinks* people act, but how they *do* act; people are not passive recipients of law – they use it, abuse it and stretch it in order to stay creatively within it and/or to frustrate its objectives. People *interact* with law.

As we discuss below, the decision by a hospital based clinician to invoke the 1983 Act[104] is one which is likely to arise only following a failure to negotiate voluntary admission. The doctor–patient interaction is therefore always potentially a discussion about whether to invoke the rules, which, for the patient, may

---

[100] McBarnet (1981).
[101] Policy Studies Institute (1983); see also, more recently, Dixon (1997).
[102] For further discussion see Reiner (1992).
[103] See Caldicott, Conlan and Zigmond (this vol.).
[104] At this stage we are confining ourselves to the dyadic relationship between doctor and patient, even though technically other parties, an ASW or the patient's family and the GP, will be involved. But, as Richardson and Thorold note (this vol.), these other parties may play a role primarily as 'ratifiers' rather than as equal partners.

be either coercive or at least perceived as such. This largely untrammelled exercise of discretion by the doctor about whether there is a need to use the rules,[105] and then a similar exercise of discretion about the application of the rules (to wit, satisfying herself of the criteria for admission) invests the clinician with considerable power and concomitant authority. Cast in this light, the clinician's authority, although ostensibly deriving from statute-based rules (positive law), takes on the appearance of Schneider's 'Khadi' discretion, where 'wise' decision-makers, with knowledge of the parties involved, decide individually on an *ad hoc* basis, taking account of legal, ethical, emotional, political and resource considerations.[106] Thus, involvement with the patient, rather than judicial distance, is central to the 'application' of the rules.

It is unusual for there to be such an imbalance in a legally regulated relationship, for, although the patient can challenge the authority to detain, this will largely occur only if the patient invokes the process and only at some considerable point in time after the decisions to admit and detain. (Notably, damages for unlawful detention at the police station are calculated per hour of detention; for psychiatric patients, days will necessarily pass by before any review of the legitimacy of the authority for their detention.) Moreover, in the other obvious area where a power imbalance is marked, namely the law relating to children, section 1(1) of the Children Act 1989 makes plain that, in the determination of any question with respect to the upbringing of a child, "the child's welfare shall be the court's paramount consideration".[107] No similar provision exists in the 1983 Act. The revised Code of Practice[108] does advise those making admission decisions to consider (amongst many other matters) "the patient's wishes and view of his own needs". It also invokes as a broad principle the notion that people should "be treated or cared for in such a way that promotes to the greatest practical degree, their self determination and personal responsibility consistent with their needs and wishes"[109]. However, as the Code expressly states, it provides *guidance* and imposes no additional legal duties; indeed, the 1983 Act does not even impose a legal duty to comply with the Code, albeit failure to follow it could be "referred to in evidence in legal proceedings"[110]. In this context, the Code arguably broadens and makes legitimate the clinician's discretion, it does not constrain it. Nor, where conflict arises between the Code and the common law, will the former be given any effect by the courts, as was highlighted in *Bournewood*. Thus, although the Code records in grandiose terms the importance of informal patients understanding their *right* to leave hospital,[111] the

---

[105] Technically, of course, the doctor's role is to decide whether to recommend detention, but she still 'uses the rules' in these terms.

[106] Schneider (1992).

[107] Even where practice shows that the principle may not be achieved, there remains merit in setting out the main goals in legislation; see, e.g., Day Sclater and Piper (1998); King and Piper (1995).

[108] Department of Health and Welsh Office (1993), para. 2.6.

[109] *Ibid.*, para. 1.3.

[110] *Ibid.*, 1.1.

[111] *Ibid.*, para. 14.1.

House of Lords has endorsed limitations on that right as justified by the common law principle of necessity.[112]

Given the considerable discretion embodied within the Act, it is curious that mental health professionals as a whole do not use the Act more than they do. Equally, decisions by some practitioners not to section where others would do so (with all of the resource consequences – positive or negative) require some explanation. For, where section 117 after-care is substantially resourced by local authorities, obtaining a bigger slice of that cake for a patient can be easily achieved through a short period of detention, since detention of any length under section 3 creates an entitlement to section 117 aftercare. Such questions, which can only be answered empirically, focus on the way in which legal criteria come to be perceived as useful means to include within, or exclude from, scarce resources those deemed to be 'worthy' recipients.

Pursuing further the relationship between mental health law and the professionals who operate it, clearly the attitudes of the latter (for example, 'libertarian' or 'paternalistic/authoritarian') are likely to be of great importance in determining both how they operate existing law and what reforms in the law they call for. Their (varying) levels of knowledge will also influence how they operate the Act, although attitudes are also likely to influence knowledge. Attitudes are determined both individually and corporately by way of professional training and contact. Indeed, it is likely that there is 'mutual reinforcement' of particular attitudes through peer interaction such that corporate attitudes, sometimes verging on stereotypes, emerge; this may be the case even though there may be more than one type of corporate attitude arising as responses to professional experience.

Anecdotally there seems much to suggest greater frequency of incongruence between clinical attitudes and civil rights legal constructs amongst doctors than other mental health professionals. For example, paradoxically, given the under-use of the 1983 Act for admissions (compared with the number of situations where its use would be legally justifiable), it is doctors, and corporately the Royal College of Psychiatrists, who have most frequently called for greater restriction of patient freedom, and correspondingly greater medical power, in relation to community care. Indeed, less recent mental health law history, and particularly the period immediately preceding passage of the 1983 Act, was marked by a clear confrontation between psychiatrists and lawyers around the extension of 'legalism' into mental health practice, fought largely around Gostin's seminal work, *A Human Condition*.[113] It is probably not too extreme to suggest that Gostin, in fact, became for many psychiatrists (but few social workers, for example) something of a pariah. Why should professional hostility, albeit not amongst all psychiatrists, have been so widespread and vehement? One possible answer might be that doctors are, as a group, particularly strongly inclusive of 'paternalistic/authoritarian' attitudes and that they merely come

---

[112] *Bournewood* at 308.
[113] Gostin (1975), (1977).

together to express such attitudes corporately through a wish for greater clinical (and therefore civil rights) power over patients. However, even if it be the case that many doctors do tend in that direction individually, there is much about the nature specifically of psychiatry as a discipline, and its status within medicine, which would suggest that, *amongst* doctors, psychiatrists are likely to be amongst the *least* authoritarian or paternalistic. So why the (probably continuing) fairly widespread confrontation?

One plausible hypothesis runs as follows. Although the law is applicable to all doctors and to all medical practice, most doctors practising currently have little training in it at medical school or beyond. The same applies to medical ethics. Indeed, it was in recognition of this, and of the importance of its reversal, that the GMC recently required the conjoined subject of 'medical law and ethics' to become part of the 'core curriculum' for undergraduate medical training,[114] now reflected in a nationally agreed medical law and ethics core curriculum.[115] The previous absence of the subject from medical training must clearly reflect an establishment view of what is (or was) seen to be 'important' but it also probably reflects more subtle factors. These might include the previous domination of medical training (and practising cudos) by both the hospital model of treatment (more than care) and 'reductionist' scientific method, as well as a form of professional defensiveness which is common where the person feels unskilled. The latter seems particularly likely to be relevant since law and ethics, as well as, for example, social sciences, require such different skills from those of the natural sciences, which students are required to pursue (effectively) exclusively in order to enter medical school at all. Once *in* training they understandably cling to that which they have been told they are good at and, supported by a medical educational establishment which is largely similarly minded and on whom they model themselves, they reject that which seems unfamiliar. The effect of such defensiveness is probably to 'avoid' law and ethics, except where it is perceived that the law is threatening to the doctor and, therefore, requires that she be 'defensive' in another sense. Further, the ethical dominance of beneficence in medical practice, arising understandably from the imbalance of knowledge between 'patient' (not 'client') and 'clinician',[116] is bound to be accompanied by an aversion to any force which contradicts it. Finally, when all of the foregoing is focussed on medical conditions and on medical contacts where the patient commonly says "thank you", at least until they perceive that something has 'gone wrong', the effect is to reinforce the approach. There is essentially joint enjoyment of the patient's consent, largely with devolution of authority from patient to doctor.

Psychiatrists are, like their medical colleagues, trained in 'consensual medicine', with only the vague background threat of legal intervention if something goes wrong with, or within, the consensus. Many are probably then drawn into

[114] General Medical Council (1998).
[115] Doyle and Gillon (1998).
[116] See Caldicott, Conlan and Zigmond (this vol.).

the speciality by way of an interest in the social aspects of medicine and a wish to adopt a more holistic approach to practice. As we have already suggested, they are also probably amongst the least 'authoritarian' of doctors. What happens next? First, where they will probably have entered psychiatry in order to treat a wide range of psychotic and neurotic disorders (they are doctors with 'broad' interests), increasingly they are required to focus more narrowly on the 'seriously mentally ill'[117]. This, in turn, tends to de-emphasise a holistic approach even to *those* patients, because, with limited resources, they can be helped largely through treatment narrowly for their psychosis. Secondly, there is great difficulty experienced by psychiatrists in fully exploring social and other aspects of 'the person' rather than 'the illness'. Thirdly, psychiatrists feel less bolstered than do their medical colleagues by the usual supportive mechanisms of medical practice. In particular, unlike with physical medicine conditions, the patients often do not acknowledge any greater knowledge of their 'condition' as vested in the doctor, emphasising rather their *own* greater knowledge of 'themselves' as a person. Carers may similarly claim both greater detailed knowledge of their relative's illness and a better understanding of their needs. Further, psychiatrists, unlike other medical colleagues, experience (at best) variable relationships with relevant pressure groups. Whereas neurologists can expect, and do experience, an unambiguous commonality of purpose with voluntary organisations supporting patients, and their carers, with (say) chronic neurological conditions, the psychiatrist can expect very different, and varying, types of relationship with MIND, SANE, Survivors Speak Out and the National Schizophrenia Fellowship (each of which adopts a particular position in relation not only to the status of mental illness but to the balance of ethical rights and duties between patients and others, including carers and society at large). At times, the various relationships, not only between psychiatrists and these voluntary organisations but also between the organisations themselves, can resemble a battleground, and a very public battleground. Also, in organisational terms, psychiatrists observe increasing 'managerialism' within the very stuff of clinical practice which challenges even their clinical authority.[118] Finally, unlike many medical patients, psychiatric (and particularly psychotic) patients do rarely say "thank you", at least not in clear and unambiguous terms.

In the face of these seemingly difficult challenges, however, the psychiatrist is granted one overriding route to, or tool of, authority, that of legal compulsion over some of their patients. Here society offers something not given to other doctors namely the right to overrule the civil right to liberty of their patients, albeit in the pursuit of a mental health outcome. Yet, being essentially a doctor

---

[117] The thrust of recent government mental health policy has been strongly in this direction, pursued, e.g., through the 'supervision register' (DoH (1994b)) and 'supervised discharge orders' (Mental Health (Patients in the Community) Act 1995); the direction has been more subtly encouraged by mandatory inquiries after homicides (DoH (1994a)).

[118] After the Bristol pædiatric surgery investigations there seems likely to be increased managerial responsibility for clinical performance in general medicine and surgery, and so the trend is perhaps spreading beyond mental health care.

by training she has no training in the nature of the law or how to use it. The situation is somewhat akin to giving a surgeon a gardening implement and expecting her to know how to use it in theatre. Coupled with increasingly being felt to be held responsible not only for their only actions but also for the actions of their patients (unique within medical practice),[119] a 'wagon circle' mentality tends to develop. This involves a 'reversion' to increasing authoritarianism, expressed, for example, through requests for "one more and better legal rifle" (for example, a CTO) in order to restrain the effects of their patients' attitudes; opposition to (as it is seen) ill-informed and over-legalistic decisions of MHRTs; expression of anger at social workers "who will not section patients as they should"; and rejection of any legal instruments directed at patient control which lack sufficient 'teeth' to master patients, who are perhaps themselves percieved to have sufficient teeth to 'gobble up' the psychiatrist. Such reversion is juxtaposed inconsistently, however, with an understandable unwillingness to enforce 'mental health public hygiene laws' (for example, the introduction of both 'supervised discharge orders' and 'supervision registers' was resisted by the Royal College of Psychiatrists[120]). Hence, 'new rifles' from the legislative gun store are pursued by even the most authoritarian of psychiatrists somewhat ambivalently (they would probably rather not be fighting the Indians at all, let alone having to be in a wagon circle).

Essentially, therefore, psychiatrists are probably ambivalent about at least three matters. First, whether, in fact, to ask for more powers to control the encircling 'Indians', be they patients, inquiries after homicides, MIND or patient advocates *or* whether to resist more powers, in order to try to limit the implied range of their own liability for the actions of their patients (perhaps whilst ultimately recognising that this is a futile objective, perhaps because they 'feel' responsible). Such ambivalence may even explain any 'under-sectioning' which occurs in a context of asking for *more* powers in the community (although the latter may reflect a wish to convert what powers they have to be consistent with a new model of care[121]). Secondly, psychiatrists are unsure whether to welcome or to resist the diversifying of responsibility into the multidisciplinary team. To welcome it seems a good clinical idea and, indeed, a substantial proportion of inquiry after homicide reports have pointed to inadequacies of multi-disciplinary and inter-agency co-operation as significant in determining care failures; it would also perhaps spread responsibility. However, to resist it would also seem sensible, both because there are insufficient resources fully to implement community care and because, ultimately, the

---

[119] See Eastman (1996b).

[120] As regards supervised discharge orders see Thompson (1995); as regards supervision registers see Caldicott (1994).

[121] This reflects a common justification offered by psychiatrists for the introduction of a community treatment order. See, e.g., Dyer, J. (1998). However, the approach ignores counter-approaches which suggest that the two circumstances, hospital and community, are dissimilar both legally and ethically; see, e.g., Hoggett (1996) who describes "a deep divide" legally between hospital and community mental health law. Ethically, see, e.g., Eastman (1997).

psychiatrist is (or feels) responsible; in any event she *likes* being responsible, because she was trained in medicine *into* it.

All of this ambivalence could perhaps have been tolerated by professionals when public policy focused largely on the risk of patients harming themselves, since what was at stake seemed essentially to fit the medical model (suicide can be seen as a direct expression of mental illness). However, when the Tarasoff factor crossed the Atlantic and a small number of homicides began to dominate the public agenda, walking what Mackay calls "the Tarasoff tightrope"[122] feels both extremely uncomfortable and professionally culturally inappropriate; after all, a training in medicine is directed at helping people and not controlling them, and certainly not controlling them by using legal tools which seem unfamiliar and potentially capable of rebounding on the clinician so that it may be *she* who is held responsible for the actions of her patients, whom she is trying to help.

The foregoing could be no more than a possibly plausible hypothesis. However, if there is any truth in it, then it infers that the effectiveness of mental health law will best be maximised, at least as regards *psychiatric* practice, not merely by training doctors in mental health law, and in the legal discourse, in a bolt on fashion, but by *integrating* it into clinical practice so that, like pharmacology or behavioural psychology, it becomes 'part of' the clinical model, or rather the ethico-lego-clinical model. This implies, to use psychiatry's own terminology, that psychiatrists must 'own' law. It also implies that they must own it as a whole, rather than demanding the odd new legal weapon with which to protect themselves from the encircling Indians.

Ownership of the law by psychiatrists is, however, probably becoming increasingly difficult. Any natural anti-bodies that all doctors may have to law are likely to be reinforced by law and public policy which emphasises not their clinical function but a duty of social control. Albeit not law *per se*, one *de facto* function of inquiries after homicides, which are invariably chaired by lawyers and conducted forensically, is that of potentially allocating blame to individual clinicians or services. Aside from the fact that the process of such (non-statutory) inquiries may be damagingly informal, the allocation of blame amounts to what might be termed 'proxy culpability'. This occurs even though the perpetrator has been found criminally liable (either by way of murder or manslaughter) for the killing. Although it might be suggested that a verdict of 'diminished responsibility' manslaughter could leave some moral responsibility 'spare', potentially to be allocated to any clinicians who might be seen as at fault in the care they offered, it is hard to see how anyone else might be even partially culpable by proxy if the conviction is for murder. Even on a manslaughter conviction, the basis of *diminished* responsibility is, in law, that the defendant, by virtue of an 'abnormality of mind', lacked full responsibility,[123] and not that someone else was partially to blame. Indeed, although a service may be respon-

---

[122] Mackay (1990).
[123] S.2 Homicide Act 1957.

sible for allowing circumstances to arise in which a patient commits a homicide, it is ultimately the patient who is responsible for the offence *per se*. In any event, what occurs in inquiries is the reverse of that observed in mental health review tribunals,[124] in that, in inquiries, the legal process tends to 'take over' from otherwise appropriate clinical or service audit. Such inquiries are, therefore, by their nature, legally tinged, or some would perhaps say legally tainted; albeit, paradoxically, an obvious critique of such a process is represented by the argument that the alternative to inquiries allocating blame should be through resort to the legal standard embodied within the negligence *Bolam* test. On the other side of the argument, by using informal methods inquiries can wholly avoid any legal insularity from mental science constructs which otherwise might occur.

In the widening search not only for homes for culpability but also for maximal public safety, a recent statutory development, presaged in the 1996 White Paper on Sentencing[125] and enacted in the Crime (Sentences) Act 1997, combined introduction of a 'hospital direction' with a custodial penal sentence (the so-called 'hybrid order'). This was reinforced in a similar policy direction by the extension of the mandatory life sentence to defendants found guilty of a second serious offence in a way which includes within its terms mentally disordered offenders, representing a novel and conceptually important shift in English psychiatric jurisprudence. It is a novelty which appears to contradict centuries of English sentencing practice based on a welfare approach to the mentally disordered; this mirrors, in policy terms, the continuing lack of a 'primacy of the patient' principle equivalent to the that adopted in the Children Act and the change in function of agencies dealing with children represented by curfew orders for children under the Crime and Disorder Act 1998 (both described earlier). However, a core question which lies behind any analysis of such implications is whether there is, in any event, a profound distinction between 'welfare' of the mentally disordered, as it is defined legally and as it is defined by 'mental welfare science'. Otherwise, it is a novelty which also has major implications, both practical and ethical, for mental health clinicians and services. Similarly, section 2(2)(b) of the Criminal Justice Act 1991, which allows imposition of a 'longer than normal' sentence on the basis of risk to the public, has practical and ethical implications for psychiatrists.[126]

The shift in the nature of psychiatric involvement in the criminal justice system is intimately linked to the change in psychiatric jurisprudence away from the traditional welfare model and towards a model which focuses particularly on (public) protective sentencing. The latter is linked, in turn, with changes in ethical and legal rules of medical (including, and perhaps especially, psychiatric) confidentiality which have served further to emphasise both elements of the

---

[124] Peay (1989).

[125] Home Office (1996).

[126] Notably, s.2(2)(b) does not exclude a hospital order, which s.2 of the Crime (Sentences) Act 1997 does; see Eastman and Peay (1998b).

'dual functioning', as professional and citizen, of all mental health professionals in a forensic context. Indeed, there is an obvious muddying of the distinction itself because information gained under one cloak can be emitted from another. This is particularly represented in the decision of the Court of Appeal in W v. *Egdell* (1989) but is reflected in aspects of the Crime (Sentences) Act 1997 and section 2(2)(b) of the the Criminal Justice Act 1991, where information may be gained for a clinical evaluative purpose, with a view to possible therapeutic sentencing, but then used by the court to increase punishment, by virtue of judicial perception of increased risk arising out of the same (originally clinical) information.[127]

Effectiveness

Questions of effectiveness are similarly neither simple nor unidirectional. This is hardly surprising since deciding whether a goal has been achieved requires, first, that those goals be spelt out (which the 1983 Act signally fails to do) and, secondly, that the goals should not conflict with one another. Law frequently embodies, implicitly or explicitly, conflicting objectives; for the 1983 Act these include providing treatment, providing effective treatment, containing high-risk patients, securing patients' rights, and, more controversially, promoting public health and protecting the public from the risk of attack. Not only are some of these goals mutually contradictory, some are also pursued formally within the Act and others informally outwith it. To note that 'law' *rarely* has a unidirectional impact on practice and to argue that it may have either a counter-intuitive impact or no impact at all is, therefore, particularly apt with respect to mental health law.

Thus, law may be problem-inducing rather than problem-solving. Questions about effectiveness are accordingly complex. Could the existing body of mental health legislation be used more effectively (or less ineffectively)? What are the impediments to its appropriate usage? Does *effective* use of the Act mean more or less use of the Act? For example, if patients are prepared to use services on a voluntary basis and present themselves early, this may obviate the ultimate need for sectioning. Effective use of the Act thus needs to be assessed not only in terms of how well it works when resort is had to it, but how its presence facilitates decision-making outside its ambit. Thus, questions of 'effectiveness' and of 'consequences' necessarily interact with, and may adulterate, one another.

To illustrate: legal processes can serve both to raise people's expectations of redress and then to dash them. An example of this paradox arises out of Jean Ritchie's Inquiry findings in respect of the care and treatment of Christopher

---

[127] See Solomka (1996). One ethical model for dealing with issues of medical confidentiality in a 'non-privileged' legal situation emphasises the role of the defendant in taking his/her own 'confidentiality risks' based upon being given by the clinician full knowledge of his/her legal situation during psychiatric assessment (Eastman (1987)).

Clunis.[128] This report helped to create the basis for an action in negligence on behalf of Clunis, an action which was thereafter struck out by the Court of Appeal as contrary to public policy and revealing no cause of action.[129] Thus can one body of quasi-legal findings have an impact upon the behaviour of affected parties, but equally be impacted upon itself by a body of higher-order law. Mental health law was not designed to secure the rights of (secondary) victims of (former) patients; tort law is designed to secure redress for injured parties, but when applied it can adopt a narrow perspective out of keeping with those entrenched in a (welfarist) perspective on mental health law.

The effectiveness of the 1983 Act may also be undermined by its attempt to reconcile the demands of civil and forensic patients who may pose very different problems and whose responsible practitioners enjoy different facilities under the Act. Forensic psychiatrists can face acute difficulties in respect of questions of risk, whilst they enjoy the equivalent, or near equivalent, of a CTO in respect of 'conditional discharge'.[130] General psychiatrists may accordingly have a different view of the problems, and thus of the practical solutions deemed necessary. Similarly, and paradoxically, forensic psychiatrists who have the opportunity to establish long-term relationships with their patients may have less need for coercive powers in the community than general psychiatrists who are required to deal with more patients and patients whom they may know significantly less well (or not all) in times of crisis; hence, the question posed by Caldicott, Conlan and Zigmond of whether resort to sectioning occurs less in the context of long-standing doctor–patient relationships and more where patients represent unknown challenges. The introduction of a CTO into the general psychiatrist's armoury of powers, although superficially attractive as a means of securing a longer-term relationship between doctor and patient, may in practice often make the establishment of an effective therapeutic relationship more, not less, problematic. Whether, and in what circumstances, that may be the case deserves to be established either by empirical research or perhaps at least by clinical trial and error.

Where services are provided on a *quasi*-coercive basis outside the Act, a further problem arises, namely, that patients may be ineligible to use those parts of the Act designed to safeguard the interests of the coerced, making the Act 'ineffective' in another sense. Thus, one reason why thinking about 'effectiveness' is so problematic is that the Act embodies two contrary notions which stretch in completely different directions. On the one hand, patients cannot gain the *safeguards* without compulsion and use of the Act; on the other, they only receive treatment within the Act once they are sufficiently ill to merit compulsion – and needing to be sufficiently ill to be made an involuntary patient carries both

---

[128] Ritchie *et al.* (1994).

[129] See Peay (1999).

[130] Patients conditionally discharged from detention under ss. 37 and 41 can be recalled to hospital for non-compliance with treatment and supervision.

stigma and coercive long-term consequences for patient and doctor which encourages non-use of the Act.

Consequences

Given these considerations it is entirely conceivable that one Act may not suit all purposes; nor may it be possible successfully to re-engineer one Act to make its use more effective. Partial solutions may include allowing safeguards to extend to the informal arena and monitoring coercion there implying perhaps a much extended role for the MHAC; *or* extending compulsion to the informal group, thereby taking safeguards with them; *or* reducing the need for compulsion by de-stigmatising patients and making more resources user-friendly and accessible outside the ambit of the Act. Alternatively, complete re-engineering of the Act itself may be required; splitting its various provisions into different statutes addressing particular needs (for example, in relation to capacity-consent) or the problems posed by particular categories of patients who find themselves subject to mental health intervention not because of their mental health needs but because of other behaviour, for example, offending (or even self-harm). What may be needed in legislative terms is not another legal high-rise block, but some low density, low rise housing.

One radical approach would be to argue that specialist mental health legislation should be abandoned[131]; curiously, this may not be as controversial as it first appears. For example, Norman Sartorius, the President of the World Psychiatric Association, is a powerful advocate for the view that we should be working towards the abolition of specialist mental health legislation (as stigmatising and problem inducing rather than problem-solving) whilst putting physical and mental health problems on the same footing.[132] Similarly, Rob Gordon argued in 1993 that recent legislation reflected:

> "a false dichotomy – care and treatment vs. rights and liberties – which deflects attention away from a more critical issue: the pursuit of the resources necessary to facilitate the creation and use of the most effective but least restrictive way of providing care and treatment for patients, and as chosen by patients whenever possible".[133]

Dealing with Canadian mental health legislation, Gordon argued that the time had come to retire such legislation in favour of general consent to health care provisions, together with enduring powers of attorney and Ulysses agreements.[134] For the problematic but tiny group of competent patients who pose a

---

[131] Szmukler and Holloway (1998); Campbell and Heginbotham (1991); Rosenman (1994), 560–5; Campbell (1994), 554–9.

[132] Personal communication.

[133] Gordon (1993a) at 42.

[134] A Ulysses agreement is a plan setting out clear guidelines for actions to be taken by a patient's support team in the event that the patient exhibits signs or symptoms of, e.g., mania or serious depression. The document is signed by both the patient and all the members of the agreed support team (friends, family and professionals) at a time when the patient is well; it contains provisions for cancellation of the agreement.

clear risk to others, but who refuse treatment, protective laws analogous to those used to contain people with infectious diseases on public hygiene grounds might be developed. Of course, the two risks are not strictly comparable since for infectious disease the certainty of communication may be very high, but the probability that it would happen 'wilfully' low; whilst for violence associated with mental disorder, the certainty of infliction is much lower, but the risk that it might occur carelessly arguably higher. But, it might be preferable to address the desirability of such an approach, rather than needlessly to taint the community of the mentally disordered with inappropriate and unjustified notions of risk.[135]

Changing the law is a laborious and time-consuming process, albeit it is much easier than changing people's practices. However, reform of the law is an activity in which it is possible to measure the extent to which the objectives of policy-makers and of the legislature are matched by the ultimate skills of parliamentary draftsmen or are corrupted in the process of the passage of legislation. So, at the end of the process there is something in black and white – whether it be a statute, regulations, directives or guidelines – against which the realisation of one's objectives can be tested. This said, and as discussed above, whether the new body of law then goes on to achieve its intended impact in practice is much more difficult to assess. Since the effectiveness of law reform is highly vulnerable to the prior need to change practitioners' views, without such change practice itself will not change and law reform will have its aims distorted or neutralised.

Finally, it would be counter-productive to adopt too negative a view; the law can set an agenda and determine resource allocation, as well as facilitating good practice by specifying for decision-makers factors of which they should take account, the sequence in which this should be done and the weight to be attached to them. Similarly, law can be sufficiently flexible to be both mandatory in its allocation of resources and discretionary in their subsequent distribution. Overarching these allocative and facilitative functions, the law has an important symbolic function.[136] In summary, therefore, changing the law may be necessary but not sufficient for achieving improved national mental health.

Law without enforcement

The themes which have pervaded this chapter and which will play themselves out in those that follow include, therefore, the inherent 'marginality' of mental health law; how to integrate the achievement of mental health and justice; the tendency of professionals to operate informally and unchecked by an Act vesting enormous discretion in their judgement; the pervasive ambiguity of the role expected of mental health professionals, namely, whether they should be interested primarily in their patient's health, public health or the protection of

[135] Steadman *et al.* (1998).
[136] E.g., the history of race relations law.

unidentifiable members of society; the public's (irrational) fear of mental disorder and the mentally disordered; the absence of clear objectives, and/or the presence of conflicting objectives and the incompatibility of those objectives with the roles and responsibilities of mental health professionals; and finally, the level of resources, their relative absence and the demand for effectiveness and value for money. In a similar vein to our assertion that law reform may be necessary, albeit insufficient, setting an agenda for that reform needs to be preceded by raising the questions it must to address. In so doing, we pursue an honourable tradition of asking, if not always answering, questions.

2

Mental Health Law: Objectives and Principles

WILLIAM BINGLEY and CHRISTOPHER HEGINBOTHAM

The purpose of mental health law has changed over the years as society's attitudes towards mental illness have changed. The 1890 Lunacy Act, seen in conventional historical assessments as creating legal obstacles to the early and effective treatment of mentally disordered people, was regarded as the height of 'legalism'. It was concerned as much with providing a protective framework for people perceived as vulnerable due to untreatable illness as with regulating the custodial context in which to detain those whom society found intolerable. The 100 years since that Act have seen three major milestones in mental health legislation, each seemingly appropriate for the time, namely the Mental Treatment Act 1930 and the Mental Health Acts 1959 and 1983. The 'jurisprudential trace' which these Acts have left appear to demonstrate a steady shift away from the care of those lacking capacity towards control of those able to consent, and then, perhaps, back again towards caring for those unable to care for themselves.

Law is often the 'trailing edge' of social morality and the enactment of legislation usually follows changes in society's attitudes. The shift away from defining the person by their illness towards a recognition of their human worth became particularly apparent in the 1930s and 1940s and was reflected by renewed concerns for human rights and, in the field of mental health, the establishment of bodies such as the World Federation for Mental Health and the National Association for Mental Health (MIND).

The Mental Treatment Act 1930, with its provision for voluntary admission, foreshadowed the seminal recommendations of the Percy Commission,[1] many of which were enshrined in the 1959 Act. With its enactment, the law and national policy changed to encourage voluntary patients and the provision of a legal regime whose emphasis was on the health of the patient, and the protection of the patient and others from harm, rather than custodial care. The emphasis on potential harm – the 'dangerousness' test – led inexorably to an individualist perspective which became firmly anchored in the subsequent mental health legislation of the 1980s (England and Wales 1983, Scotland 1984 and

[1] Royal Commission on the Law Relating to Mental Illness and Mental Deficiency (1959).

Northern Ireland 1986). All legislation is a compromise, but these Acts enshrined as far as it was possible additional procedural rights and remedies for the protection of the 'negative' freedoms of individual patients.

By 1983 the swing back towards an alternative emphasis had probably already begun, though masked by the media coverage of publications such as *A Human Condition*[2] and the celebrated cases taken by MIND to the European Commission and Court of Human Rights which preceded the enactment of the 1983 Mental Health Act. Since then there has been a steady movement towards a new paradigm, one concerned to achieve a proper balance of care and control offering maximum freedom to patients through the provision of community services. There is thus a trend back towards emphasising care for people who are in the clinical sense of the word incapacitated.

As a result of very significant advances in treatments, the trend is unlikely to be a return to custodial involuntary arrangements, which applied especially before the Second World War, but to a new formulation recognising the dual objectives which law is required to perform; namely, to recognise, preserve and enhance the self-determination of individual patients whilst at the same time providing a framework for the care and treatment for those who are genuinely and seriously disabled as a result of mental illness. The legislative framework must be established in a way which emphasises and encourages the provision and development of mental health care, sustaining patients within the community wherever possible and providing opportunities for patients to receive, if necessary, accessible and local compulsory care including, if really necessary, detention in hospital. In this chapter we set out some of those objectives and principles, as well as examining some of the legal mechanisms that could contribute to their achievement.

AIMS OF LEGISLATION

It has been argued[3] that if separate and distinct mental health legislation is needed it should have three principal aims:

1. the establishment of a legal basis for the provision of services, wherever possible offering effective individual enforceable entitlements;
2. the provision of legal authority for involuntary compulsion for treatment and to enable appropriately qualified persons to direct patients and service users to receive particular forms of services, whether in institutions or in the community, and to provide appropriate safeguards for service users in relation to the exercise of this authority by professional staff; and
3. to protect and enhance the civil and social status of persons labelled, diagnosed or treated as mentally ill.

[2] Gostin (1975) and (1977).
[3] Gostin (1975).

These aims encompass the full scope of mental health legislation which, simply put, requires a balance of, first, services; secondly, compulsion and safeguards; and thirdly, negative and positive rights. From these three aims spring a number of significant questions which will be considered further below, but which are worth identifying at this stage. These are:

(a) to what extent can there be, and should there be, effective individual enforceable rights to care, support and treatment?

(b) to what extent should legislation provide the necessary framework that will enable patients to require certain services to be made available to them?

(c) should law be restricted to the protection of negative rights, i.e. the zone of protection around the individual patient, or should law enshrine positive rights, on the one hand, to services, care, support and treatment and, on the other, to those additional resources which enable, catalyse or support the wider scope of individual autonomy?

(d) to what extent can (or should) the law set limits to and provide safeguards or controls over the exercise of professional authority or clinical judgement?

(e) can a legislative framework be established which enables community provision whilst ensuring treatment is given to those who need it?

OBJECTIVES OF LEGISLATION

The three aims may themselves be contentious. In any event, they suggest a number of specific objectives for mental health legislation of two sorts; those objectives that enshrine a principle, and those that are concerned with practical implementation.

Objectives incorporating principle

The following objectives establish key principles on which legislation might be founded:

1. to ensure that care, support and treatment is provided to mentally ill persons in their best interests;

2. to ensure that services maximise the autonomy of the individual and that the authority vested in professional staff of mental health services is used to co-ordinate the best possible care for the individual concerned;

3. to provide a legal framework within which to protect the fundamental rights and freedoms of persons with mental illness liable to civil detention for care and treatment; and

4. to ensure that as far as possible the risk of harm to the individual or other persons is minimised.

Objectives concerned with practical implementation

5. to achieve a balance of care and control and to ensure that, as far as possible, mental health services focus on the needs of the patient rather than on the needs of the service or the wider society;
6. to provide a context for offering care in the least restrictive environment/non-custodial environment and to provide effective community care services;
7. to provide appropriate procedural safeguards and considerations for the protection of persons with mental illness and the staff of mental health services; and
8. to provide a controlled and audited environment for professional conduct and within which individuals may have confidence in the mental health service.

Implicit within these principles are two distinct ways in which mental health legislation can relate to the needs of individual patients, first, using a 'best interests' test, and secondly, using a 'dangerousness' or 'harm' test. Neither is entirely desirable; the best interests test may fall short of providing the most therapeutic care under especially challenging circumstances; the dangerousness test requires patients to demonstrate potential harm to themselves or other people and identifies mental illness with dangerousness. An alternative approach is to develop a capacity-competence test that offers a more flexible option for which appropriate criteria can be developed, dependent on circumstances and the location of care. This will be described further below.

ASSUMPTIONS AND IMPLICATIONS

These aims and objectives contain a number of assumptions and suggest various lines of enquiry. As we noted above the objectives of mental health legislation are contentious, and can be broadly or narrowly drawn dependent on wider public policy objectives. For example, should mental health legislation incorporate systems for regulating the authority of mental health professionals that go beyond the need to provide safeguards for individual patients? More fundamentally, should mental illness and thus mental health care be accorded a higher degree of priority than other areas of healthcare? What is distinct and special about mental illness in comparison to physical illness such that it therefore requires special legislative powers?

There appear to be a number of reasons why mental illness, *prima facie*, is perceived differently. Those reasons include, first, the fact that persons suffering mental illness are, in certain circumstances, subject to compulsion. It might be argued, as we will see below, that such compulsion should not necessarily be applied only to persons with mental illness; but for the purposes of argument here we can note that, if people with mental illness are subject to forms of compulsion which do not apply in relation to other illnesses, this creates a complementary duty of care. Moreover, that duty of care implies responsibilities for the patient and for society and is thus a two-edged sword. Compulsion may deny physical freedoms to persons suffering mental illness, but the fact of compulsion can be used to argue for the necessary resources to ensure that it achieves some desired health outcome. Involuntary treatment for civil detention requires that services are provided. Here we must make a distinction between the 'treatability' test in relation to particular sorts of illness or disorder and the more general issue that civil detention requires a minimum level of caring provision if it is to be justified.

The second reason why mental illness is perceived differently concerns the notion that, while people with mental illness are not alone in displaying behaviour which may be harmful to themselves or others (or more likely indulging in behaviour which is considered anti-social), persons with mental illness *are* more likely to be perceived as dangerous, irrational and unpredictable than people not obviously suffering from some sort of mental health problem, such as football hooligans. Persons with mental illness are the only group subject regularly to civil detention in the interest of controlling potentially harmful behaviour. This raises a fundamental question about the nature of mental health law and the possible desirability of legislation concerned with the preventative detention of persons liable to cause harm to others.

The third reason is that mentally ill persons are always at risk of harming themselves, either deliberately or non-voluntarily. We recognise that under certain circumstances a person with a severe mental illness may be unable to reason effectively and their competence may be limited. The Mental Health Acts recognised this; for example section 58 of the 1983 Mental Health Act requires the patient's consent or a second opinion in relation to some treatments. Mental illness appears to reduce a person's competence to make decisions even if their underlying intellectual capacity is not affected.

Capacity and competence should not be confused with one another, although the recent Law Commission Report, *Mental Incapacity*,[4] treats the terms as more or less inter-changeable. For our purposes, capacity is the fundamental intellectual ability to reason; competence is a variable function dependent upon age, socialisation, education, information, fluctuating ability to comprehend (for example as a result of mental illness) and so forth. A test of competence offers an alternative way to the present (best interests and harm) basis for decisions about compulsion. By and large we should not treat patients on an involuntary basis unless they are unable to consent to or refuse treatment.

Mental illness of itself does not necessarily reduce an individual's capacity or competence. Consequently a test of competence to consent or refuse may be a better benchmark for deciding on compulsion. A test of competency also has the

---

[4] Law Commission (1995).

advantage that the criteria for competency can vary, depending on the nature and extent of care, support or treatment which professional authority suggests should be provided to the patient. Non-invasive community support would require a lower level of competency for consent or refusal than compulsory administration of neuroleptic medication.

Such a capacity or competence test is not without its difficulties. Defining capacity and competence is not straightforward, and the potential conflation of capacity and incompetence for legal purposes undermines the opportunities that the distinction might offer in clinical circumstances. A determination of the point at which capacity has been lost is a challenge which physicians face now, when managing services such as those for people suffering from dementia. Where capacity fluctuates and where competence may vary depending upon education, information and so forth, the determination of the extent of that competence may prove to be a 'challenge too far' in day-to-day professional practice. That is not to say that the general approach is unworthy of serious investigation. Simple and direct criteria may be achievable for two or three levels of competence, given there is a basic sufficient intellectual capacity to make at least simple decisions.

However, once we have a test of competency it is a short step to proposing radical revision of present procedures for involuntary detention and compulsion. It becomes possible to propose a separation between (i) the mechanism for dealing with those with a diagnosable mental illness who do not have the competence to consent or refuse treatments, and (ii) the disposal of those who may be at risk of causing harm to other people but have the capacity/competence to make decisions for themselves regardless of the nature of their mental disorder. In relation to the second group, a possible way forward would be the introduction of 'compulsory intervention panels' similar to the system of children's panels in Scotland.[5]

In this proposal the courts would act as the appropriate form of disposal in relation to persons charged with actual offences or where potential harm to others was predicted. The panels would aim exclusively to question, within a framework of statutory regulation, whether or not compulsory intervention would be in the interests of the person affected. If the panel felt that the person was a potential danger to other people as well as requiring compulsory intervention in his or her interests the case would be referred in one of two ways; either via the Crown Prosecution Service to an appropriate court (if an offence has been committed) or by taking advice from a second panel, the 'Preventive Detention Panel'. The purpose of this latter panel would primarily be to advise the courts on disposal of any person brought before the court charged with some sort of threatening behaviour or criminal offence.

One of the implications of this approach would be a radical re-think of current mechanisms for civil detention, which might then meet more effectively the

---

[5] Campbell and Heginbotham (1991).

objectives established for mental health law, i.e. to provide care for individuals in their best interests without falling into the trap of using mental health law to palliate society's anxieties about the potential harms which might be caused by persons with mental illness.

CONTRACT AND TORT: DEVELOPING A THERAPEUTIC RELATIONSHIP BETWEEN LAW AND SERVICE PROVISION

Current public policy in mental health care is to emphasise the importance of mental health services entering into forms of contract with patients or service users for the care that they are to receive from the various agencies that provide such services. This contractual approach finds expression in the Patient's Charter, in the demands that all mentally ill patients who require psychiatric treatment or care must have a care programme,[6] and that carefully constructed protocols are developed for referral between services. This 'contractual' position is presently relatively flexible but the principles established above suggest that it could become more rigid, at least ensuring that a minimum set of services, agreed with all those involved, are provided to service users.

The other side of this coin is the use of the law of tort to challenge breaches of contract and negligent provision of care. In commercial litigation the use of tort is becoming more flexible and tortious claims are being made when remedies exist under contract law. It has been suggested that the more rigidly contract law is applied the more flexible tort will become. The application of this type of thinking to mental health services suggests another balance is required, between (a) the establishment of effective contracts between services and service users for the types of care to be provided in a way which provides a legally binding set of duties and responsibilities, set against (b) the use of tort law to right the wrongs which occur both to patients and to the public. Increasingly patients and the public are suing health authorities and Trusts for failures by mental health services to provide adequate care and control of service users. If we are to avoid the extension of such negligence actions a compromise arrangement may be valuable.

Recognition that both contract and the application of tort can be more or less flexible, suggests that mental health law might usefully provide a framework which:

- establishes and maintains a form of contract or service agreement between the Mental Health Service and the service user (and significant others such as informal carers, general practitioners, etc.);
- focuses legal remedies and positive rights through the contractual mechanism as far as possible; but

[6] Health Circular (90)23.

- achieves as much certainty as possible without offering perverse incentives only to fund or provide those elements of care to which tort might apply;
- allows a controlled evolution of law and policy, but in a way which extends and preserves the rights of service users whilst providing suitably wide boundaries on professional authority;
- encourages and enhances users' rights and entitlements within a properly constructed legal framework; and
- provides tortious remedies where necessary without over-burdening the system or encouraging vexatious and unnecessary claims.

If accepted this formulation suggests that an important objective of mental health law is to achieve the balance suggested by maximising both negative and positive freedoms for service users, in a context which provides as great a certainty as possible about the availability and delivery of care, but without unnecessarily undermining the proper authority of mental health professionals to provide adequate care and reasonable controls on behaviours liable to cause self-harm or harm to others.

CONCLUSION

Reform of mental health legislation has been likened to the swings of a pendulum[7] between providing clinicians with broad discretion or prescribing detailed regulation.[8] Some would argue that the rights approach, pursued to a limited extent in the 1983 Mental Health Act, has principally resulted in the greater regulation of treatment and has not made any significant contribution to ensuring that appropriate treatments are delivered to those who stand in need of them.[9] If such an analysis is correct then, maybe, amongst other things, it represents the results of a rather narrow approach to the role and potential of the law in mental health and a failure to appreciate the breadth of the contribution that the law in general can make to securing the policy objectives set for mental health services.

[7] Jones (1972).
[8] Carson (1996).
[9] *Ibid.*

3

Mental and Physical Illness – An Unsustainable Separation?

ERIC MATTHEWS

The very name 'Mental Health Act' ought to make us pause for thought. It implies that the domain of health and illness can validly be divided into separate categories of 'mental' and 'physical'. Furthermore (since we do not have a 'Physical Health Act') it suggests that those human ills classified as mental ill-health share some common features which make them, unlike those classified as physical ill-health, in need of particular legislative attention. The assumption that there is need for a special legal framework to regulate mental illness does indeed seem to have a long history,[1] going back to the time when it was more usual to speak of 'madness' or 'insanity' than to use the medicalised conception of illness.

Many of the characteristic features of mental health legislation seem to fit better this ancient concept of madness than present-day thinking about mental illness. 'Madness' is an essentially non-technical term, a term of everyday language that, like most such expressions, is difficult, if not impossible, to define with any precision. Mad people are thought of as different from the rest of us, out of touch with reality as most of us conceive of it. They are seen as liable to engage in anti-social behaviour, for which they are not (or are not fully) responsible; but also (to the more compassionate among us, anyway) as being particularly in need of protection from others. Madness in this traditional sense is certainly seen as very different from any physical illness. Those who have a physical illness are people like ourselves who are suffering: we help them as equals and respect their wishes about how and how far they should be helped. Mad people, on the other hand, have suffered an even greater misfortune which actually sets them apart from the community of normal human beings: kindly people will show their kindness more by *protecting* them than by *helping* them in the way we help our equals. Given this conception of madness, it is not surprising that there should be thought to be a need for special legislation to regulate society's dealings with mad people, but not with those who are physically ill: we have a moral duty to protect them from themselves and to protect the rest of society from them.

[1] Fennell (1996).

The modern concept of 'mental illness' has undoubtedly developed histori-cally out of this ancient concept of madness, and the ways in which we think of the mentally ill, not only in popular and journalistic discussions, but also in the law and even in psychiatry itself, still bear the marks of these historical origins. For example, the stigma that still tends to attach to mental illness (but not to most forms of physical illness) is surely a relic of the exclusion of mad people from normal society. But most striking of all, and most relevant to our present theme, is the existence of special legislation for mental illness, based on the assumption that those suffering from mental disorder, unlike the physically ill, have to be cared for whether or not they themselves wish it.

It is significant that there is seldom any serious attempt to say what is meant by 'mental disorder': it is taken for granted that we all know already what it means, and that makes it easier to assimilate the term to an older and so more intuitive notion of madness. The most recent piece of mental health legislation in England and Wales, the Mental Health Act 1983, does not offer an explicit definition of 'mental disorder', contenting itself with a list of synonymous expressions.[2] But the terms used in many sections of the Act suggest a view of much mental disorder (at any rate of the kind that merits the attention of the law) which comes close to the popular picture of 'madness' sketched above.[3] Mentally disordered people, in particular, are clearly considered to be particu-larly liable to be unaware of, or maybe unconcerned about, their need for treat-ment, to such an extent that they may require to be compulsorily admitted to hospital or to be given treatment without their consent, for their own good and/or for the protection of others.[4]

It may seem that the point of the preceding paragraph is to argue the need for a clear definition of 'mental illness', but that is far from being the case. I shall in fact argue that much trouble has arisen out of the fruitless quest for definitions. Conceptual clarification is certainly needed, but philosophically, clarity comes sometimes from a recognition of the *diversity* of terms like 'mental illness', including definition by virtue of usage, rather than from attempts to discover what all these terms have in common.

Seeking essentialist definitions tends to lead into rarefied realms of abstrac-tion, whereas achieving conceptual clarity from definitions based on usage can have important practical advantages. If we can develop an understanding of mental illness that better fits what goes on in the practice of psychiatrists, we shall thereby separate out from it the remaining residues of ancient ideas of madness. In turn, this will enable us to see what we refer to as 'mental disorder' as covering a spectrum of human conditions. I shall argue also that a clear dis-

[2] Mental Health Act 1983.

[3] Indeed, even where the law has been constructed apparently with the intention of incorporating a medical concept, namely 'psychopathic disorder' introduced into the 1959 Act on the recommen-dation of the Royal Commission (1957), the definition of the disorder, essentially repeated in s.1 of the 1983 Act, pulls it far away from its medical origins and towards a behavioural or social con-struct.

[4] Mental Health Act 1983, ss. 2, 3, 58, 62 and 63.

tinction between 'physical' and 'mental' illness is impossible to draw in a way which would justify a separate legal framework for the latter.

THE RIGHT TO REFUSE TREATMENT

Before we can really begin to consider the social construction of mentally ill people and their rights, we need to think about the question of patients' rights more generally, and about the basis for the widespread assumption that mentally ill people have fewer rights than those with physical illness. Philosophers and medical ethicists have tended to base the right to accept or refuse medical treatment on the concept of autonomy. But this essentially Kantian concept seems unsatisfactory for this purpose. Kant justified respect for autonomy by reference to human rationality, that is, by our capacity to choose an end on the basis of impersonal principles of reason rather than of our own individual self-interest. But that was because he was concerned with our choice of *moral* goals: a goal was not truly moral in Kant's view unless it was autonomously chosen, i.e. chosen on the basis of a rational recognition of its moral worth. In making treatment decisions for ourselves, however, we are not concerned with what is morally right from some impersonal perspective, but what will suit our own personal preferences. Our alleged possession of a capacity to judge in terms of impersonal rational principles is therefore scarcely relevant to our right to have our own preferences respected in regard to treatment.

This is particularly important in the present context, because it is all too easy to use an alleged irrationality to conclude that those who are mentally ill are by definition less likely to be capable of autonomous treatment decisions than those with physical illnesses. It was suggested earlier that those who are sick only in body are considered to be people like ourselves, people whose membership of the community of reasonable beings is not diminished by their illness. But why not? The underlying assumption seems to be that membership of the community of the reasonable depends on being a certain kind of *person*, and being the kind of person one is cannot be dependent on what happens to one's *body* alone. The illness is seen as an extraneous factor that invades the body but not the essential self. Physically ill people are not supposed, in virtue of their illness, to have 'lost their reason'. In terms of the doctrine of autonomy, therefore, they are still entitled to be allowed to decide whether the harm of going on suffering, or even of dying, outweighs or is outweighed by the harm of going into hospital or submitting to medical or surgical treatment.

One reason why it has traditionally been felt that mental illness requires separate treatment in this respect is the continuing influence of ideas about madness. Madness is seen as something that takes over our essential self and changes it. It is thought of as undermining our very reasonableness, and so as invalidating our judgements about the relative harms of going on as we are and receiving treatment for our condition. Hence the normal respect which we owe each other as fellow-members of the community of the reasonable is no longer necessary. A mad person is not 'one of us', and we do not need to treat him or her in the way we should like to be treated ourselves.

But there is another reason for the assumed need for separate legal treatment of mental illness. Philosophy itself has reinforced social and legal tradition by appearing to give it the backing of quasi-rational argument. In the idea that the ills of the body are external to the essential self, while those of the mind invade its very core, we can see, I think, the baleful influence of Cartesian mind-body dualism. Descartes' distinction between mind and body as separate *substances*, the first characterised by 'thought', the second by 'extension', entails a division of the human being into two heterogeneous domains, each with its own specific mode of operation: the mind operates in rational ways, the body in mechanical. And his conclusion that "this 'I' – that is, the soul by which I am what I am – is entirely distinct from the body . . . and would not fail to be whatever it is, even if the body did not exist"[5] identifies only one of these domains with the essential self.

On Cartesian assumptions, bodily illnesses are the expression of purely mechanical breakdowns in the functioning of bodily organs and systems, as when the heart, essentially a pumping device, fails to function efficiently as a pump. Such mechanical failures in a body which is only contingently connected with us cannot, obviously, affect our essential selves, and so our awareness of our long-term interests. The mind, on the other hand, is not in the Cartesian view merely a mechanism by means of which we realise our conceptions and intentions: it is our self, the being which formulates those very conceptions and intentions. Anything which may be called 'mental' disorder, therefore, cannot be seen as a mere mechanical breakdown in a peripheral instrument: it is a disorder in our very selves, a breakdown in the reasoning powers by which we formulate our awareness of what is good for us in the long run. It is *essentially* different from bodily illness, and so needs different kinds of treatment, both in the clinical and in the legal sense.

BEYOND CARTESIANISM

Once we abandon Cartesian assumptions, however, the conception of mental illness as essentially different from physical, in ways relevant to the need for legal regulation, comes to seem much less self-evident. It is, after all, *people* who are ill, not 'bodies' or 'minds', and any kind of illness may affect *both* bodily *and* mental functioning. There may be good pragmatic reasons for distinguishing conditions best treated by psychiatrists from those best dealt with by, say, nephrologists or cardiologists, but this pragmatic distinction does not seem to imply any principled difference in the need for legal regulation. If we forget *a*

---

[5] Cottingham, Stoothoff and Murdoch (1985).

priori divisions into 'mental' and 'bodily' disorders, and simply examine one of the standard classifications of mental disorder, such as the *Diagnostic and Statistical Manual of Mental Disorder (DSM)* or *Classification of Mental and Behavioural Disorders (ICD)*,[6] what is most likely to strike us is the sheer *variety* of the human misfortunes collected there. Cognitive disorders such as dementia, psychotic disorders such as schizophrenia, mood disorders, anxiety, identity disorders, sexual disorders, eating disorders, personality disorders, alcohol abuse, and the rest, do not look like a homogeneous group united by a common essence, but at best like a collection unified by a Wittgensteinian "family resemblance", with "a complicated network of similarities, overlapping and criss-crossing: sometimes overall similarities, sometimes similarities of detail".[7]

Wittgenstein's example was the concept of a game: what leads us to call, say, chess a 'game' is significantly different from what leads us to apply that term to, say, ring-a-ring-a-roses. A similar point could be made about our use of the term 'mental disorder'. What leads us to call a condition 'disordered', and what leads us to distinguish between mental and physical disorders, seem to vary considerably from case to case. Consider some examples from the *Diagnostic and Statistical Manual DSM-IV*.[8] First, the cognitive disorders are 'mental' in that they consist in a failure to perform, or to perform effectively, certain characteristic human operations which are generally classed as mental rather than physical – thinking, reasoning and remembering – and which play some part in our ability to make decisions about our own welfare. But we know full well that in most, if not all, of these cases, these deficiencies in mental capacity are the result of *physical* causes – deterioration in, disease of or injury to the brain. They could, therefore, with equal propriety be classified as *physical* illnesses. Furthermore, people suffering from undeniably physical conditions such as cancer or intoxication may equally experience problems in thinking, reasoning and remembering. Cases of this kind therefore do not support any claims about relevant differences between physical and mental disorders.

A second example might be psychoses like schizophrenia, often seen as the paradigm case of 'mental illness', and so seemingly the most promising examples to choose if we wish to make a sharp distinction of a relevant kind between mental and physical conditions. But closer inspection suggests otherwise. The diagnostic criteria for schizophrenia are listed in *DSM-IV* as follows[9]:

> "Characteristic symptoms: Two or more of the following. . . . (1) delusions; (2) hallucinations; (3) disorganised speech (e.g. frequent derailment or incoherence); (4) grossly disorganised or catatonic behaviour; (5) negative symptoms, i.e. affective flattening, alogia, or avolition."

---

[6] American Psychiatric Association (1994); World Health Organisation (1992).
[7] Wittgenstein (1963).
[8] American Psychiatric Association (1994).
[9] American Psychiatric Association (1994), 285.

These are all mental or behavioural symptoms, affecting thoughts, perceptions, feelings, intentions and like, and so may have a bearing on our capacity to weigh up what is for our own good. Delusions and hallucinations, for instance, by definition distort our sense of reality in ways which may adversely affect our judgements about our own needs: in particular, someone who is deluded may not be (though they may well be) aware that he or she is deluded, that is, that he or she has a problem for which help is needed. It is a familiar enough situation to psychiatrists and others dealing with the mentally ill that the person in question denies that he or she is ill. If someone is in denial in this way, then clearly they will not freely consent to treatment for their problem. But note that such denial, though a 'mental' symptom in that it involves thought, is not confined to those suffering from psychiatric disorders; nor are all those suffering even with psychosis necessarily unaware that they need help, and help of a specific kind.

Delusions and hallucinations of this kind are anyway symptoms of only some of the wide class of human conditions we now describe as 'mental illness'. Other serious disorders, such as depression, are marked by disturbances of *mood* rather than by any deficiency in reasoning powers. According to *DSM-IV*:

> "The essential feature of a Major Depressive Episode is a period of at least 2 weeks during which there is either depressed mood or the loss of interest or pleasure in nearly all activities . . . The individual must also experience at least four additional symptoms drawn from a list that includes changes in appetite or weight, sleep, and psychomotor activity; decreased energy; feelings of worthlessness or guilt; difficulty thinking, concentrating, or making decisions; or recurrent thoughts of death or suicidal ideation, plans or attempts".[10]

All these indices of depression in mood or behaviour could be described as 'irrational' in one sense of that very fluid word. But what irrationality means here is not deficiency of logical capacity (depressed people seem to be neither more nor less logical than the average), but inappropriateness of response to the facts of the person's situation (where inappropriateness is judged by the standards prevailing in 'normal' society). Anyone for instance might feel driven to think of suicide in the face of, say, the breakdown of an important relationship or the death of someone very dear to them or seemingly insuperable financial problems: suicidal feelings seem at least an intelligible response to such situations. The depressive's "suicidal ideation, plans or attempts" seem irrational only in the sense that they are not motivated by anything which seems to the rest of us sufficiently serious.

Irrationality in that sense, however, does not seem to have any bearing on the individual's ability to make decisions about his or her treatment. The depressive is not prevented by his or her mood from recognising that he or she has a problem, and needs help: the very lack of energy, lack of pleasure in activities, problems with sleeping or concentrating, which are concommittant symptoms of

---

[10] American Psychiatric Association (1994), 320.

depression, are likely to be experienced by the depressive as undesirable and as something needing help, in just the same way as the symptoms of a bodily illness. The person may, of course, misunderstand the nature of the problem, e.g. seeing it as physically caused: but again, it is surely not unknown for a person suffering from a physical illness, likewise, to misunderstand the nature of the problem. Once again, there does not seem to be any reason here for contrasting mental and physical illnesses.

But what of the seemingly overwhelming urge of some depressives to take their own lives? Do we not have a humane duty to seek to prevent the realisation of such tendencies? If we fail to do anything to prevent someone committing suicide, when we are perfectly well able to do so, have we not failed, not simply as psychiatrists, but even as human beings? If the urge is so overwhelming, however, then any such attempt will have to be carried out against the wishes of the would-be suicide. But, first, such compulsive suicidal urges are not universal features of all depression, and any justification which there may be for frustrating them does not extend to other expressions of this condition. Secondly, some bodily illnesses may raise similar moral dilemmas: they may not create an urge to suicide, but they may result in avoidable death which sufferers themselves may not wish to avoid. Later in the chapter, I shall examine the moral issues involved in such cases, but, to anticipate, I see no reason to regard the issues as any different in the case of a mental illness from those which arise in dealing with bodily illness.

Similar considerations hold for most of the other types of mental illness listed in *DSM-IV*. Some, like the phobias, affect the behaviour of sufferers in distressing (and in some sense irrational) ways: but just because of that, sufferers are as likely to be aware of the problem from which they suffer as anyone with a physical illness, and therefore freely to consent to treatment. In other cases, such as eating disorders and perhaps alcoholism and drug abuse, the problem which creates the need for treatment is the self-destructive, ultimately suicidal, nature of the behaviour in question. If patients, as they may well do, themselves recognise that they have a problem which needs treatment, then the question of compulsory treatment clearly does not arise.

But what if they at least appear to embrace voluntarily their own self-destruction? In that case, it seems to me, we have a parallel to the persistent suicidal attempts of some depressives, and the dilemmas will be the same as in that case. Alternatively, what if the anorexic or the alcoholic denies that their behaviour is self-destructive? The anorexic may say, for instance, that she does not want to kill herself, she just does not want to be fat; the alcoholic, that he is not seeking suicide, but just likes a drink. These are in many ways the most difficult cases of all, but they are no more difficult than cases of physical illness in which the patient denies that he or she is in fact ill. Once again, this is a difficulty which must be addressed in the next section of the chapter, where I shall try to show how the principles involved do not distinguish between mental and physical disorders.

Finally, there are some conditions classified as mental disorders in *DSM* (though they are often distinguished from mental *illnesses*) in which the harm caused by the disorder is not, or at least not primarily, to the disordered person, but to others. The various sorts of sexual deviation called "paraphilias", such as pædophilia, represent good examples. These disorders seem to have no parallel among physical illnesses: someone who is physically ill suffers him- or herself, and any harm caused to others (e.g. through infection) is contingent. But a pædophile does not himself suffer from his pædophilia (except indirectly, in that he suffers social disapproval): those who suffer are the children he abuses. There is therefore good reason for distinguishing between this sort of mental disorder and 'illness', whether mental or physical.

The important distinction here, therefore, is not one between mental and physical *illness*, but between illness in general and a particular kind of mental disorder which is not an illness in any sense. Secondly, precisely *because* these disorders are not illnesses, the question which arises with them is not to do with compulsory *treatment*. Paedophiles are often said to be 'untreatable': but that is rather misleading. They do not *require* treatment in the medical sense, since their condition is not an illness, not something which causes them suffering contrary to their own wishes. It is their personality itself, and the wishes which emanate from it, which are said to be disordered. The treatment which they require is that which would prevent this disordered personality causing harm to others, not something which they would either choose or reject on the basis of their own self-interest. The questions which arise here, therefore, are of a completely different kind from those which concern the compulsory treatment of an illness, whether physical or mental, and so require separate discussion below.

CONSEQUENCES FOR LEGISLATION

It is important to be clear what is being argued here, and even more what is *not* being claimed. It is no part of the aim of this chapter, first of all, to defend a view of the concept of mental illness as a 'myth', *à la* Thomas Szasz.[11] The assumption on which the argument of the chapter is based is that the human ills with which psychiatrists and related professionals deal are every bit as real, every bit as much the cause of human suffering and distress, as those with which their colleagues in 'bodily' medicine have to do. Equally, however, it is not being claimed that there are no significant differences between mental disorders and physical illnesses – that all the disorders we call mental are simply symptoms of diseases of the brain and nervous system. It is an empirical matter, on which I am not qualified to pronounce, how far future research will show that mental disorders have physical causes (neurological, biochemical, genetic or whatever). But even if it were to be shown that *all* the conditions listed in *DSM-IV* were caused by

[11] Szasz (1974).

lesions to the brain and nervous system, it still would not follow that there were no significant differences between at least some of them and the conditions treated by cardiologists, renal specialists or otorhinolaryngologists.

So what *is* the contention of this chapter? It is that the field of illness does not neatly divide into two sub-fields – 'physical' and 'mental' – which are different in their very essence. The idea that it does, I have argued, is in part a product of lingering Cartesianism, and it is in part a product of the continuing influence of ancient concepts of madness. Once we have freed ourselves from these cobwebs, I have argued, and looked straight at the phenomena, a rather different picture emerges of the conditions we call 'mental disorders' as a collection of different sorts of human distress with only loose and varying relations between them, and unified into a class by pragmatic clinical considerations rather than by any underlying essence of 'mentality'.

This has an important bearing on the question of mental health legislation. For once we have abandoned the notion that there is a separate and homogeneous category of mental illness (and correspondingly of mental health), then the need for specific legislation to regulate that category to say the least becomes less obvious. This is not to say that many of the problems historically regulated by mental health legislation are not real and pressing. But it is to say that it may be more helpful to cease regarding these problems as exclusively arising in relation to mental illness, since they are neither confined to the field of mental health nor arise in all sorts of cases of mental illness. Furthermore, to set them in this wider context may both end the segregation of 'the mentally ill' as a group apart (encouraging, for instance, ideas about 'care in the community') and lead to a more holistic approach to illness of all kinds, in which the mental and the physical are not ultimately separated.

What are these problems? Existing mental health legislation, as indicated above, clearly rests on the assumption that there is a special problem about the hospitalisation and treatment of mentally ill people without their consent (or even against their explicit wishes) whether that be done for their own good or for the protection of others. The argument of this chapter has been that there is no such *specific* problem about mental illness as such: but that leaves open the possibility that there may be a problem or problems in certain cases of illness which may include some cases of mental illness. Mental illness, as I have suggested, is held to justify the waiving of a patient's right to consent to treatment on the basis of the following argument: only those who are autonomous (rational) have the right to consent to or refuse treatment which is judged by others to be for their own good; but mental illness typically diminishes autonomy by affecting rationality; therefore, those with mental illness have a necessarily restricted right to refuse treatment deemed by others to be for their good. (Sectioning for the protection of others raises different problems, and so will be considered separately later.)

In view of what has been said in this chapter, the argument just set out is open to criticism at virtually every stage. Consider first the alleged connection between the right to consent and rationality. The trouble here is in the slipperiness of the concept of rationality, which may have at least three different senses. In Kant's philosophy, as mentioned earlier, rationality means possession of the capacity to recognise and act upon universal and impersonal moral principles, if necessary in defiance of our own emotions and impulses. But it has already been argued that the right to consent to or refuse medical treatment does not depend on any such capacity to recognise impersonal moral principles, but only on one's ability to judge what is in one's own interest. That right, therefore, does not depend on possession of 'autonomy' in Kant's sense.

'Rationality' may also mean possession of the capacity for logical reasoning, and possession of at least some degree of that capacity can obviously be relevant to the clarity and detail of one's perception of what might be in one's own interest, and so to having the right to decide about one's own medical treatment. Some ability in logical reasoning, for instance, seems necessary if one is to recognise a causal connection between the treatment on offer and a future improvement in one's condition. But logical ability is an aspect of general *intelligence*, and it surely cannot be contended that being intelligent is a necessary condition for having one's wishes respected.

Thirdly, someone is often said to be 'rational', as was said earlier, to the extent that his or her responses, attitudes, values, conceptions of self-interest, etc., correspond to what is regarded as normal or intelligible by most people. We say that someone is 'irrational' in this sense when their behaviour, feelings, thoughts etc. seem *incomprehensible* to most of us. But this kind of rationality surely cannot be a requirement if one is to have the right to consent to treatment. The deviant nature of one's conceptions of one's own self-interest cannot justify others in imposing their own, more 'normal' conceptions on one. Think how monstrous it would be if, for instance, deeply religious people who chose to fast to death in obedience to what they believed to be God's command were to be force-fed, simply because most of us who lack the relevant beliefs find it unintelligible that someone should knowingly starve to death.

For these reasons, the first premise of the argument seems unacceptable. In a sense, this makes the second premise irrelevant. But it is worth saying that mentally ill people are no more likely to be irrational in any of the three senses than other members of society, including those with physical illness. Few people anyway have much awareness of impersonal moral principles, whether 'sane' or mentally disordered; and such awareness as we may have is as likely to be affected by intense physical pain as by mental disturbance; and, in regard to the second meaning, mentally ill people exhibit the same variations in intelligence, including logical capacity, as the population at large. Finally, although many forms of mental illness may result in deviant conceptions of what is in one's own interest, by no means all do; moreover, such deviant conceptions are as likely to result from other causes as from mental illness (as in the case of religiously-inspired fasting referred to above, or in the Jehovah's Witness's refusal of blood transfusions).

If rationality is not the basis for patients' rights, then what is? It can surely only be that human beings have a right to decide what is to be done to them for their own good simply because it is *their own good* which is in question. My life and well-being are my own: that is a truism, but it embodies a central moral conception of a liberal society. I therefore have a right to choose how far my life is to be preserved and in what way my well-being is to be promoted, in the light of my own conceptions of the value of life and of what well-being consists in. And that right does not depend on my degree of mental health, only on my being human and so worthy of respect.

Of course, my ability to *exercise* that right presupposes that I have such conceptions and that they are before my mind when I have to make my choice. The morally difficult cases arise when there is reason to doubt whether those preconditions have been met, but there is nothing particular about mental illness as such which gives such reason to doubt. Reasons exist, not only in some (but not all) cases of mental illness, but also in many cases of physical illness, especially those which involve intense pain, anxiety, temporary lapses in consciousness, or other forms of vulnerability. Human beings, whether mentally ill or not, are often liable to mistake their own good: fear of the immediate pain or distress caused by the treatment on offer can always lead someone to reject that treatment, even if, in calmer moments, they may realise that it is worth putting up with that pain for the sake of a longer-term benefit. Nothing in the brief survey of types of mental illness given earlier seems to suggest that mental illness, just because it is *mental*, is particularly likely to lead to such mistakes.

Humane and respectful treatment in all such cases requires an effort to balance whether the good to be achieved by the treatment is sufficiently great to justify the harm of overriding the patient's expressed wishes. In part, this requires an attempt to establish whether the doubts are really justified–whether there is any reason to suspect that the expressed wishes do not correspond to the patient's underlying sense of what is for his or her own good. It may be possible, at least in a few fortunate instances, to discover by discussion with patients how deep-seated in them are their expressed preferences about treatment or non-treatment. Secondly, if this is not possible for any reason, proxies or advance directives may give a clue. Finally, if all else fails, doctors may need to make treatment choices themselves, but these must be limited to what is most likely to save life and to restore the patient to a position in which he or she is clearly able to make genuine choices on the basis of his or her own values and preferences, however deviant. The important point is that these problems arise for physically as well as mentally ill patients, and only for some in each category. What is needed, therefore, is not a 'Mental Health Act', applying only to the mentally ill, but a general legal framework for making decisions on behalf of patients of any kind in such circumstances.

Finally, we must consider the very different problem of compulsory hospitalisation for the protection of others. As suggested above, this problem has traditionally been dealt with by mental health legislation because some of the disorders classified as mental have included as major (or even sole) symptoms *behavioural* deviations from what is considered socially acceptable. To the extent that some mental disorders are of this kind, I argued earlier, they are not strictly *illnesses* at all, since the suffering they cause is not primarily to the disordered person, but to others. This suggests that what is legally required to deal with such cases is, again, not a 'Mental Health Act', which among other things has the unfortunate effect of reinforcing popular prejudices about the allegedly violent and dangerous character of all mentally ill people (remember the significant ambiguity of the colloquial phrase 'a sick mind'). Rather, we need to address the difficult issues involved in the containment of people who behave in anti-social ways, but who are not what might be called 'rational criminals' whom one might hope to deter by imprisonment or other standard forms of punishment, or who may in some cases be deemed to need to be detained in advance of having committed any offence. The horrendous balancing act involved, between regard for civil liberties and the protection of the vulnerable, is, however, a matter for the criminal law, not for mental health legislation.

4

Public Policy via Law: Practitioner's Sword and Politician's Shield

CHRIS HEGINBOTHAM and TONY ELSON

The translation of public policy into practice does not always follow the original intentions of those who formulated the policy proposals; and this is equally true of policy implementation via law. This chapter considers therefore the way in which public policy is implemented and seeks to answer relevant questions. For example, how do good intentions become translated into good actions? What are the influences that can work against successful outcome?

Law has a limited role. This arises both because it is only one contributor to the effective achievement of public policy and because of its own inherent limitations. Hence, law provides a context in which public policy is framed, albeit new or revised legislation can also provide 'levers' towards achieving specific change. Law can also be seen as the trailing edge of public morality, even though it may not always be welcomed by those most affected by it. This implies the question, how can law shape social action rather than always be perceived as at best slightly dated? Conversely, is that somewhat conservative element of law in practice an important bulwark against fads and fancies, 'flavours of the month', short-lived ideas (of politicians especially) dreamt up to satisfy this or that vociferous constituency?

The translation of policy into practice via law infers that in many, but not all, cases a national–local tension is at work. Decisions taken at a national level may seem to be based on clear and well-articulated issues of principle. But, when these have to be interpreted at a local level they can, for a variety of reasons, become much more confused. So, whereas Parliament and national policy-makers may perceive issues with great clarity and with a commitment to perfection, the real world is much muddier and murkier. At best the real world of policy implementation is one of competing attitudes and claims on resources, and at worst it is made more complex by local political and organisational anxieties. We can see this particularly in the accountability of public bodies to Select Committees of the House of Commons. Such accountability is essential, but can become counterproductive to effective policy implementation if public servants focus almost entirely on the things they know that politicians will examine, rather than on the broad range of policy for which they are responsible.

Aspects of the latter may well be more important in responsible public administration.

Two particular reasons can be cited for this problem of interpretation. First, policies must be justified to ordinary people who may not share the same value base and are very likely not to share the same knowledge base as those making policy. The effects of lack of a shared value base were well illustrated in the early 1990s following NHS reforms when many 'ordinary' staff of the NHS were clearly uncomfortable with the internal market approach adopted by the Conservative Government between 1991 and 1997. As a result, many sought to filibuster developments that they perceived as unreasonable and inequitable. This encouraged a psychological context in which difficult decisions had to be taken, some of which with hindsight may seem to have been inappropriate or unwise. At the time, those taking the decisions had to balance the demands of a legitimately elected government with the aspirations and concerns of local politicians, local people and the staff of the service; it is unsurprising that tensions erupted into outright conflict over changes to service configuration.

Second, different policies emerge from the differing sections of central government: at a local level these may appear contradictory and create conflict and confusion. For example, demands of the Home Office may not always sit comfortably with those of the Department of Health or the Department of Environment, Transport and the Regions. Similarly, differing imperatives which seem perfectly reasonable at central government level may cause significant tension locally. One well-known example is seen in the disparity between social services' departments charging for care, whereas provision by the NHS must be free at the point of delivery.

TRANSLATING POLICY INTO PRACTICE

Government sometimes also under-estimates the speed with which public bodies such as the NHS can react once policy direction has been made clear. The Labour Party in opposition was critical of NHS and local government managers for implementing the various reforms, on the ground that such public servants were not acting 'independently' but had become 'party political'. It is thus ironic to note the surprise of the newly elected Labour Government to the same speed with which the same public servants began to implement the White Paper, *The New NHS*,[1] almost before the ink was dry, and certainly before the full implications had been worked through. In this instance 'law' *per se* is unnecessary, only legitimacy in the policy-maker.

Where reframing of the law is to be used towards achieving mental health policy objectives, it must sit within the broader philosophical approach that the government takes to social policy generally. The approach currently prevailing

---

[1] DoH (1997b).

reflects the underlying values of a communitarian perspective. This emphasises individual and community responsibility as a major theme within the development of social policy; such values are seen to be a proper approach to social policy development. However, there is nested within such terms a lack of clarity and a further potential for conflict between the rights and entitlements of individuals and the legitimate aspirations of the larger social group. Also, politicians who have been out of power for a generation, or who are inexperienced, may perceive the need for stronger central direction than is either necessary or desirable. Such 'naïve authoritarianism' can be seen in various ways; for example, demands on teachers for further curriculum changes; pressure to reduce waiting lists linked to threats from senior politicians to health service staff if they do not or cannot perform quick miracles; criticism of local authorities for being insufficiently democratic; curfews on adolescents; and, in the 'welfare to work' provisions.

When a communitarian emphasis is interpreted by the Home Office as a crack-down on social disorder and crime, and leads to an encouragement of community activity to drive out wrongdoing arising from mental abnormality, then the potential is evident for what were the best of intentions to become a repressive force against those who suffer from mental disorders. Recent community action to identify and exclude any person with a history of pædophilia may at first sight appear not unreasonable: communities do not want within them individuals who have demonstrated that they are a danger to children. However, those individuals also have rights, including the right to seek to overcome their past and wherever possible to rebuild as normal a life as possible, or at least to be provided with safe accommodation and assistance not to re-offend. There is then a danger that individuals with diagnosable mental disorders will get caught up in the 'folk panic' about pædophilia, the flames of which are fanned by people's perception of the government's policy interpretation.

Welfare to work is another example. Helping those who can to move from welfare dependency to open employment is a laudable aim. But when welfare to work is promoted as the socially responsible alternative to welfare dependency for the sick and disabled there is bound to be weakening of traditional sympathy and tolerance for those with mental disorders, which will have the effect of reinforcing their exclusion from the labour market.[2] The result is therefore paradoxical and may run counter to the policy objective. Hence, whilst the needs of mentally disordered people may be included in the small print of policy initiatives they are too often lost in a media-dominated presentation of policy which cannot cope with the complexity of the debate.[3]

---

[2] See, e.g., the recent Green Paper on welfare reform, DSS (1998).

[3] The reverse can also be true. The Disability Discrimination Act 1995, which, amongst other matters, makes it unlawful to discriminate against disabled persons in connection with employment, the provision of goods facilities and services, includes those with "mental impairments" in the meaning of "disability" in s. 1 of the Act. However, categories of mental impairment can be excluded through the making of regulations via the small print of Sched. 1 to the Act.

Both local authorities and health authorities are often aware of these conflicting pressures. However, elected members of local authorities are more widely exposed to such tensions by comparison with members of health authorities. Such members have legislatively backed responsibilities for caring for those individuals who are socially excluded. The dysfunctional family, perhaps with many children, or the mentally disordered individual, has the right to expect support from the local authority. However, local tenants, residents' associations and other community groups will expect the local authority to protect *their* interests. In practice, and in reality, it is not always possible to do both. Similarly, health authorities have a duty to provide the most effective community care for people with mental disorders, and again this does not always sit easily with their opposing responsibility to ensure the safety and health of local residents. Hence, social inclusion as a policy goal is welcome, indeed we would argue it is essential; but its implementation and implications are anything but straightforward.

Both local authorities and health authorities may experience conflict, not as a result of differing policy interpretations but as a result of incompatible responsibilities. A local authority member may be faced with having to support the individual rights of a 'problem' family against the not unreasonable demands of neighbours who do not like to suffer racial abuse, threats of violence or increased criminal activity in their area. Reasonable demands can very quickly become unreasonable demands, such as are represented by the pressure that a member of a social services committee might face from constituents who want her to encourage the health service to have an inadequate mother sterilised compulsorily and/or to have her children locked up for the convenience of the rest of the community. The thoughtful local authority member may be deeply distressed by these demands whilst at the same time recognising the need to manage competing rights.

Current social policy places an emphasis on the importance of tackling social exclusion, yet it has the paradoxical potential for increasing the level of threat to excluded individuals, especially those with a mental illness. A major plank in the revitalisation of civic life is the new government's emphasis upon democratic renewal. But democracy, like law, is a two-edged sword. It is, of course, essential both for the proper and full involvement of citizens and to ensure that public bodies are accountable directly to local people. Conversely, such democracy incorporates a utilitarian ethic, achieving the greatest 'happiness' for the majority, sometimes at the expense of minority groups.

One aspect of democratic renewal is represented by the extent to which local authorities and health authorities are being encouraged more and more to consult with a wide variety of individuals and agencies and to create action zones or networks which draw on the normative views of community groups.[4] Hence, public sector investment is being adjudicated according to the ability of local

---

[4] DETR (1998).

authorities to demonstrate that they engage in active and responsive consultation with their communities. Similarly, public health policy places an emphasis on the need to engage communities in identifying both the policies that should be adopted and the solutions provided to local health problems. Health action zones and education action zones are just two examples. The White Paper, *The New NHS*,[5] requires health authorities to develop a health improvement programme (HImP) and to consult widely on the contents of the plan. This policy direction places a new emphasis on views of community groups, potentially at the expense of individuals who are socially maladjusted or excluded from normal social discourse. This may have the unintended effect of reducing the scope for elected members to play a facilitative role in resolving intractable clashes of civil and political rights.

In framing the problem in this way we make no criticism of the new government's approach to social policy; much in the style and nature of the developments they are proposing should be welcomed. The direction of travel, however, demonstrates the requirement for stronger protection for the rights of disadvantaged and excluded individuals or families against the potential pressure from a more active or responsive form of community politics. That may be necessary both in the form of specific legislation to protect individual rights, and through safeguards within new policy enactments requiring public agencies to identify policy standards for the protection of socially excluded members of the community, embracing their needs alongside those of the majority. As we shall see below, the law has many guises; the protection of persons with mental disorder is achieved not only through mental health law, but also through the interaction of a wide variety of laws, regulations and social policy arrangements.

LAW AND REGULATION

As we have seen, law can be both protective and antagonistic. It can be used both to defend the liberties and freedoms of individuals and to undermine those liberties. Law can also provide both constraints and opportunities; it can act as a shield, or sometimes a smokescreen, behind which politicians can hide when they seek to translate policy into practice in the face of public pressure to do otherwise. Or, when it suits, politicians can use law to delimit the extent of necessary action. Of course, not all politicians want a shield; many unashamedly *wish* to promote local concern, particularly where their continued legitimacy relies on them being seen to do so.

Our use of the term 'law' is not confined to legislation specific to mental health care. The relevant legal and jurisprudential framework incorporates legislation specific to mental health and disabled persons, administrative law, other legislation with marginal but important implications for mental health care,

---

[5] DoH (1997b).

anti-discrimination legislation, Conventions and Declarations on Human Rights,[6] statutory regulations, as well as departmental guidance. This spectrum of 'law' implies variable impact. Conventions and Declarations, for example, may not be binding on UK courts; regulations, and in particular those laid down in accordance with various Acts, will be enforceable, but will not enjoy the authoritative status of the principal Act. Guidance on the other hand, which (amongst other things) includes requirements laid on health authorities and local authorities by the Department of Health, the NHS Executive and other government departments, will have a much less decisive impact in the courts. Although recent judgments have indicated the extent to which the courts will increasingly take note of such guidance in framing decisions,[7] here too there are pitfalls for unwary public servants. It can be, and has been, argued both ways. On the one hand, that guidance from government departments is precisely that and can be ignored if due-process decision-making suggests excluding the requirements of guidance; and on the other that guidance has an enhanced legitimacy over other considerations unless there is a head-on clash with legislative demands.

Law provides both opportunities and constraints for those seeking to improve the lot of people labelled, diagnosed or treated as mentally ill. As we saw in Chapter 2, the theoretical principles on which, on one view, mental health law ought to be based are rarely enacted in practice. For various social, political, cultural or economic reasons the best intentions of practitioners and politicians alike are often thwarted in achieving workable legislation. For example, countries differ in their definition of 'speedy' in relation to access to a court or similar body following involuntary detention. The UK is probably as much at odds as any jurisdiction in applying this requirement of the UN Declaration,[8] by insisting that a mental health tribunal within six months of detention accords with the Declaration's requirements. Yet, when the full panoply of law and regulation is assembled, it provides what is potentially a powerful armoury for sustaining and supporting the rights of mentally ill people and providing a policy framework within which continuous service quality improvement can occur. So, where politicians or health and local authority managers want to develop services that may not be welcomed by local people, the 'legal shelter' is extensive.

---

[6] See Richardson and Thorold (this vol.).

[7] *R. v. North Derbyshire Health Authority, ex parte Fisher* [1997]. A decision from the QBD, this case establishes that it was unlawful for a health authority to operate a policy opposed to that contained in a NHS circular. Although the circular (which concerned the prescription of beta interferon) was only advisory and not mandatory, the health authority had to take it into account in the discharge of its own functions. Having a policy to fund the drug only within a trial, contrary to the circular which requested that appropriate patients be targeted, was unlawful. Moreover, the health authority's decision to avoid the reality of a blanket ban by resorting to "creative constraints" was regarded, in the context of health care, as "surprising".

[8] In 1991 the UN adopted 25 Principles for the Protection of Persons with Mental Illness and for the Improvement of Mental Health. This Declaration is in addition to the 1971 Declaration on the Rights of Mentally Retarded Persons. It is not currently possible to test UK law against either international instrument.

In addition to the Mental Health Acts (England and Wales 1983, Scotland 1984 and Northern Ireland 1986) there are a number of relevant Acts of Parliament relating to sex and race discrimination and to the provision of services for disabled people. The Children Act 1989 is appropriate in some circumstances, as are education and local government legislation. Much specific law is then underpinned by administrative law requiring due process in decision-making, backed up by Conventions and Declarations of the UN and the Council of Europe. The European Convention on Human Rights, in particular, has influenced British legislation and British courts in many subtle ways, and post incorporation, its impact will be enhanced. Case law and precedents of the European Court concerning mental health cases[9] establish a context in which the rights of mentally ill people can be sustained.

Examples of guidance which influence the direction of care can be found in the 'care programme approach' (CPA)[10] and in the more recent stipulation placed on health authorities and Trusts to ensure single-sex accommodation. Guidance on the CPA requires mental health providers to have in place adequate assessment arrangements for patients and service users, and to provide a range of services relevant to that person's needs. This provides an opportunity to argue strenuously that those needs are best met in community settings that sustain and enhance service-user autonomy and 'valued' life styles. When this is associated with other guidance, such as Building Bridges,[11] and the Spectrum of Care,[12] it provides a powerful policy context which managers ignore at their peril.

It might be argued plausibly that international law, and in particular the European Convention on Human Rights, has done much to tackle discrimination in provision for people with mental illnesses and to provide the cloak which politicians and agencies such as the NHS Executive need in order to develop appropriate care in the face of sometimes hostile local reaction. The 1991 UN Declaration provides a further context through which to support the needs of persons with mental illness. Although such a document has, as yet, no direct legal status in UK law, UN declarations have the effect of setting a tone or framework for national mental health policies.

It is therefore regrettable that the general approach provided by the UN ignores or plays down the importance of the voluntary patient, given that the trend towards community care will mean that fewer patients will be detained in hospital on a compulsory basis. The rationale for neglecting the voluntary patient is that patients are, by definition, voluntary, and therefore not thought to be in need of special protection.[13] Voluntary patients are covered by other

---

[9] See, e.g., *X* v. *United Kingdom* [1981] at para. 52 (ECHR).

[10] DoH (1990).

[11] DoH (1995a).

[12] DoH (1996).

[13] The term 'voluntary' is problematic. It is used here in the sense explained in Ch. 1. Accordingly, there should be need for concern about the protection of some voluntary patients since the group includes patients who formally consent but who do so only in a context suffused by their perception of coercion.

declarations (notably the declaration of Hawaii of the World Psychiatric Association[14]) but many voluntary patients are not voluntary in anything but civil status. Voluntary patients are just as likely to suffer neglect and indifference. Yet the remit of the Mental Health Act Commission extends only to the detained patient, although the situation is different in Scotland where the Mental Welfare Commission has a more comprehensive remit for all persons with mental disorders.[15]

LAW AND HUMAN RIGHTS

A number of cases have now been brought from the UK to the European Commission on Human Rights and the European Court. The UK Government has been found in breach of Article 5(4) on a number of occasions. Article 5(4) requires proper 'due process' in law when any person is deprived of their liberty.[16] It can be argued that the MHRT process has that equivalent status, being set up by statute, and providing an independent and reasonably impartial review of detention. But such tribunals have difficulty in distinguishing their legal role of protecting the rights of patients from their welfare and social-protection functions.[17]

Article 5 requires that the lawfulness of detention be reviewed by a court or a body with the same level of impartiality as a court and that the rules of natural justice shall be observed in any form of administrative body or tribunal acting within the law. This is required even if, by civil detention, the law forces the status of legal incompetency on the individual detainee. Article 5(1)(e) lumps together widely diverging categories of persons – alcoholics, vagrants, persons with contagious diseases and people of "unsound mind". This mixture devalues people with mental health problems and inappropriately blurs the divergent categories of alcoholism, vagrancy and so on, together with mental illness. The conflation of these terms in the same clause of a Declaration can of itself be discriminatory. The Commission and the Court have however neatly side-stepped the problems which have confronted them by emphasising that the term "unsound mind" requires objective medical expertise and that the degree of mental disorder must be such as "to justify the deprivation of liberty". Whilst, naturally, this puts some bounds on what is meant by "unsound mind" it yet

---

[14] The World Psychiatric Association's "Declaration of Hawaii" is reprinted in the *Journal of Medical Ethics* (1978) 4, 71–3. The "Declaration of Hawaii II" was approved by the General Assembly of the WPA in Vienna on 10 July 1983, and represents a somewhat more paternalistic approach. A further declaration, the "Declaration of Madrid", was approved in 1996.

[15] Following *Bournewood*, the DoH issued a Health Service Circular (HSC 1998/112) aimed at reinforcing existing protections of patients lacking capacity in hospital. As regards reforms aimed at more fundamental protections see Eastman and Peay (1998a).

[16] *Van Droogenbroeck* [1982].

[17] Campbell and Heginbotham (1991), Peay (1989).

again emphasises the medical domination of the terminology of mental illness and does nothing to provide security for the mentally ill person.[18]

Achieving the ultimate objectives of Declarations and Conventions depend on their incorporation in some way into the ordinary law of jurisdictions. The UK government has now incorporated the European Convention on Human Rights (ECHR) via the Human Rights Act 1998. Whether incorporation will help or hinder is unclear. It may become a 'lawyers' paradise' and make much legal reasoning more opaque and uncertain; certainly there is a danger of creating a 'conflict of laws' *within* UK law.

The 1978 Report of the Select Committee of the House of Lords on a Bill of Rights came to the view that there were both advantages and disadvantages to such a Bill and, by extension, to the incorporation of ECHR.[19] The advantages include making the individual citizen better off; providing a positive and public declaration of the rights guaranteed; providing a local remedy rather than requiring a trip to the European Court, which is not established as a 'court of first instance'; reinforcing the value of the ECHR; and providing a constituent framework for human rights in the United Kingdom.

Ranged against these advantages are a number of clear disadvantages. Incorporation of the Convention serves to graft onto existing law an Act of Parliament in a form totally at variance with any current legislation. Not only will such an Act be potentially incompatible with existing legislation, but it will also introduce into UK law a substantial and wide-ranging element of uncertainty, since the European Convention is framed in general terms capable of a variety of interpretations. This broad framing was necessary to provide a context within which many different legislative jurisdictions could operate; as with many Declarations, the Convention represents the lowest common denominator of international consensus rather than incorporating the highest common factor of agreed principle. Further disadvantages are that the ECHR, as a set of principles, could have a life of its own within UK law independent of other statutes, and it could provide at least one alternative way of arguing a case.

The European Convention, the Commission and the Court have been valuable in laying down minimum standards of human rights which, it is assumed, will be in accord with the spirit of all legal systems. The machinery of the Commission and Court is intended to deal with conflicts that arise from time to time between the domestic laws of the signatory states and the Convention. Appeal to the Commission is one way of seeking arbitration arising out of such domestic law disputes. Incorporation of the ECHR may lead towards much wider uncertainty in many spheres of law. This is not an argument against incorporation. Rather it emphasises the need for careful consideration by Parliament of the advantages and disadvantages in order to ensure that nothing is lost by incorporation and that legal process does not become distorted to a point where arbitrary decisions emerge.

[18] *Winterwerp* [1979].
[19] Janis (1995), 460–3.

CONSTRAINTS ON THE ROLE OF LAW

Although law in its many guises provides support to those seeking improvements in mental health care and an enhancement of the rights of persons labelled, diagnosed or treated as mentally ill, there are nonetheless many constraints on the action that can be taken. Those constraints reside partially in the nature of law itself, which can discriminate against those whom it is intended to protect. The Mental Health Acts and international standards such as the European Convention on Human Rights contain within them paradoxical seeds of discriminatory opportunity. As we have seen, Article 5 of the European Convention uses the term "unsound mind" and thus perpetuates confusion about various forms of mental disorder. Given the existence of prejudice against mental illness it would not be surprising if courts showed a tendency to use the concept "unsound mind" to down-grade the perceived value and significance of those with mental illness. Not only is "unsound mind" conflated with terms such as vagrancy (with pejorative overtones) but also those of "unsound mind" are excluded from general rights to liberty. People with mental illnesses are unequally liable to compulsory detention because mental disorder is routinely made a precondition of liability to civil detention in hospitals. Article 3 of the Universal Declaration on Human Rights is similarly open to interpretations that license discrimination against persons with mental illness. For this reason it will be important in future to recognise mental illness as a status which is explicitly excluded from the grounds on which full human rights may be legally denied.[20]

Many other constraints on social and political action for improvement in the status and rights of mentally ill people can be found in legislation and case law. Section 117 of the Mental Health Act 1983 provides for aftercare for detained patients. Unfortunately, aftercare is not defined and, while the general right of patients to appropriate aftercare is not denied, the necessary components of effective aftercare cannot be enforced through recourse to this section. It has been argued that because some benefits, such as those under section 117, can only be obtained by those who have been detained, patients would be better off being deprived of their liberty via the Act, at least temporarily, such that these benefits might accrue. Thereby, their rights would be protected better. Whilst we applaud the intent to enhance the rights of patients it seems particularly perverse to deprive patients of their liberty, usually against their will, in order that such benefits may follow. The disadvantages are all too obvious, not least the stigma of being a detained patient. Some alternative way of enhancing and protecting patients' rights and benefits is desperately needed. Similarly recent case law has upheld a local authority's discretion in determining what continuing care can be provided, given the resources available to the local authority.[21]

---

[20] Campbell (1994).
[21] R v. *Gloucestershire County Council and Another, ex parte Barry* [1997].

During 1997 another mental patient was *denied* the opportunity to sue a health authority for inadequate care even though the lack of effective hospital and community services could be argued to be both directly and indirectly related to the homicide committed by that patient.[22] Patients have been unable to insist on a minimum range of services being provided either through determination by the courts on the package of care, or by bringing a case in tort for negligent care. Defining a minimum service may be difficult, and potentially extremely expensive, but the establishment of clear criteria governing the level of care to be provided to an individual patient should be considered.

MANAGEMENT IN PLACE OF LAW

Continuous changes in the management and organisation of mental health services over a decade from the mid-1980s have fragmented care provision, exacerbated the difficulties faced by health and social services managers in achieving coherent services, provided confusing messages to patients and carers, and offered perverse incentives for service development which have not achieved the desired degree of local integration. The Local Government Act 1988 and the 'enabling' approach that this fostered forced local authorities into compulsory competitive tendering. Sometimes this has provided improvements in value for money; in other cases fragmentation of care has simply been reinforced. Choice for patients and service users of the most appropriate form of care must be balanced by effective co-ordination of relevant services.

Similarly, the purchaser/provider split institutionalised in the health service following the implementation of the NHS and Community Care Act 1990 has been a doubled-edged sword. Separating the planning of healthcare from its provision has enabled hospital and community health service managers to focus on the business of healthcare; but separation has also encouraged a blame culture in which different parts of the health service are able to abdicate responsibility for patient care and to find scapegoats in other organisations. Also, the use of extra-contractual referrals provides a good example of perverse incentives at work.[23] Where health authorities retain a sufficient contingency fund in order to deal with emergencies and the few cases requiring high-cost specialist care, there is an implicit encouragement to mental health providers to refer patients for out-of-area specialist care rather than retain those patients in local units. This has had a number of effects: first, taking the pressure off local management to use resources as efficiently and effectively as possible; second, fragmenting the patient's experience of the service, with detrimental effects on professional, familial and social continuity; and third, creating significant organisational and practical problems where patients are returned, given that often the distant

---

[22] *Clunis* v. *Camden and Islington Health Authority* [1998]. See also Ritchie *et al.* (1994) and Peay (1999).

[23] Richardson *et al.* (1997).

provider has no arrangements for developing a care programme for community and continuing care provision.

Risk management, especially for patients discharged to community care, is another area in which the law and professional practice can demonstrate perverse effects. Effective risk management requires a sharing of information between all those involved in providing some component of the potentially complex array of services needed by individual patients. This is particularly true for those patients or service users where there is any continuing concern about violence or harm to themselves or to other people. Risk management arrangements demand a sharing of information about the service user on a 'need to know' basis. Confidentiality of personal information and protection of the patient from unnecessary 'exposure' are essential, but equally, effective co-ordination of care requires that individual professions recognise the contribution which all others bring to the caring task. The Data Protection Act 1984, and similar legislation, is sometimes a constraint on the extent to which information-sharing can be achieved in order to enhance the care of the patient and to achieve maximum protection of society. The key word is 'confidence'. It is essential to ensure that the public have confidence in the service's ability to provide safe 'containment' for the patient or service user; that the patient be reassured that he or she is treated in 'confidence'; and that the patient has confidence in the competence of the service to deliver necessary care.

Confidence is undermined by the clash of cultures between different professional groups. Medicine – psychiatry – is dominant, and retains legal responsibility whilst the patient is under the care of an individual doctor, although that responsibility may be shared with other professions, notably approved social workers. However, much of the agreed care plan proposed by psychiatrists is moderated by community psychiatric nurses and other community staff (for example, occupational therapists) who bring further professional cultures to bear.

This potential clash of professional cultures is a serious constraint on the effective operation of mental health legislation. Not only are there communication problems – which persist despite problems of communication being identified in every independent inquiry report on homicides by mentally ill people – but the demands of service users, professionals and of society are frustrated by the complex interplay of professional cultures and models of mental illness. The patient's distress is reflected by multiple mirrors, literally a 'crazed' mirror of differing professional and organisational concerns. One requirement on the law therefore should be to provide a context in which multi-professional, multi-agency and multi-modal services can offer an integrated response to patient need. Instead of the 'crazed' mirror the response should be a 'tight bundle' of responses relevant to the individual patient. Law has a necessary role in constraining the extent of disintegration of services and in catalysing a re-focusing of multi-professional concern.[24]

[24] Heginbotham (forthcoming, 1999).

The recent White Paper, *The New NHS*, may both help and hinder this process.[25] Dismantling the internal market may reduce the perverse incentives that encourage fragmentation but the retention of the planner/provider split leaves open the opportunity for abdication of responsibility. More importantly the decision by government to develop primary care groups and, in the fullness of time, primary care trusts, may further divide and sub-divide the planning and commissioning of mental health services. Recognising this, the White Paper suggests that mental health services should be managed by specialist mental health providers providing both economies of scale and centres of necessary expertise. Although the continued emphasis on a primary care-led NHS is to be welcomed, the further development of primary mental health care services may not integrate easily with outreach secondary services (namely, specialist mental health care teams operating in the community) and thus provide fertile ground for further confusion of responsibility.[26] Boundary problems between services remain problematic and this may limit the commissioning of potentially highly effective assertive outreach operated by community mental health care teams. Law cannot solve many of these organisational, managerial and financial problems; but a challenge to those drafting revised mental health legislation is to provide a legal framework within which effective community care can be offered, recognising the practical realities of multi-professional multi-agency services whilst coping with constant organisational evolution and change.

The common organising principle is 'health'. By achieving both an effective balance between the health of the individual and the health of (potentially disparate) communities and an appropriate emphasis on definitions of health, it may be possible to reconcile these varying influences on service provision for people with mental disorder, whilst stressing a positive and developmental approach to individual need. Health can be broadly defined to include positive attributes of social functioning, physical and mental health, the health of interdependent relationships, health promotion and education, healthy communities, and healthy interactions between agencies and organisations locally and nationally. The Green Paper, *Our Healthier Nation*,[27] should be used as a springboard for a wider health agenda, seeking to exploit both the natural creative tension between protection of the rights of individuals against unwanted interference (negative rights) and the opportunities presented in a society otherwise focused on personal and cultural growth, thereby offering new possibilities for individual development (positive rights).

---

[25] DoH (1997b).
[26] See also Ch 1 concerning the effect of the organisation of health care on the potential effectiveness of mental health law.
[27] DoH (1998).

BUILDING MENTALLY HEALTHY COMMUNITIES

The law in all its forms – legislation, administrative frameworks, national guidance, international conventions – can be used to further opportunities for tackling social exclusion and for enhancing the rights of individuals, while concurrently supporting the community as a natural cradle in which individual growth can occur. The challenge for social policy is to help the community *en masse* both to recognise and to respond to the fact that there are individuals and there is society, but that society comprises individuals.[28] Everyone has some need for support and interdependence; everyone can offer something to others.

Recent concerns of national politicians have focused on the development of community care for mentally disordered people. Community care requires much of society and places the mentally ill person, amongst the least well equipped of citizens, in the vanguard of service development, demanding his or her rightful place in a distrustful and sometimes frightened community. Community care, it is said, has failed some people; in practice community care has been starved of resources and has hardly started. Titmuss, in a famous phrase, described community care as "a myth conjured up by cheese-parers under the banner of progress". Many commentators have pointed to the 'unholy alliance' between the do-gooders of mental health policy and politicians keen to save money. In practice, community care is anything but a cheap option, as the closure of hospitals has begun to demonstrate.

In developing community care, law has, as yet, neither helped nor hindered. The legal formulation of the 1959 and 1983 Acts did not encourage community care.[29] Although the 1995 amendment legislation has established a health initiated form of 'guardianship' (that is, supervised discharge), where patients can be required, amongst other things, to attend at a specific place for care on a regular basis, this development is one of a number of amendments of present legislation which have been undertaken over many years in an *ad hoc* fashion. This has created a somewhat confused and incoherent legislative framework.[30] As we saw in Chapter 2, one of the main principles of mental health law must be to achieve an effective framework for community-orientated, patient-focused services which encourage a revaluation of those who have been devalued by institutional experiences. Community care is, if anything, a humanising impulse towards re-establishing the personal worth of anyone whose autonomy and social integrity has been compromised by mental illness and its effects.

Many people fear mental illness because of a deep-seated and sometimes irrational belief that they too will suffer mental illness at some point in their lives.

---

[28] See Pearson (this vol.).

[29] There has, of course, been substantial debate about community treatment orders and other mechanisms to encourage individuals to accept appropriate support, care or treatment in community settings.

[30] For further discussion of the effects on both the allocation of resources and the system of care see Ch. 1.

The debilitating effects of severe mental illness, and discrimination meted out to sufferers, is not something anyone wishes to contemplate lightly. Yet the very discrimination which people fear is the same discrimination that they themselves create in excluding people with mental illness from natural social networks and community groups. Mental illness is distressing and debilitating – that is bad enough for those who are unfortunate enough to suffer from it. Then to be excluded from the ordinary but necessary everyday settings in which people lead their lives – the library, the cafe, the cinema, the shopping centre – because of occasional bizarre behaviour which is perceived by others as unwanted, only tightens the screw of discrimination and of distress.

Discrimination is further encouraged by the unhelpful funding boundary between health and social services. As patients transfer across that boundary, from health care to social care, they go from services that are free at the point of delivery to services for which charges can be made. People whose livelihoods have been destroyed by the experience of mental illness find that, as they leave hospital or a health service hostel, they not only again have to learn how to live as independent a life as possible, with continuing disability, but they also have to fend for themselves, subject often to both discrimination and a lack of money or other resources.

Welfare benefits are under attack from a government committed to individual responsibility; and social services' funds have to be supplemented by payments for some forms of care out of the meagre welfare benefits received by individuals. The individual, who may already be having difficulty coping, is required to manage on a subsistence income and to live in at best poor, and at worst sub-standard, housing. Moreover, they may be unable to buy clothes and accessories which can help to palliate the worst examples of behavioural disturbance or social mal-functioning. In that sense the law works both discriminately (against the mentally disordered) and indiscriminately (irrespective of their individual needs). Few health or social services authorities provide or fund the requisite 'domestic' environment likely to encourage maximum independence or autonomy. Is this not what is needed if mentally ill people are to rebuild their lives or to function adequately in the community, and as full citizens, with continuing mental disorder? Changing the law will not help; imposing available legal constraints will not help. Only a concerted and appropriately resourced effort to meet the morally legitimate claims of the most vulnerable in society will ensure the social inclusion of people with mental disorder.

CONCLUSION

Good mental health services result from a combination of (i) clear central policy guidance, with a willingness of local politicians to implement that guidance, (ii) expert professional practice, and (iii) resources sufficient for an adequate and responsive service. These ingredients must be set in a legal context that provides a regulatory framework that reflects current formalisation of social and political attitudes. But law, *per se*, has not been, and is unlikely to be, the only impetus for change. Rather, law sets the bounds within which policy, practice and resources can be used to achieve as good and as caring a service as those intimately involved would wish it to be. Some limitations to poor practice must be set, but the law often has little to offer of relevance to day-to-day management. Much good work is done in spite of the law; and where the law is perceived not to be of great assistance, it is usually quietly ignored as long as certain basic procedures are followed. This is not to condone but to describe.

Law can catalyse changes in behaviour. However, the likely effects of any change in the law require careful consideration, since behaviours may often change in unexpected and counter-intuitive ways.[31] Law has an essential role in providing boundaries, instituting rights and clarifying responsibilities. But at root the effectiveness of mental health care stems not from the law but from the attitudes and training of staff, and from available resources. Perhaps the crucial distinction is that law can *prevent* (or at least provide sanctions against) the worst abuses of patients or neglect of good practice; it is much more difficult for law to *promote* effective care and ensure best practice is always followed.

---

[31] A non-mental health example would be the introduction of the suspended sentence of imprisonment. Designed to take offenders from the prison population, it was used by sentencers primarily as an alternative to a non-custodial sentence. Breach was accordingly likely to lead to an increase in the prison population.

5

Client and Clinician – Law as an Intrusion

FIONA CALDICOTT, EDNA CONLAN and ANTHONY ZIGMOND

"Schizophrenia cannot be understood without understanding despair".[1]

"Madness need not be all breakdown. It may also be break-through. It is potential liberation and renewal as well as enslavement and existential death".[2]

"A lunatic, in law language, is civilitus mortuus. If committed unduly, he receives in his single person nearly all the civil injuries that can be inflicted; for not only is his liberty thereby taken away and his property removed from his control but he suffers an imputation which operates with all the force of a libel. . . . A party detained on a charge of insanity may be acquitted and restored to liberty; but we all know that this is a question of such a nature that it cannot even be raised without attaching suspicion ever after to the individual to whom it relates".[3]

Although this chapter has been prepared on the basis of the views expressed by three parties, a psychiatrist, a service user/patient's advocate and a psychiatrist member of the Mental Health Act Commission (charged with, amongst other matters, protecting the rights of detained patients), there is a good deal more commonality than might be expected in such views. Moreover, the first two quotations above, from the 'radical' psychiatrist, R.D. Laing, also suggest that psychiatrists are not inherently insensitive to the realities of, and distress caused by, mental illness and to resultant tensions in the sufferer; indeed, given that they are first trained as doctors, it would be surprising if they were. Sensitivity can co-exist with a recognition that disorder brings with it a conflict between the desire of the sufferer to be free of negative symptomatology, but still to retain control over when and how that alleviation occurs, for alleviation brings its own negative consequences. In short, the clinician's desire to treat needs to be tempered with respect for patient choice. This is one central theme of this chapter.

Earlier chapters have already indicated that, for those suffering with mental disorder, the doctor–patient relationship is distinctive; the peculiar legal framework which can impinge on that relationship provides knowledge on both sides

---

[1] Laing (1960) at 39.
[2] Laing (1967) at 110.
[3] *The Spectator* (1839) cited by Peter McCandless in Scull (1981) at 342.

that resort to coerced care is potentially always on the agenda – a sort of 'take my advice or have it thrust upon you'. In practice, this manifests itself in the medical notes as "section if tries to leave" or "will need to section if refuses ECT". The spectre of compulsion thus hangs over all psychiatric patients. How does this context affect either the patient's willingness to seek and continue with treatment or the doctor's preparedness to offer care outside a statutory framework? Does the law impact negatively by ensuring that treatment, when it takes place, only takes place at a relatively late stage in the development of an illness? Is the treatment regime thereby contrary to all other areas of medicine where early preventive care is encouraged and the notion that, for example, one's cataract had to 'ripen' before treatment would be given would be perceived as both anathema and anti-therapeutic? Moreover, for those who do present themselves early with their symptomatology and are articulate in their explanations, some assert that the response is not 'here is an opportunity to intervene in an effective way', but 'here is a member of the "worried-well"', since they fail to fit the stereotype of the need for crisis intervention which more usually typifies the doctor's experience of the mentally ill in need.

The third quotation at the start of this chapter is from *The Spectator* in 1839. It illustrates another theme which pervades this chapter; namely, that the stigma associated with mental disorder and the view that unjust confinement is one of the greatest indignities individuals can suffer are both damaging and enduring. Indeed, the formation in 1853 of the "Alleged Lunatics Friends Society" campaigning for "the protection of the British Subject from unjust confinement on the grounds of mental derangement", indicates that the primary fear was *not* of a failure to obtain treatment but of compulsory detention. This fear of compulsory detention led to the 1890 Lunacy Act, perhaps the most legalistic in our mental health history[4]; this was an Act designed to prevent hospital admission unless two doctors thought the patient was so ill that there was no choice and was passed at the end of an era in which there had been a massive increase in the population of the asylums. Other than the Maudsley, hospitals were *not permitted* to take informal patients. It took the Percy Commission[5] in 1957 to reverse this philosophy. One of the central premises of this Royal Commission's recommendations was that patients suffering from mental disorder should be treated on the same basis as those suffering from physical disorders. Informal admission was to be encouraged wherever possible.

> "We consider compulsion and detention quite unnecessary for a large number, probably the great majority, of the patients at present cared for in mental deficiency hospitals. We strongly recommend that the principle of treatment without certification should be extended to them. Such a step would help to alter the whole atmosphere of this branch of the mental health services. We have no doubt that the element of coercion also increases the resentment of some feebleminded psychopaths, and of their parents, when they are placed under 'statutory supervision' . . . and this makes it even

[4] Bingley and Heginbotham (this vol.).
[5] Royal Commission (1957).

more difficult than it need be to persuade them to regard these services in the same way as other social services and other types of hospital treatment, as services which are provided for their own benefit. Equally important, if the procedures which authorise detention become the exception rather than the rule, the attitude towards compulsion on the part of those administering the services should change. It will be possible to consider the need for care and the justification for compulsion as two quite separate questions".[6]

It is ironic that the vestiges of compulsion retained by Percy and embodied in the 1959 and 1983 Acts should have continued to have such a pervasive influence on the practices of doctors and the perceptions of patients.

Although this chapter revolves primarily around the doctor–patient relationship, looking first from the perspective of patients, then from that of doctors and finally trying to reconcile the two, it makes no pretence to be comprehensive and focuses largely on issues of coercion and compulsion. It does so in the knowledge that considerable power is vested in mental health professionals over the lives of those suffering from mental disorder. It is inevitable that such an approach will not reflect well on the parties involved; yet, we recognise that some of the negative attitudes reviewed here are not confined to mental health practitioners. Indeed, patients will come into contact with all sorts of other professionals and officials, whether they be court staff, local authority personnel or post office clerks. Some of these people are likely to be less well informed about mental health issues; that they may hold stigmatising and excluding attitudes cannot be condoned, but it nonetheless needs to be understood in context where local and national media, and public opinion generally, are informed by a culture of blame and fear.[7]

PATIENTS LOOKING AT DOCTORS

From the user's perspective there can be a deep suspicion, sometimes founded on past experience, that those with mental disorders are not treated with equal respect and dignity by the medical and nursing professions. Making oneself understood can be sufficiently difficult when, for example, seeking to explain the nature, occurrence and consequences of back pain. But here one starts from the presumption (even if ill-founded) that patients can describe their symptoms with clarity and accuracy. As Eric Matthews has illustrated,[8] those with mental disorder are perceived as having an impediment which goes to the core of their ability to separate out "having an illness" from "being an illness". So, when patients with mental health problems speak, their voices are not always heard; and if they are heard, the meaning attributed to their concerns, descriptions and explanations – the phenomenology of their illness – can be differentially

[6] Royal Commission (1957), para. 289.
[7] Pearson (this vol.).
[8] See this vol.

perceived because of the attributions that are made about people who suffer from mental disorder. They are, in short, potentially in a cleft stick. Emotion or inappropriate emotion can be understood as a symptom of the illness; the absence of appropriate emotion can also be a defining diagnostic feature. The power imbalance necessarily faced by all patients disadvantaged by illness, pain or ignorance in their dealings with professionals is simply shifted up into another gear, where the professionals can cruise comforted by the knowledge of professional and personal superiority. And, should the patient fail to see the situation from the doctor's perspective, there is always the safety-net of legal coercion on which to fall back to ensure that the doctor's view holds sway.

In hospital

The possibility of legal coercion, together with a parallel, but fundamentally different, system for determining when treatment should be given without consent as regards physical and mental illnesses, marks out the mentally ill patient. Although the physically ill can decline treatment because they do not like the doctor, do not like the food, believe that the treatment is worse than the disease or because they wish to die, detained mentally ill patients have no similar discretion – even though they may, in fact, be just as capable of deciding for themselves as is the physically ill patient. How this plays out in practice is complex. Some practical examples may help to illustrate the powerlessness of the mentally ill detained patient (and thus the likelihood of their subsequent refusal to countenance unnecessary exposure to doctors or 'treatment'). First, in the process of admission there may be an unnecessary loss of confidentiality; a patient's details may be shared with social services and relatives (leading to fears about the viability of continuing parental responsibility where children are involved); the balance of power with relatives will shift where patients come to recognise that their spouse or parent or child may enjoy the power to 'have them put away'. The relationship with staff for detained patients is a particularly vulnerable one. Although in conditions of detention the patient may complain to the Mental Health Act Commission, and may even be visited by a Commissioner, such inspectorial functions as the Commission enjoys are peripatetic; once the Commissioner leaves, the patient is again wholly dependent on the staff to fulfil all of their needs. Similarly with respect to the relationship between doctor and patient, the doctor does not have to listen to the patient with regard to the potential benefits or side effects of medication, even though she may do so; consent need not be sought and, when sought, need not be given; even patients who are consenting can be subject to continuing coercion; patients can be made to take treatment they regard as harmful; and patients lose the choice (because of the fact of detention) to make some of the most basic decisions about their lives – when to go to bed, what to watch on television, whether to have sexual relationships or drink alcohol, to walk in the fresh air or take other exercise. Many patients develop the belief (not always erroneous) that permission is required to go to bed early or to get up in the night and read. Finally, there are no minimum standards as there are even for convicted prisoners (albeit that these are unenforceable, there is at least the recognition that with detention comes some responsibility on those doing the detaining to meet certain standards). In short, many patients probably experience the workings of the Act as a depersonalising, degrading gateway to care and treatment, which seems particularly to value compliance and passivity, and being a patient patient. It is hard to justify these terms and conditions as likely contributors to the patients' health; indeed, they are there for reasons of detention. Yet, whilst all patients compulsorily admitted have health needs, a proportion are thereafter detained in the interests of their own safety or for the protection of others.

In the community

The prospect of coercion does not, of course, evaporate when patients leave hospital. Some will be subject to the quasi-coercive features of supervised discharge orders; others may find themselves placed on a 'supervision register'. Although the ability of the medical profession to 'enforce' its will through use of these provisions is, in practice, extremely limited,[9] patients may nonetheless feel obliged to co-operate. Moreover, persistent discussion of the possibility of introducing a community treatment order (CTO) (like the many-headed hydra this debate refuses to die) providing for compulsory treatment of patients not currently detained in hospital, further skews the balance of power in favour of the medical profession.[10] Patients rightly fear the associated reduction in their autonomy and the increased stigma of being made subject to such an order, where patients suffering from physical illnesses are not compulsorily medicated in the community. Patients ask why it is that any prospective deterioration in their condition through failure to follow medical advice should be subject to compulsion? If the answer seeks justification in the risk that such failure poses a danger to the well-being of others, why is it that diabetics or epileptics who fail adequately to follow a prescribed medical regime should nonetheless still be able, for example, to drive their cars (until such time as their licence is removed based on a report from their doctor), without them being removed to hospital for forcible administration of a sticky bun or insulin (as appropriate) or of an anti-convulsant? Were this the case, is it not likely that even more patients suffering from disorders that might bring them within the ambit of state control would find ways to avoid contact with the medical profession in order never to risk being subject to such coercive care? In summary, such a response runs a high risk of being anti-therapeutic. If the argument is so readily understood in respect of HIV and sexually transmitted diseases (i.e. that we need confidentiality if

[9] Baker (1997); Cohen and Eastman (1996).
[10] Eastman, Zigmond and McIver (1998).

patients are to volunteer themselves for treatment and thereby reduce the aggregate risk and extent of suffering) why is it seemingly so hard to understand that marking out those with mental disorders as suitable for subjection to a coercive regime is likely, in the short term in respect of that patient and in the long term in respect of the body of patients, to reduce overall patient compliance? This is particularly likely to be the case if coercive law is substituted for high levels and quality resources. Whilst patients with mental disorders who value their 'right to autonomy' more highly than their 'right to health' cannot ultimately effect their preference, those with physical disorders can do so. On what basis is such a distinction justifiable?

These observations also need to be set in the context of patients' experience of care in the community. As one person suffering from manic-depression observed:

> "Twenty-five years ago on the first occurrence of my illness, admission to hospital on a compulsory basis was the only option—I did not know what was happening to me and was resistant—now, managing my illness is all about me and my family taking responsibility and, together with help from the Community Psychiatric Nurse, avoiding hospital admission by those around me being alert to any deterioration in my condition and responding quickly".[11]

It has been strongly argued that a programme of care in the community is likely only to be capable of substantially helping those who are prepared to volunteer for it[12]; the potentially negative impact of a regime of coercive care is all too evident.

It would be encouraging to think that this person's experiences reflect a genuine shift in the understanding of the clinical team that patients need to maintain and regain control over their lives – even if that control is sometimes lost by patients and sometimes removed from them by others. For, as Peter Campbell observed some ten years earlier, loss of control is "a major feature of life for those diagnosed as mentally ill".[13] The disenchantment with the psychiatric professional was all too evident; for, as he continued:

> "no psychiatric professional has ever advised me on how to cope with a breakdown beyond the blanket exhortation to keep on taking the drugs. My own experiences suggest that once I start to lose control again I am expected to admit powerlessness, hand myself over to the experts and count to 15,000".[14]

However, the dependency which he describes is a "double dependency", since the caring team also bases its operations on an expectation of inequality. This, in turn, can have a detrimental impact on the aspirations of staff; not only may they underestimate (in the patient's mind) the patient's capacity to change, but they may also ignore the potential that they as professionals have to assist that

---

[11] Personal communication.
[12] Eastman (1997).
[13] Campbell (1989) 11.
[14] *Ibid.*, 13.

change. As Campbell notes when describing the difficulties he has encountered over the years, at times when he found himself in severe mental distress, the network of provisions is "designed to make it difficult for me to receive the help I may need and almost impossible to seek out the help I want".[15]

The extent to which mental health services are acceptable to those who use them, and a growing recognition that taking account of users' views of health care is critical as a route to ensuring social acceptability and legitimacy of those practices, should properly drive mental health policy. Moreover, services that are not used, or are used reluctantly, are likely to generate the justification for more (not less) coercive services. This can be strongly reinforced by the recruitment of users as staff, and the involvement of users in drafting informative clinical and legal literature. Conversely, 'coercive services' run the risk of being counterproductive to the wider health needs of the community. Poignantly, as one study revealed, when the views of psychiatric in-patients are sought, the "thing psychiatric in-patients value most about being in hospital is their ability to leave".[16] Surveying, taking seriously and responding to the views of users is crucial.[17]

DOCTORS LOOKING AT PATIENTS

From the doctor's perspective much of the foregoing may appear a bleak portrayal. However, Zigmond's description[18] of how conditions in special care wards can depart so markedly from an acceptable standard, brutalising the staff and making it "harder to maintain standards of humane care", is telling. One feature which marks out patients on special care wards is that, by and large, they are all compulsorily detained. As such, they represent the extreme of a continuum in respect of the potential impact of law on patient care; and, as Zigmond illustrates, this regime has negative consequences for both staff and patients. He gives the example of how there can be an increasing acceptance of a deteriorating ward environment – to the extent that when, as a Commissioner, he complained in relation to one such ward that "patients were being made to sleep in a dormitory smeared with faeces it was pointed out to me that one of the patients had done this". Regrettably, as Nick Bosanquet illustrates when he draws upon the work of the Sainsbury Centre/Mental Health Commission, such appalling standards are by no means exceptional in acute wards.[19] Since we would not tolerate such conditions on wards for the physically ill, and throw our hands up in horror when we see them in 'third world' or former Eastern block countries, how is it possible for them to persist in psychiatric wards if it is not mediated via some process of subtle de-humanisation of the patients?

[15] *Ibid.*, 14.
[16] McIntyre, Farrell and David (1989) 298, 159–60.
[17] Rogers, Pilgrim and Lacey (1993).
[18] Zigmond (1995), 19, 310–12.
[19] See this vol.

In turn, the context of coercion may modify in subtle ways the choices doctors make about treatment. And the presence of coercion may be made manifest by the mere existence of a seclusion room, for such facilities, even if rarely used, nonetheless ensure the ever-present threat of coercion. Since drugs and ECT can be given compulsorily, but talking/behaviour therapy is not so amenable to 'a quick fix', are the former more likely to be administered? There certainly is evidence that very large dosages of drugs, way above the British National Formulary range, may be given.[20] Given that such dosages are most likely to be prescribed in the early stages of illness, relapse and admission, when section 58 does not require consent or a Mental Health Act Commission Second Opinion Appointed Doctor, do staff slip too readily into forgetting, or forgetting how, to ask for consent or to take no for an answer? As Zigmond has illustrated[21] this attitude can be passed to new nursing staff and junior doctors who, unfamiliar with the particular drug regime, seek advice and guidance on the needs of 'special care' patients about the standard of acceptable practice. Ultimately, deteriorating standards can lead to a siege mentality, magnifying resistance to change. Sedation is advantageous in both controlling patients and reducing complaints. This is an issue which cries out for the application of clinical audit, with protocols developed at a Trust level and in agreement with senior pharmacists.

Doctors' choices may also be constrained by the crisis nature of much mental health intervention (in turn, partially attributable to patients' reluctance to volunteer themselves for preventive care). Hard information is not yet available about the frequency with which compulsory admission occurs where the admitting doctor has no long-term relationship with the patient. However, experienced practitioners suspect that it is the very absence of this relationship which may often contribute to the resort to compulsion. Where the patient is known to the mental health team, crises can often be contained, addressed and managed in a way that does not require resort to detention under the Mental Health Act. Another reason why crises may develop in a service where resources are stretched is that staff have insufficient time to listen to patients' worries about the progress (or deterioration) in their illnesses or about their desire for other kinds of drugs which may suit them better. So, in much the same way that the 'worried-well', referred to earlier, may fail to obtain the attention they need, the 'worried-unwell' equally may be sidelined by a service stretched by trying to cope with the 'not worried but manifestly unwell in crisis' and having to resort to compulsion (with all of its bureaucratic costs) to make any intervention effective.

Law, coercive relationships and resources

At the heart of all these matters is, however, the clinico-legal nature of the relationship between client and clinician. The quality of the relationship affects the

---

[20] See Richardson and Thorold (this vol.), drawing on the work of Fennell.
[21] Zigmond (1995).

likelihood that legal compulsion will be used *and* the use of compulsion affects the relationship, and not just on the particular occasion when compulsion is used but in an enduring manner; compulsion has a long memory. Indeed, the clear, and perhaps at first glance surprising, difference of view between many general and forensic psychiatrists as to the desirability of enacting some form of CTO seems likely to derive, at least in part, from the typically longer-term relationship with their patients experienced by forensic clinicians.[22] Although general colleagues may retort that the forensic psychiatrist has the 'legal luxury' already of a *de facto* CTO, through the frequent presence of conditional discharge consequent upon original detention under a restriction order, forensic psychiatrists seem to value at least equally the longevity of any admission which precedes discharge, resulting in greater 'clinical closeness'.[23] The latter, in turn, reflects substantially more than average resourcing of forensic services; this is not restricted to in-patient care in that, anecdotally, there seems little doubt that the community case loads of all forensic clinicians (perhaps best reflected in CPNs) is likely to be substantially less than those of their community mental health care colleagues.

Whether or not this explanation of common differences of view between general and forensic psychiatrists is valid, few would disagree that resources affect the clinical relationship and that fewer resources almost inevitably implies more 'sectioning'. This is likely to arise in several ways. First, inadequate in-patient beds will determine that admission is offered later in the development of an illness or relapse, such that the likelihood that it will have to be accompanied by legal coercion is increased. Secondly, lack of community resourcing will determine that relapse is either identified later or, if it *is* identified early, that both treatment, and the encouragement of the client into treatment, will be less effective. Thus, lack of resources to sustain and make maximally therapeutic the relationship will result in both unnecessary coercion now and the possibility sometimes of the relationship being damaged in relation to the next period of care in the community. The likely cumulative effect of this is obvious. Hence, it may not be that the clinician either wishes to, or believes, that she has to wait for a patient's psychosis to "ripen"[24] but that gardening resources both in the community and in the in-patient greenhouse are inadequate to do otherwise. Although some evidence points to greater resourcing of 'assertive outreach' as resulting in either as frequent or more frequent hospital admissions, there is little evidence to suggest that such in-patient admissions are overly inclusive of legal detention and good reason to believe that such admissions may well be accompanied by less legal coercion. Ultimately, using the economist's framework, it seems likely that the marginal contribution of law to mental health outcome will be greater the less is the resourcing of the care to which it relates. That

---

[22] Eastman, Zigmond, and McIver (1998).

[23] See comments attributed to Snowden, current Chairperson of the Forensic Faculty of the Royal College of Psychiatrists, in *ibid*.

[24] Blom-Cooper *et al.* (1995).

is, the marginal 'value added' contribution of law will be high, but only because the resourcing contribution is low. This is perhaps one central tenet upon which most clients and clinicians are likely to find unanimity of view. Such unanimity is likely surely to extend to the belief that substituting legal coercion for resources is unethical and socially unacceptable. It might also extend to agreement with the principle of "reciprocity"[25] and with the required inclusion within mental health law of "rights to treatment resources".[26]

There may also be agreement that the presence and use of law are discriminatory between clients and types of clients in that, for example, increasingly it is via 'sectioning' that resources are achieved (be it an in-patient bed via hospital detention or community resources via a 'supervised discharge order'); or at least that sectioning is an accompaniment to gaining resources. Indeed, the over-representation of ethnic minority patients amongst those who are detained may reflect not coercive racism, as is sometimes suggested, but resource racism, through the differential availability of resources to different social groups. Certainly, such a factor may reinforce any effect on patterns of care reflective of inadequate numbers of ethnic minority clinicians, reflected, for example, in the very low numbers of Afro-Caribbean medical students, and therefore doctors.

The effect of resources on the necessity of resorting to law extends crucially to types of medication. Albeit most psychiatrists would argue that it is common for chronic psychosis inherently to be accompanied by lack of insight, either or both into the illness *per se* and/or into the need for medication, accessibility to (ethical) 'persuasion' is clearly likely to be highly influenced by the nature and degree of any drug side effects. Hence, if (so-called) 'atypical' antipsychotics which have significantly better side effect profiles than their 'typical' ancestors[27] are unavailable because of additional cost then the loss of any therapeutic advantage they can confer will tend to result in greater legal coercion.[28] So, it is not all about insight but also about resources.

Finally, the resource availability of time sufficient for public and individual education of the 'reality' of legal coercion would greatly assist patients with relapsing illnesses to have less fear of the possibility of coercion. Indeed, even calls by some psychiatrists for CTOs would be less 'feared' if they were not (falsely) perceived as 'injecting people on the kitchen table'.

---

[25] Eastman (1994).

[26] See Bingley and Heginbotham (this vol.).

[27] The term 'atypical' actually refers to atypicality of side effect profile and not to any therapeutic atyplicality or advantage; albeit, at the time of writing, *one* atypical antipsychotic has been shown to be more 'efficacious' in relation to drug resistant schizophrenia and it is likely that many other atypical antipsychotics will be more 'effective' or 'efficient' because of greater patent compliance.

[28] See above.

Confidence in and within the relationship

Confidence, or its absence, within an intended therapeutic relationship is bilateral, albeit any relationship between a doctor and a patient may tend inherently to be distorted away from equality and mutuality.[29] The greater the client's confidence in the clinician the more likely will she listen to (even if not necessarily adhere to) advice; and the more the patient listens (and perhaps adheres) the more confidence has the clinician that the client can be trusted at least to make informed and reasonable decisions (even if they amount to rejection of advice). Confidence of this type is also influenced by the client's perception that the relationship is 'in confidence', in the sense of private. Indeed, 'private' is importantly used here not only to indicate that it is a relationship properly with secrets, but also that the relationship is concerned with matters personal to the client and not matters which are 'public', in the sense of the public having a natural interest in them as an ethical party. But the latter sense of 'the private relationship' is increasingly being eroded, through the client's benefit being subjugated to the benefit of the public, by way of control of the client's behaviour. This 'social control' agenda should not, however, be of the type 'the (direct) purpose of treatment is public safety' but, rather, 'the purpose of treatment is patient benefit, albeit that it *may* confer (indirect) public benefit'. To admit otherwise is to lay the foundation for profound *lack* of 'confidence' in the therapeutic relationship, in every sense; indeed, it is to lay the foundation for the relationship not only to be non therapeutic but to be *defined* as such.[30] The profound professional concern which attended the introduction of supervision registers[31] nicely illustrates the fact that lack of confidentiality is likely to result in less confidence within the client–clinician relationship. Ultimately, however, what is most likely to be influential on the client–clinician relationship is the nature of mental health law *per se*, both in terms of its effect on individual clients in individual circumstances and in terms of the effect of its 'image' (and reality) on all clients, including those who will never become subject to it.[32] This emphasises the enormous importance of careful consideration of legal reform *in terms of* the therapeutic relationship. Law cannot be 'bolted on' to mental health care and on to the therapeutic relationship but, rather, must be written in terms of it. It follows that research into the operation of law, as a necessary prelude to law reform, must be similarly focussed, and therefore inclusive of audit of the experience clients, as well as carers, have of it. This also implies that reform must be set publicly in that context and not within an agenda for social control and safety.

---

[29] See Chap. 1.
[30] Increasingly clinicians may wish to avoid encouraging the public perception that mental health care can be of substantial influence in achieving greater public safety.
[31] See Caldicott (1994).
[32] See above.

The ethical relationship

Mental health law forms a major part of the core of the ethical relationship between client and clinician, both when it is used and when it is merely a background presence which might be used. Apart from issues of confidentiality, the framework of law allowing coerced care clearly affects some clients' willingness to seek care; while it is also possible that clinicians may wish to avoid using the law, both because of its perceived stigmatising effect on clients and because it may be damaging to the relationship (although some argue that there can be a good yet unbalanced relationship centred partly around authority[33]). It is also possible (perhaps likely) that clinicians may import their own ethical stances into their application (or not) of the Act.

If there is an ethical debate amongst psychiatrists about coercion *per se*, it is particularly well represented by the debate concerning the ethics specifically of a CTO (leaving aside questions of its likely efficacy or effectiveness).[34] One view is that clients have the 'right to be well' and, in pursuing that, they have the right to the 'least restrictive' means of achieving it.[35] However, such a view is usually predicated on a notion that the client is unable fully to decide for herself. It follows, therefore, that only if the latter is satisfied can it be right ethically to override a client's stated wishes. Of course, what may still be at issue is the definition and threshold for being 'unable', and whether it is merely equated with 'lack of insight', as well as how either lack of capacity or insight is interpreted in the context of a fluctuating mental state. This perhaps goes to the heart of the ethical debate, and ultimately the ethical relationship.

Perhaps of further crucial importance in this context are the importance both of training *per se* and of joint training of mental health staff. This is not to encourage or require uniformity of ethics but at least uniformity of understanding of the ethical issues, as well as of the substantive law and of its interface with clinical data and care. Such joint training would not (and perhaps should not) achieve uniformity of views about the threshold for detention under the Act but it would elaborate and make clear the bases of any differences of thresholds.

RECONCILING PERSPECTIVES

Building into service delivery a proper respect for the views of users and patients is not likely to be easy. However, if the resultant clinico-legal framework is to be culturally and socially sensitive, it is imperative that incorporation of users' views be achieved. Moreover, where service users are thought of as one undifferentiated group, further discrimination occurs against the very young, the very

---

[33] Burns (personal communication).
[34] Again see Eastman, Zigmond and McIver (1998).
[35] Dyer, J. (1998).

old, women, ethnic minorities, the disabled and the deprived. As Conlan has remarked, service users should not be protected from information and involvement in decisions which directly affect them; this is neatly summarised in her personal credo 'Nothing About Us Without Us'. The incorporation of service users' views should not be perceived therefore solely as a means of trying to shore up and protect patients against services that might be detrimental to their well-being; for many of the improvements in mental health services in recent years have been driven by the service user/survivor movement. These improvements include extended visiting hours, easier access, home treatment, emphases on the importance of quality of life and good therapeutic relationships, links to housing, benefits, employment, the involvement of people in planning and monitoring their services, and, of course, the establishment of independent advocacy aimed at redressing the balance of power. Even some of the organisational changes and homicide inquiry recommendations have served users well; the care programme approach has also enabled some psychiatrists to negotiate flexibly on leave arrangements; community mental health teams do co-ordinate support arrangements; joint assessments and training have simplified much of the paperwork.

The negative impact of special legislation is only one element in the kaleidoscope of factors which influence how doctors and patients perceive one another. Independent advocacy can serve not only to help patients leave hospital when there is no basis for their detention but can also, and equally importantly, help them to get into hospital, or into treatment, at a stage when treatment can be offered and accepted on a voluntary basis. Regular service users and those with long-term mental health problems have independent knowledge about what services and which drugs suit them best (in much the same way that those with long-term back problems may have learnt that a maintenance trip once every six months to a chiropractic can prevent the onset of problems or that, for those with persistent headaches, ibuprofen rather than Aspirin does the trick). How to ensure that this knowledge is both conveyed to and valued by those offering health care is another matter. For, as one articulate service user remarked "I've 30 years in the system, and it's taken me 25 to get an agreement not to be given Melleril rather than chlorpromazine".

The justification for the individual use of detention might also be clarified, to advantage; patients may accept the use of compulsion where it is designed to keep them safe, but resent its use where the primary purpose is to administer treatment on a compulsory basis. In conditions of detention the notion of genuine consent is untenable; even mere assent by the patient may leave them with a memory of de-personalisation, which may subsequently influence their decisions about future treatment. The confusion between decisions being taken which properly reflect the patient's interests, and those giving primacy to his or her family or carers, or of the ill-defined interests of wider society, needs to be laid bare. Moreover, the public health costs of imposing treatment on one individual, arising from the potential alienation of future patients, should not be underestimated. That a Mental Health Act Commissioner can describe the use of rooms for the seclusion of patients, when they are at their most disturbed, as miserable, dirty and bare is sufficiently galling. For that Commissioner further to be able to describe practices where patients are told that if they leave unlocked 'seclusion' areas without permission they will be deprived of their meals clearly demonstrates unacceptable procedures.[36] Such practices reflect an attitude to the mentally ill which should have been consigned to history long ago. Like previous attitudes to slavery and to the export of children to the colonies, it devalues both those practising within and those subjected to such regimes.

[36] Zigmond (1995).

6

Law as a Clinical Tool: Practising Within and Outwith the Law

IAN BYNOE and ANTHONY HOLLAND

The Mental Health Act 1983 brings with it unique powers within the field of medicine. It gives special powers to a particular group of medical specialists, 'psychiatrists', to override a fundamental principle within our society, that of autonomy. The Act, and its use and abuse, is inevitably open to different interpretations, which can be at their most striking when the different perspectives of clinicians and lawyers are involved. This chapter deliberately attempts both to polarise and to reconcile these diverse perspectives.

It is the implication for an individual's liberty that quite rightly focusses considerable attention on mental health legislation. Yet, most people either receive treatment for their mental disorder out of hospital and with their consent or, if necessary, come into hospital voluntarily. Fundamentally, the Act serves to enable the lawful treatment of people who have a mental disorder and are unwilling to accept treatment for that disorder. In contrast to the treatment of physical illness, where a competent adult can decline treatment even if the consequences for them are serious, in the case of mental disorder individual autonomy can be overridden. As we discuss in more detail later, the criteria for its use go beyond the issue of the person's mental health but also include matters concerning the individual's general health, his/her safety and public safety. Furthermore, the criteria do not fundamentally relate to the question of an individual's capacity to determine for him/herself whether to accept or reject treatment advice.

When considering how this Act is used and misused and how it might be reformed, we need to place our observations in their appropriate context. This context is shaped by the recent past and present-day political and economic climate, and by attitudes engendered in society, such as retribution for those who offend, public fear of the mentally ill, and the wish to allocate blame when things go wrong or are perceived to have gone wrong. Furthermore, mental health is concerned with human feelings and behaviour, both notoriously difficult to ascertain and predict. It is also concerned with the experiences and actions of many professionals who make good and bad judgements under varying conditions. For clinicians there are many grey areas, but the clinician's view of the law and of lawyers is that it and they assume that something or somebody has to be either right or wrong, lawful or unlawful, guilty or not guilty. There is no room for greyness. The issues we address below need to be seen in this context.

THE 1983 ACT AND THE CLINICIAN

What purpose does using the Act serve for the clinician? The superficial answer is that it enables him/her legally to treat an individual's mental disorder within the safeguards of an appeal system. However, two cases recently decided by our senior appellate courts illuminate the issues raised by this question.[1] In the *Bournewood* case, the statutory regime for the admission and treatment of a patient with mental impairment was not used by the professional carers of a man with autism. Instead, they relied on their understanding of a common law principle – supported by legal academic opinion and a long-standing practice affecting tens of thousands of admissions – that someone whose mental disorder was such that they could not consent to admission could nevertheless be received into a psychiatric hospital and treated there as an in-patient without legal formalities.

By his next friend and carer, the patient challenged this assumption, arguing that the only means by which medical and nursing professionals could admit and treat him in hospital in the way they planned was under the 1983 Act. When the Court of Appeal accepted this argument, ruling that the patient was unlawfully detained unless he was admitted formally under the Act the ramifications for clinical practice became suddenly apparent. Many thousands of admissions undertaken without formality would now need to be effected using the statutory procedures and criteria of the Act. Many thousands of inpatients would need to have their status reviewed and, if necessary, changed to reflect this new interpretation of the common law and of the role of the Act. The Court of Appeal did not question that the patient's doctor had acted according to her judgement of what was in his best interests. However, in the future, it decided, those contemplating such clinical interventions would need to fit them within the statutory regime before they could be lawfully implemented. The NHS Trust involved appealed and the House of Lords unanimously disagreed and ruled that the admission had been lawful.[2] However, one of the judges drew attention to what he considered was a serious gap in current law. Lord Steyn expressed his misgivings as follows:

[1] *L v. Bournewood Community Mental Health NHS Trust* [1998]; *R. v. Bournewood Community and Mental Health NHS Trust, ex parte L (Secretary of State for Health and others intervening)* [1998]; *St George's Healthcare NHS Trust v. S* [1998], *R. v. Collins and Others, ex parte S* [1998].

[2] Two out of the five judges decided that the patient had been detained, albeit lawfully. The matter may now be pursued under the European Convention on Human Rights (ECHR). If the majority had found a detention took place, it is hard to envisage the European Court of Human Rights (ECtHR) not then requiring formal protections and a judicial review of the need for it, as provided in the ECHR.

"If the decision of the Court of Appeal is reversed almost all the basic protections under the Act of 1983 will be inapplicable to compliant incapacitated patients. The result would be an indefensible gap in our mental health law . . . how we address the intractable problems of mental health care for all classes of mentally incapacitated patients must be a touchstone of our maturity as a civilised society. . . . Given that [compliant incapacitated patients] are indistinguishable from compulsory patients there is no reason to withhold the specific and effective protections of the Act of 1983 from a large class of vulnerable mentally incapacitated patients".[3]

The key issues in the *Bournewood* case were the following. The purpose of admission was said to be for assessment of the person's mental disorder; the person concerned lacked capacity to consent; and the admission was opposed by his main carers in the community, who wished for him to return home. There can be little doubt that, if admission was required, the Act was there to enable such a course of action to take place, and therefore in this case should have been used. Most importantly it would also have enabled an appeal to take place (which is what eventually happened). The wider concerns raised about the numbers who would be affected, were practice to change, partly reflects the current state of services: people with severe learning disabilities or dementia, in parts of the country, still live in places designated as hospitals or mental health nursing homes rather than in group homes. If living in the former, the Act might have to be used; if in the latter the common law 'best interests' principle would be the justification. For many, hospital would have been their home and admission would have been for respite, not fundamentally for the treatment of a mental disorder. It was these inconsistencies, together with concerns over the representation of vulnerable people in whatever the social care setting, that *Bournewood* brought to public consciousness.

The *St George's* case concerned not bypassing the Act but its controversial use. Here, the Court of Appeal decided that section 2 of the Act had been improperly and unjustifiably used to admit and detain a pregnant woman who refused to allow the delivery of her baby by cæsarian section. Once she was admitted the NHS Trust sought and obtained (in her absence and without her being represented) a High Court order permitting the delivery to go ahead despite her objections. The appeal court did not doubt that the health care staff and social worker were motivated by a genuine desire to act in the woman's best interests. However, its decision reminded health-care professionals that even the best of ethical motives for a clinical intervention will not assist them if compulsion steps beyond accepted boundaries. Lord Justice Judge expressed this principle as follows:

The Act cannot be deployed to achieve the detention of an individual against her will merely because her thinking process is unusual, even apparently bizarre and irrational, and contrary to the views of the overwhelming majority of the community at large. . . . Even when used by well intentioned individuals for what they believe to be

[3] R v. *Bournewood Community and Mental Health NHS Trust, ex parte L* [1998] 3 WLR 107 at p. 124.

genuine and powerful reasons, perhaps shared by a large section of the community, unless the individual case falls within the prescribed conditions the Act cannot be used to justify detention for mental disorder.[3a]

These two cases throw into sharp relief how the Act may be currently understood by practitioners and also highlights the value which a clinician may place on a statutory regime in order to sanction treatment. Though each arose from particular facts, unusual ones in the latter case, the cases and their outcomes demonstrate the potential gap which may emerge between the law's expectations and a clinician's intentions. In both cases the courts did not question the honourable intentions of the clinicians concerned. However, what was striking was that these intentions did not extend to ensuring that a mechanism existed for putting an alternative point of view by means of a formal appeal procedure.[4] Examining this gap, analysing what may cause it and its significance, is the subject of this chapter.

Throughout, we contrast how the aim of using the law effectively may differ from the concept of clinical effectiveness. In some circumstances, these ideas may exactly correspond and be seen to do so in practice. Other situations will present a more complex and confusing picture. For, on occasions, a doctor may regard the law's requirements as irrelevant or counter to the objectives of planned therapy, and the best ways of providing it. Our investigation aims to pinpoint the factors which affect clinicians' relationships with the law; these include the law's own distinctive qualities, medical knowledge about the law and its philosophy, and practitioner confidence when using it.

It focuses on the following main questions. What is the 'fit' between clinical practice and law? Where clinical practice diverges from Parliament's apparent intentions expressed in statutory mental health law does this show the law to be ineffective or the doctor's judgement poor or ill-informed? If the former, this may amount to evidence of the need for changes in practice *or* for the law to be amended and to be given fresh and more relevant roles. If the latter, then where are medical training and continuous professional development failing? Perhaps it does it not have to be one or the other: an apparent divergence may be a reflection of how difficult some decisions can be, being dilemmas with no clear or right answer. Lastly, are there new approaches which might revive the usefulness of law in the clinical setting and give it a fresh relevance?

The questions which we raise are timely in view of policy proposals being currently considered and the increasing importance given to questions of capacity, consent and professional accountability. The Law Commission's work on mental incapacity, and the Government's acceptance of much of what it recommended,[5] create the prospect of major law reform in the field of mental disorder and medical treatment. There is a wide-ranging consensus on the principles

---

[3a] See note 1 above.

[4] In the *St George's* case, the Hospital sought a High Court order permitting the cæsarean but did not inform either the patient or her solicitor of this application, which was made *ex parte*.

[5] Lord Chancellor's Department (1997).

which should drive such changes and on the system of rights and duties which should be established to implement them.

If this happens, and new legislation is enacted to run in parallel with the 1983 Act, there will be many striking differences between the new system governing decision-making for adults lacking capacity and that provided by mental health legislation. The former is likely to adopt a functional, decision-specific approach which is in stark contrast to the status approach found with the latter. Here the assessment and treatment of mental disorder, in the absence of an individual's consent, is singled out for special consideration if their health or safety, or the safety of others, is judged to be at risk. Unless the gap between these two quite different approaches is bridged, there is a risk of a two-tier system developing, giving greater rights protection to one group of patients than to another with equal needs.

During the last ten years, a series of medical law cases[6] and other innovations[7] have highlighted the significance of consent to treatment and the role of the clinician in determining decision-making capacity. On the one hand, this unprecedented development has emphasised the need to win the co-operation and agreement of the patient who is able to provide valid consent. On the other, it has reinforced the power of the medical practitioner to determine what treatment would be in the 'best interests' of a patient unable to do this, and accordingly encouraged demands for greater professional accountability when the power is exercised.

Lastly, politicians have revived the possibility of introducing a community treatment order to extend the compulsory powers found in the Act to people after they have been fully discharged from hospital and from liability to detention under the Act. How relevant is the new focus on incapacity to the arguments for and against a community treatment order, and would such powers be used if the law was changed to provide for this?

THE CONTEXT FOR USING THE LAW

Law in the field of psychiatric practice is fashioned with certain ethical assumptions in mind. Before describing how legislation is, or is not, used by clinicians we need to outline these broad principles. We shall see that it is to define and limit these that an explicit statutory regime is required at all.

---

[6] See *Re F* [1990] (sterilisation of adult learning-disabled woman); *Airedale NHS Trust* v. *Bland* [1993] (withdrawal of feeding to adult man in PVS); *Re C* (Refusal of medical treatment) [1994] (declaration preventing amputation of mentally ill man with gangrene refusing treatment); In *Re MB* (Cæsarean section) [1997] (refusal of cæsarean section delivery by woman with needle phobia).

[7] See e.g. Mental Health Act Code of Practice (DoH and Welsh Office (1993)), chap. 15, containing explicit guidance on the provision of medical treatment to people suffering from mental disorder; Department of Health Guidance issued following recent rulings: EL(97)32 "Consent to Treatment—Summary of Legal Rulings"; the Patient's Charter standard on consent and information: Department of Health (1995).

Medicine is not practised in isolation from the system of prevailing social values which sanction private and public behaviour. Our society, in particular, promotes the importance of individual human value and worth and its major ethical principles – of privacy and personal autonomy, equal treatment and equal opportunity – flow from this idea of 'prized individualism'. The development of the notion of consent, and the presumption that an adult person has the capacity to give this, directly express these principles, as does the therapeutic imperative itself: to cure illness and improve health is to increase the capacity for individual autonomy, independence and achievement. These fundamentals therefore affect not just the practice of psychiatry but all of medicine and, at their best, work to the betterment of the 'patient' and the satisfaction of the health professional. There has, however, been a shift from the attitude best characterised by the phrase 'doctor knows best' to encouraging a greater independence of thinking among the general population and an acknowledgement of the need to question and challenge professional opinion. For the medical profession there has been the need to adjust to such changes, and with it the recognition that people may make different decisions from those the doctor him/herself has recommended, or might have made if in the same position. Health professionals may therefore have to face wanting to treat a patient, and having the means to do so, but not being able to because the patient him/herself does not wish for the treatment and therefore will not consent.

However, psychiatrists, uniquely, can step outside this ethical framework and both initiate and utilize the effect of procedures by which someone may be detained in hospital and receive treatment specifically for a mental disorder without their consent and without even any need to consider the person's capacity to decide whether or not to agree. And, since the House of Lords' decision in the *Bournewood* case, where capacity is tested and found to be wanting, the common law permits a practitioner to admit and treat a person if that would broadly serve their 'best interests'. What might justify the use of such powers – and prompt clinicians to employ them?

The right to treatment

According to this principle, steps should be taken to enable someone affected by mental disorder to obtain medical treatment which he/she would otherwise not seek or would irrationally refuse. Mentally disordered people, it is argued, should not be prevented from participating in the benefits of medical treatment and care which could benefit them. The clinician becomes the advocate of their right to treatment and its facilitator.

English statutory mental health law reflects this principle in the power which it gives to medical practitioners to recommend a person's compulsory admission to hospital in the interests of their health alone.[8] The legal threshold for using

---

[8] See criteria for admission to hospital found in s. 3(2)(c) Mental Health Act 1983.

this is not that the person lacks capacity to decide for themselves whether they are ill and what treatment is called for – an 'incapacity threshold'. The test is lower and is met as soon as practitioners agree that a person's condition is serious enough to warrant the planned intervention, that treatment in hospital is needed, is appropriate and could not be given unless the person was detained there – a 'necessity/appropriateness threshold'. Given that this constitutes the current standard, a person is unable, by executing an advance directive, even when possessing full capacity, to prevent the Act being used to compel them to receive psychiatric treatment on some future date were they to lose capacity.

That the aim of the 1983 Act is not to focus on the question of capacity but the desirability and benefit of treatment was reinforced by the Court of Appeal's decision in *B v. Croydon District Health Authority*.[9] In this case the court declared that a patient detained under section 3 of the Act and held to have full capacity to consent to treatment or refuse it could nevertheless still be force fed under the Act, since this constituted "medical treatment" within section 63 and was therefore authorised by the statute.

As it is understood, the right to treatment principle would justify not any or all treatments but *only* those considered appropriate to the person's disorder or illness; which would improve it or prevent its further deterioration; and which could be administered without undue risk of adverse or unforeseen harm. For this reason Part IV of the Act regulates medical treatment for mental disorder, creating particular protections for treatments which are considered more potentially harmful or controversial.

Rescue

The second broad justification for a clinical intervention could be termed the 'rescue' principle. This would sanction intervening to prevent a person from harming him or herself when, due to their mental disorder, they are unable to control self-destructive impulses which may themselves be symptoms of that disorder.

The Act – and, to a far more limited extent, the common law – incorporate the rescue principle. Someone may be admitted under the Act to hospital for assessment or for treatment in the interests of their own safety. The most obvious example is that of depression and the associated risk of suicide. An individual's mental state might be such that he/she feels worthless and believes that they and society would be better off if he/she were dead. Such feelings would not normally have been present and will resolve when the depression responds to treatment. Similarly, under common law, someone may be physically restrained from harming themselves whilst the risk of this happening persists.

[9] [1995].

Third-party protection

This third and final principle provides justification for detaining a person for medical treatment or restraining them – by, for example, the use of supervised discharge – in order to prevent the person from acting in any way which is reckoned to create an unacceptable risk of harm to someone else. The principle is still found within our common law, though is now more fully incorporated into statutory mental health legislation. This gives health and social care professionals and courts very extensive powers preventively to detain someone 'for the protection of others'. Additional restrictions are available to regulate discharge into the community and the supervision there of patients who pose especial risk of harm to the public.

CURRENT PRACTICE: AN ANALYSIS

Such powers under the Act require that the person has a mental disorder of "a nature or degree" that detention in hospital is appropriate and that detention in hospital is required so that he/she can receive treatment (section 3). Treatment is broadly defined in the Act, and phrases such as "nature or degree" and "treatment" are open to wide interpretation. An additional factor, which all parties, particularly the approved social worker (ASW), have to consider is the question of alternative possibilities other than detention. Whether it is for the person's health, safety or for the safety of the public it is not simply a matter of the presence or not of a mental disorder and its likely effects on a person's behaviour, but also some consideration of what accommodation and support is available to the person concerned out of hospital.

Such considerations are very reasonable, but they mean that at many points in the decision-making process discretion can be exercised. These opportunities may be used wisely, or may reflect inappropriate attitudes of the staff of a particular service, or may be influenced, for example, by limited resources or poor liaison within and between services. Those clearly developing serious mental illness are not followed up, not admitted when they should have been and perhaps already have a reputation that has alienated them from the service. We further consider these factors below.

There are three situations in which it is of value to examine how clinicians approach the law, the opportunities which it provides and its requirements: first, where a practitioner declines to establish any clinical relationship at all with a potential patient; secondly, where there is a clinical relationship with the patient but the practitioner does not place this within the formal statutory framework provided by the 1983 Act; and thirdly, where a clinical relationship has been established which is supported by the Act, but where practice diverges from the standards required within that framework.

No *clinical relationship*

The mere existence of mental health legislation with a wide potential coverage does not mean that it is applied by clinicians on each and every occasion when this could lawfully occur. For example, many prisoners or persons detained in police custody who display signs of mental illness could properly be admitted to hospital and treated under the Act or, in the case of the former, even informally, but do not receive any opportunity of doing so or are assessed for and then refused it.

When practitioners decide not to admit the person to their service it follows that the Act will not be used. Though transfers of mentally ill inmates from prison custody to NHS services have risen throughout the 1990s a significant number continue to remain in settings entirely unfitted for their mental health needs leading on occasions to tragic consequences.[10] Why may this be? Perhaps such decisions reflect different tensions.

First, those working in the prison service need to recognise that a person has a mental health problem but the fact that someone is withdrawn or muttering to themselves may, at one extreme, be seen as an understandable response to incarceration and, at the other, a deliberate attempt to avoid prison. Therefore referral does not take place.

Secondly, other influences include perceptions about the relative supremacy of either treatment or containment, moral judgements such as 'bad versus mad', and the stresses experienced by, and the attitude of, psychiatrists and others in the mental health services reflected in a willingness or not to accept patients. Past experience of violence or the knowledge that someone has been 'difficult' may be sufficient for an over-stretched service to look for a way out, a reason for not having to admit. In other settings, where a bed is readily available and staff morale is good, a different decision might have been made.

Finally, a further factor that may be important is one of responsibility within the context of a culture which looks to apportion blame when something is believed to have gone wrong. If an individual is detained under the Act there are clear responsibilities placed on the psychiatrist and other staff. If it can be argued that this person does not meet criteria for detention then the responsibility for his or her behaviour remains with that person. This is particularly relevant where there are doubts about the exact nature of a person's mental disorder and the likely efficacy of treatment, for example in the case of someone diagnosed as having a psychopathic personality disorder.

Informal clinical relationship

In the second situation, a patient–doctor relationship is established and medical treatment is provided, but the clinician chooses not to use legal procedures

[10] See Coonan *et al.* (1998).

available to him or her under the Act. This is most commonly seen with the admission and treatment of incapacitated and non-consenting patients, not thought to need sectioning under statute until the Court of Appeal in the *Bournewood* case declared that they did.

In the course of the appeal to the House of Lords, the Mental Health Act Commission estimated that 48,000 admissions *per annum* were, prior to the decision, arranged informally which, if the Court of Appeal's ruling prevailed, would in future have to be completed formally under the Act. The Commission estimated that the total average number of detained patients resident in hospitals in England and Wales from time to time would rise by 22,000. The House of Lords allowed the appeal, ruling that formalities are not needed where a person lacks capacity but is compliant. Although the Department of Health has issued fresh guidance, we are bound to see a rapid return to this long-standing practice for the vast majority of admissions falling into this category.

For lawyers, the injustice is that a course of action can take place without consent (because the person lacks the capacity to give this) and without recourse to an immediate appeal procedure. For the clinician, there is the knowledge that people who may lack capacity, such as those with dementia or severe learning disabilities, have always had many decisions made on their behalf. These have concerned day-to-day matters, such as what the person should wear, to more significant questions concerning, for example, where he or she should live.

Although the legal significance of such actions is rarely appreciated, they are examples of common law 'best interests' decisions being made on a daily basis. Whilst major changes in attitudes have resulted in, by and large, better practice and greater attempts to consult the individual concerned, it is what is available and the resources which can be found that will have a major influence on where that person lives. Do those lacking capacity who still happen to live in what is designated a hospital really need to be detained? In many cases, all the necessary criteria would not be met; the person does not have to be in hospital for treatment of his/her mental disorder; he or she may not even meet the necessary criteria for any of the four defined mental disorders and for these reasons could not be detained but would remain living in hospital, as it was in his/her best interest, given that it was home; or the admission was for respite care for relatives. These distinctions are being made all the time. They are highlighted only when a case such as *Bournewood* is taken, illustrating the vulnerability of an individual to the decisions of others. Then the tussle over who determines 'best interests' comes to light. The delicate balance is to ensure, on the one hand, that vulnerable people receive the care that they need and, where specific treatment is required, it is provided and of a good standard and, on the other, that individual autonomy is respected. Where this is not possible, due to an individual's lack of capacity to make a particular decision, consultation between all relevant parties should determine what is truly in that person's 'best interests'.

To a lesser extent the limited use of either guardianship or after-care under supervision reflects a similar approach except in the community. Practitioners consciously decline to acquire and deploy statutory powers which they could obtain relatively easily under the administrative procedures provided by the Act.

Formal clinical relationship

The third and final perspective is obtained from considering what happens when the clinician treats the patient within the statutory framework. In a majority of cases, practice corresponds to the standards and expectations set by the Act, the regulations and the Code of Practice made under it. However, this cannot be said for all the occasions when the Act is used. The Mental Health Act Commission in its Biennial Reports has reported deficiencies in legal compliance which have been commonly discovered by its visiting teams during their monitoring operations. Inquiry reports into recent homicides or other untoward incidents have also highlighted where clinical or administrative practice has not met the necessary legal standards.[11] The following are given as illustrations only:

- The admission of patients under section 2 when section 3 should have been used and would have availed the patient of section 117 aftercare services when he or she came to be discharged from hospital.
- The admission of patients under section 4 on the basis of a sole medical recommendation due to the administrative non-availability of a section 12 approved doctor rather than any genuine psychiatric emergency.
- Over-use of the section 5(2) medical holding power shortly after admission, casting doubt on the grounds for believing the patient freely agreed to be admitted to hospital.
- Maladministration in relation to decisions to give patients leave of absence from hospital under section 17 of the Act.[12]
- Maladministration in relation to the detailed requirements concerning medical treatment found in Part IV of the Act, the regulations and chapter 16 of the 1993 edition of the Code of Practice.

Factors affecting clinical use of the law

It is not difficult to see why clinicians may choose to employ legal procedures under the Act in the course of their practice. Powers obtained in this way may be deployed to increase clinical authority over the choice of treatment, its administration and location and in managing restrictions on the physical freedom of a non-compliant patient, so as to protect public safety or reduce the risk

---

[11] Crichton and Sheppard (1996).
[12] Poor practice in relation to s. 17 leave was also highlighted by the report of the Inquiry into the events leading up to and surrounding the fatal incident at the Edith Morgan Centre, Torbay, on 1 Sep. 1993. See Blom-Cooper *et al.* (1995).

of self-harm. This is, of course, what is expected of psychiatrists when faced with a person clearly mentally ill, in distress and thinking and/or behaving in a manner that puts them or others at risk. Authority to enable this is necessary and its use in appropriate circumstances is expected.

Sometimes, a judicial ruling is needed to ensure that the spirit of the law is not overly stretched. For example, until it was declared unlawful,[13] the use made by clinicians of repeat section 3 admissions combined with the routine granting of section 17 leave to perpetuate a form of community treatment order provides ample evidence of clinical enthusiasm for using the law when it is seen to achieve their aims.

Sometimes the law is used to extend responsibility for decision-making beyond the clinician. The Act brings with it enhanced professional accountability and the involvement of independent parties in key decisions: hospital managers, the MHRT, the ASW and the nearest relative. This may be thought by practitioners to help to clarify for the clinician and others the respective responsibilities of agencies and individuals involved in someone's care, providing a framework within which contrary opinions or interests can be accommodated or fairly overruled. The appeal procedure is essential, but its use can be both constructive and destructive. In the former, MHRTs can be a force to focus purchasers and providers on the task of providing appropriate after-care. In the latter, services see MHRTs as usurping powers that are rightfully theirs and respond with resentment if the MHRT arrives at a different opinion to that of the clinical team.

What may explain the reason for divergent practice is far harder to uncover. A more complex and varied picture emerges. Some variations are seen in the individual practice of many different psychiatrists and other professionals. Other approaches are widely, even universally, observed. At least five separate factors can be readily identified.

General characteristics of mental health law

The main purposes served by the law in the practice of psychiatry can be summarised as follows:

- It can provide authority for clinical decisions and actions where otherwise this would be lacking.
- Where it is engaged, it provides a review system capable of overruling practitioner decisions (the MHRT) or investigating complaints of improper use of the law (the MHAC).
- Legislation and regulations, as well as guidance can establish a threshold standard or approach (for example, in rights to consultation, information,

[13] *R. v. Hallstrom, ex parte W; R. v. Gardner, ex parte L* [1986]; see now also *R v. BHB Community Healthcare NHS Trust and Another ex parte Barker* (1998) CA which held that S.3 detention *could* be renewed pursuant to S.20, where the patient had been granted lengthy leave of absence, provided that treatment, viewed as a whole, involved in-patient treatment.

reasons for decisions etc.), especially important where third-party interests such as the need for public protection are claimed to justify restrictions on a person's liberty.

- Systems of legal accountability in general require objectivity and formal openness. This can help to make explicit all relevant factors leading to decisions and help to reduce or avoid bias or unfair discrimination.

In attempting to fulfil these objectives, mental health law has developed distinctive qualities. A number of its characteristics clearly help to explain how it comes to be used in practice. Substantively, it is drafted in a fairly general and adaptable fashion. Terms such as 'health', 'mental illness', 'treatment' are either not defined or are very broadly defined.

The criteria needing to be fulfilled for interventions under the Act, such as for admission to hospital, are vague. Most patients enter hospital via the administrative, civil route, not from the criminal courts. Thus, the decision to use or not to use the law is now almost exclusively the responsibility of professionals. In these circumstances, the Act assumes that the specifics needed to determine whether or not to apply its provisions will emerge from a combination of professional judgement and discretion, not the operation of a comprehensive body of prescriptive regulations.

Even standard civil admission forms call for little in the way of full and thorough explanation. No formal agreed risk assessment or individual care plan has to accompany the medical recommendations supporting an application for inpatient admission. Professionals are trusted not to exercise their skills carelessly or improperly.

Procedural duties are more precisely described, but even these are mainly administrative and, compared to other systems regulating the deprivation of liberty,[14] can hardly be considered onerous or excessively bureaucratic. Most of the detail is delivered in administrative practice guidance found in the Code of Practice, not in mandatory regulations.

This is how the law has been written: to be used pragmatically and flexibly in order to cover a vast range of differing situations. It is permissive rather than prescriptive, accommodating individual professional and service variations and approaches. As a result, it is possible that alternative and parallel criteria – drawn from professional, not legal, perspectives – are used to aid the practical interpretation of uncertain legislation. Thus, medical practitioners may use rule-of-thumb tests such as a patient's possession or lack of 'insight' to indicate whether or when to seek the legal power to compel treatment or solely "danger to self or to others" to establish the risk justifying forced detention in hospital.

It would be hard to deny that the latter test has been widely applied in practice as a criterion for using the Act to admit to hospital. In 1993 the Department

---

[14] See, e.g., the elaborate provisions regulating the detention of suspects in police custody found in the Police and Criminal Evidence Act 1984 and the mandatory Codes of Practice made under it, breach of which may lead to disciplinary action.

of Health introduced changes to the Act's Code of Practice specifically designed to remind social work and medical practitioners of the criteria for possible admission to hospital and that concerns for safety did not have to be present if the interests of the person's health were sufficient to justify making an application.[15]

Clinical autonomy

By training and vocation, medical practitioners and other health and social care professionals will perceive their personal authority resting on foundations other than the law: a body of expert knowledge and an ability to understand, explain or communicate technical information and to judge its relevance to human experience and the prediction of behaviour.

This may lead the practitioner to have little affinity for the law and its ways. It represents unfamiliar territory where the use of concepts, deployment of argument and weighing of evidence differ greatly from how each of these is done in medical practice. However much the law may offer the clinician a useful reinforcement to their authority, it is still regarded by many as something 'out there' rather than fully integrated into practice. Its methods, the completion of standard documentation or written reporting, for example, are regarded as cumbersome and bureaucratic.

This deep-seated attitude is no more clearly seen than in clinicians' reactions to the recent clarification by the courts of the constituent elements of decision-making capacity according to common law.[16] For the first time there is now a degree of certainty about the respective legal powers of the doctor and the corresponding rights of the patient. Yet, how many clinicians could be said truly to welcome these latest results of judicial activism? Furthermore, the fact that common law provides a defence for a particular course of action, not an authorisation (as is the case with the Act), creates further anxiety.

The limits of law

One reason for variation and 'under use' of the Act may be that the law is still seen as only peripheral to what matters in the doctor–patient relationship. Using a process of negotiation, the relationship is seen mainly to depend on winning the co-operation of the patient in their therapy, not compelling them to have something they object to. The potential contribution which the use of legal procedures can make to this endeavour may be limited or even negative. Law may be the solution of last resort, with its own damaging adverse effects on working relationships.

The law is seen by others as limited, in an entirely different respect – it does not enable the clinician to compel treatment where this is deemed to be neces-

---

[15] Department of Health and Welsh Office (1993).
[16] See the cases referred to in n. 6 above.

sary, in relation to patients living in the community. The 'soft' powers available to the appointed guardian or after-care supervisor under the Act are perceived as inadequate for managing such patients' compliance with the medication prescribed for them.

The practical difficulties of using legal powers are also seen to limit its usefulness, particularly in community settings. This is one of the objections which is made to the introduction of a community treatment order (CTO). Although the law might provide for a community nurse or doctor to have powers to compel treatment, practical considerations would inhibit the use of those powers away from hospital settings. No-one, for example, suggests that a non-compliant patient, subject to any new treatment order, should be forced to be injected in their own home.

The resources template

As discussed earlier, mental health law is not practised in a textbook vacuum but largely within a public sector possessing only finite resources. Their availability in a general sense and the services provided in individual cases are therefore likely to influence how legislation is interpreted and applied. The level of in-patient bed occupancy may determine in practice whether or not an application is made for compulsory admission; the demand for scarce accommodation may influence the time when someone will be discharged on leave or from section.

It was vigorously argued in *Bournewood* that the resources required to admit and treat incapacitated patients under the Act rather than informally would severely test local services, consuming a wholly disproportionate share of their limited staff resources. Concerns mainly focused on the additional paperwork associated with use of the Act, extra visits and liaison with and attendance at, hearings and meetings of the hospital's Mental Health Act Managers. In the same case, in the Court of Appeal, the Bournewood NHS Trust opposed the use of the Act, on the ground that if this were required routinely, it would create an unforeseen and intolerable demand for section 117 after-care services. Such an emphasis on services and practices rather than principle is clearly regrettable.

Stigma and social discrimination

A reluctance by clinicians to resort to law is sometimes justified due to the stigma believed to be associated with this – a perception probably shared by patients, family and the wider public. The Code of Practice draws attention to this. It specifically obliges professionals conducting an assessment prior to admission to have regard to "the impact that compulsory admission would have on the patient's life after discharge from detention".[17] Concerns centre on the

---

[17] DoH and Welsh Office (1993) at para. 2.6.

difficulties which someone who has been detained will face when travelling abroad, applying for insurance or seeking work, particularly in sensitive employments.

We cannot measure accurately what unfair disadvantage results from use of the law to add to the stigma which arises simply from diagnosis, in-patient admission and treatment. There can be no doubt, though, that fears about stigma, particularly expressed by family members, influence practice in the treatment of adolescents and in the hospital admission of compliant adults who nevertheless lack capacity.

NON-CONFORMING PRACTICE: WHOSE PROBLEM?

We have outlined above a number of ways in which psychiatric practice could be expected to avoid what the law might intend or require. Is this is a problem? If so, is it practitioners' behaviour which needs to change, or should the law be reformed?

It would be wrong to attempt any generalised answer, valid for each of the three different situations outlined above. Where no clinical relationship exists, it may be regrettable if the law inhibits in some way the provision of a service where one could be beneficial but its contribution to this happening could only be marginal. A shortage of resources, competing priorities, the current configuration of services and individual clinical considerations are singly, or in combination, far more likely to be significant in this situation. Changing the law could do little or nothing to change practice if these other factors remained unchanged.

Where treatment is given under the Act and poor compliance with the law or maladministration is identified, it is not hard to suggest how this might be tackled: first, a better and sounder grounding by all concerned in the legal principles highlighted in this chapter and a genuine appreciation of the various tensions and dilemmas in the field is essential; secondly, improved monitoring by bodies such as the MHAC. Other changes could also play a part in raising performance: more effective, initial and in-service practice training; clearer guidance; and tougher standards required by NHS purchasers.

What of the situation where a clinical relationship exists but this is not affected by the current Act. Here, most clinicians would regard the legislative framework provided under that Act as neither relevant or necessary: a scenario highlighted by what happened in *Bournewood*. Yet ensuring that psychiatric treatment for any patient who may lack capacity is only given according to a set of clear and contemporary legal standards and procedures would fulfil some well-recognised objectives:

- It would identify more clearly where it is justified to intervene without authority derived from the person's own consent – against defined standards which incorporate only those widely recognised ethical principles which permit professionals to make medical treatment decisions on behalf of their patient.

- It would introduce a system of independent and objective review for a vulnerable patient group, unable on their own to hold professionals to account.
- It would encourage minimum standards of fairness in the process of decision-making, especially important where the views of significant family members or carers may differ from those of the clinical team.

That the current Act is not used in these circumstances suggests to us that it may not be appropriate to this task. Clinicians, managers and many carers voiced objections to taking the route signalled by the Court of Appeal's decision in *Bournewood* and in the guidance from the MHAC which followed it. Lord Steyn in *Bournewood* warned that: "[p]rofessions are seldom enthusiastic about protective measures to guard against lapses by their members. And health care professionals are probably no different." However, such reactions cannot just be dismissed as the predictable complaints of professionals preferring informal practice to working to legal standards and procedures. What is needed is a new legal code which reflects modern expectations of professional accountability and rights protection, and yet which is also practical, easy and inexpensive to operate and non-stigmatising.

WHERE NEXT?

In a number of respects, the Act does not meet these requirements. Its necessity/appropriateness threshold for interventions reflects an earlier, more paternalistic age when medical practitioners could assume their decisions would carry authority simply for being those of an experienced professional. The ethical debate has moved on, in parallel with common law developments that highlight the crucial importance of capacity and in government policy towards those unable to make valid decisions because they lack it.

In future, non-volitional treatment should only be justified in two situations: first, where a person, because of demonstrated mental disorder, lacks the functional capacity needed to agree to that treatment and where such treatment would be in that person's best interests, bearing in mind their life style, cultural ties, preferences, responsibilities etc.[18]; secondly, where a person, because of their mental disorder, exhibits a demonstrated risk of physical harm to the public; the disorder is treatable and the proposed treatment would be in their best interests.

---

[18] Some libertarians might argue that even this formulation is unacceptable. On this, it is noteworthy that even though John Stuart Mill forcefully rejected any interference with personal liberty on grounds of paternalism or concern for someone's welfare, he expressly excluded those unable to decide for themselves what could benefit them or meet their needs. See Monahan (1977).

For some situations, the current Mental Health Act is both inflexible and over-elaborate. A range of different legal solutions should be incorporated into new legislation so that the most appropriate one can be found for each situation. The Law Commission's work on incapacity and the measures proposed in its draft Incapacity Bill demonstrate how a flexible and practical approach can be designed in similar circumstances to provide a range of options to suit varying needs.

The separation of 'incapacity' from 'public protection' grounds could be further reflected in the choice of procedures for determining whether or not they have been sufficiently established to warrant detention in hospital and treatment or supervision in the community. For the former, administrative procedures similar to those currently used could be supplemented by more formal, possibly court-based, arrangements to approve the appointment of substitute consent-givers, the nomination of advocates or to validate any directions which the patient may have given in advance.

It would be desirable and surely possible to include all the necessary legislation in a Medical Treatments Act, rather than in a specific piece of *mental health* legislation. This would help to encourage a similar approach in the provision of psychiatric treatment to that adopted for treating physical illness where the justification for acting in the absence of consent is that the person lacks capacity. Such a fundamental break with past practice would help to reduce the stigma associated with special psychiatric legislation.

Shifting to this new approach will undoubtedly challenge professional cultures if these are not yet ready to apply this more sophisticated justification for treatment. Unfairness will result if uneven and inconsistent approaches to capacity are employed in practice. Effective national guidance, in-depth training and careful monitoring will be needed if the new legal code is not to fail.

Where the risk of harm to others is the basis for coercion then a more formal, due-process system should be used to test the basis for such judgements. This could involve the use of independent decision-makers to sanction the taking of powers, not just to consider the discharge of them. For example, measures leading to supervision in the community should be imposed following application to an independent body able to hear representations from the patient, in addition to those from the clinician. At the least, procedures need to ensure that formal written risk assessments are used to support opinions concerning risk of harm to others and that these are soundly and reliably based on good quality information obtained and interpreted without bias.

How would these fundamental changes to mental health law affect the arguments around the need for a community treatment order? Discussions to date have been largely influenced by the present legislation and its necessity/appropriateness threshold. If the law were to develop in the ways we have suggested then the arguments for – and possible objections to – a community treatment order would become simpler.

Where there was no evidence of possible harm to others, the only basis upon which law could be employed would be to provide medical treatment to someone who was unable to consent to this themselves. Instead of the common law being used to sanction this, a formal statutory procedure would do so, with safeguards to ensure that treatment was appropriate and monitored. Such arrangements could only be regarded as providing a CTO in the sense that they would authorise and regulate the provision of medical treatment for mental disorder to someone unable to consent to this themselves and who did not need to be in a hospital for that treatment.

For a person judged to be capable of consenting to or refusing treatment, we cannot envisage any circumstances in which any form of CTO could be applied to compel them to co-operate with treatment *unless* that person could be shown to be a serious risk of physical harm to the public and the provision of such treatment would demonstrably reduce or remove that risk.

Mental health law reform offers no panacea for the deep-seated problems of profesional morale, of scarce resources and public ambivalence which currently affect services. Changes should not be undertaken in order to distract attention from the need to tackle these other challenges. They should be seen as only one element in a comprehensive strategy to equip services, as well as to support those running them.

7

Law as a Rights Protector: Assessing the Mental Health Act 1983

GENEVRA RICHARDSON and OLIVER THOROLD

In this chapter we examine the ways in which law seeks to protect the rights of patients subjected to compulsion within the mental health system. Modern statutory mental health law arrived in 1959, sweeping away a thicket of lunacy legislation dating from the nineteenth century. The 1959 Mental Health Act put in place most of the essentials of the present legal system, including the consensus necessary to 'section', the three civil powers to admit, admission criteria relating to "health, safety or the protection of others", hospital orders, the mental health review tribunal system and the role of nearest relatives.

The 1983 Mental Health Act was a reform rather than a revolution. It codified and regulated the power to impose treatment in hospital, extended tribunal rights to restricted patients and those detained for assessment, introduced automatic tribunals and doubled the frequency of rights to apply to tribunals, removed a treatment power from guardianship and created the Mental Health Act Commission. The underlying legal structure remains late 1950s, though with extensive modern additions.

We propose in this chapter to review the legal protection which patients enjoy under domestic legislation, placing particular emphasis on the position of detained patients, to consider what evidence exists to show that this protection is effective and finally to consider the impact of the ECHR. However, before moving to the substantive sections we need briefly to introduce three preliminary but central issues: the limits to legal intervention, the relationship between law and psychiatry and the meaning of rights.

THE LIMITS OF LEGAL INTERVENTION

It is important at the outset to be realistic about law's ability to change behaviour. The socio-legal literature on the topic is extensive and predominantly pessimistic with regard to law's capacity 'to make people good'.[1] Two issues of particular relevance to our present topic emerge. In the first place the general

---

[1] For a clear discussion of the relevant literature see Cotterrell (1992), chap. 2.

arguments concerning the chilling effects of legalism are well known and there is growing evidence that the introduction of legal regulation can have unexpected and possibly counter-productive consequences.[2] Secondly fundamental reservations are expressed about law's ability truly to influence behaviour. These reservations are strongest when law seeks to regulate in areas where alternative value systems exist. Studies of police decision-making, for example, frequently refer to the apparent conflict between legality and order, while discussions of the relationship between law and psychiatry dwell on the differences between medical and legal values.[3] The problem of communication between cultures is most vividly presented by the proponents of systems theory.[4] According to this approach society is divided into autonomous sub-systems, law being one and medicine another. While each system is influenced by the environment around it no system can directly incorporate the norms of another. So, while medicine can be influenced by the law it can never adopt legal norms as its own. In such a world law's ability to effect real change within another system is severely limited.

LAW AND PSYCHIATRY

Even without reference to systems theory the differences in values and approach between psychiatry and law are well recognised in the literature. The lawyer's concern with the autonomy of the individual is contrasted with the doctor's pursuit of beneficence and non-maleficence, the promotion of the welfare of others and the avoidance of harm.[5] In certain situations the demands of patient autonomy may run counter to both the pursuit of beneficence and the therapeutic goal, and conflict can occur, for example, in the context of consent to treatment. Thus, unless the clinical context within which it is to operate is understood, the legal regulation of psychiatry runs the danger of being either counter-productive or irrelevant.

RIGHTS

Finally it is necessary to say something about the notion of rights. We are concerned here primarily with the legal recognition of rights. It is customary to see the 1983 Act as strengthening the safeguards available to patients and as effectively protecting patient autonomy against the incursions of psychiatric

[2] E.g., there is concern that informal disciplinary measures within prisons emerge as a direct consequence of what is seen by staff as the over-legalisation of the formal structures: see Loughlin (1993), Livingstone (1994).

[3] As early as 1966 the tension between 'law' and 'order' in police work was well recognised: Skolnick (1966). For a discussion of the differing values of law and psychiatry see Peay (1989).

[4] The literature is extensive, but with particular reference to law see Teubner (1993).

[5] Peay (1989); Faden and Beauchamp (1986); Richardson (1993); Appelbaum (1990).

discretion.[6] To that extent the Act adopts the orthodox British approach to civil rights: such rights fall to be asserted because someone has trespassed on the autonomy of another, "[t]he notion is essentially negative, a right not to be interfered with".[7] This negative notion of rights implying a correlative duty in others not to interfere can be distinguished from the positive notion which would imply a correlative duty in another to act. The distinction is not absolute, but it is useful for our purposes since the rights protected by the 1983 Act are primarily negative in nature: the right not to be detained unless suffering from a mental disorder, for example. One significant exception might be provided by section 117 – the duty to provide after-care. It is clear that this section imposes a duty on the relevant authorities to provide after-care services to the individual patient, and it might be assumed that that duty would entail a correlative right in the patient to the appropriate facilities. In a world of scarce resources such a positive right to services would have immense value for the individual. However, it is unclear whether the courts would in practice uphold a patient's individual right to after-care through an action for damages in private law and, in the one successful public law challenge brought against a defaulting authority, the court stopped short of ordering the provision of the required facilities.[8]

We turn now to the protection provided by the Mental Health Act 1983 in relation to three central decisions: compulsory admission to hospital, discharge from hospital and compulsory treatment.

COMPULSORY ADMISSION TO HOSPITAL

The 1983 Act authorises the restriction of individual rights by providing for compulsory admission to and detention in hospital. In so doing it also provides safeguards against abuse. Historically judicial involvement in the process of compulsory admission was regarded as an essential safeguard; however, with the passage of the 1959 Act the last vestiges of judicial involvement in civil admission were removed. The current framework relies instead on express admission criteria, the requirement of consensus between medical and non-medical opinion, and the provision of powers to the nearest relative.

The admission criteria

According to the traditional legal values of certainty and predictability, criteria used to justify the removal of liberty should be as precise as possible. Unfortunately in the context of compulsory admission to hospital this is not the

---

[6] Unsworth (1987).
[7] Laws (1996), 627.
[8] R. v. *Ealing District Health Authority, ex p Fox* [1993]; Hoggett (1996), 206-10; Gordon (1993b).

case. The 1983 Act uses a wide variety of qualificatory expressions in the course of setting the criteria for compulsory admission. For example, for a section 2 admission for assessment the mental disorder must be of a nature or degree which "warrants" detention for assessment, and it must be possible to say that the patient "ought to be so detained in the interests of his own health or safety or with the view to the protection of other persons". By contrast, when an approved social worker (ASW) and psychiatrist assess with a view to admission for treatment under section 3 they must consider first whether the nature or degree of the patient's mental disorder renders it "appropriate" for him to receive medical treatment in a hospital, secondly whether it is "necessary" for his health or safety or for the protection of others that he should receive such treatment, and thirdly whether the treatment cannot be provided unless the patient is detained under that section. The ASW has a duty to apply where, after heeding the wishes expressed by relatives, he or she is satisfied that it is "necessary or proper" for the application to be made, and that detention in a hospital "is in all the circumstances of the case the most appropriate way of providing the care and medical treatment of which the patient stands in need".[9]

"Appropriate", "necessary" and "proper", "warrant" and "ought" are not synonyms, and it is hard to understand why the Act uses so many variants of word and phrase in closely analogous contexts. Canons of statutory construction might say that significance must be found in difference of wording in different contexts, but an ASW could be forgiven for concluding that the legislature has simply found it difficult to express its true intent, and resorted to a sequence of reiterative criteria with overlapping shades of meaning to cover its embarrassment. We should not be surprised if an ASW, faced with such draftsmanship, treats the statute as one which permits a high degree of subjectivity.

In exercising their powers and duties in relation to admission ASWs are offered little formal legal guidance and have no conclusive means of assessing whether or not their practice conforms to the intentions of the statute. Since tribunals consider the merits of discharge on the day of the hearing, a decision to discharge cannot be assumed to imply criticism of the initial admission. Further, the existence of a right to apply to a tribunal has tended to discourage judicial review of decisions to admit.[10] Consequently the admission criteria have received little judicial elucidation, although a section 2 admission was recently declared to have been unlawful by the Court of Appeal on the ground that, although the patient was suffering from a mental disorder, it was not necessarily of a nature or degree which warranted detention in hospital.[11]

---

[9] S. 13(1).

[10] Tribunals do not consider the legality of the initial detention, but their power to order discharge provides a more immediate remedy.

[11] *R. v. Collins, ex parte S* [1998]. The court was concerned that no adequate distinction had been drawn between the patient's need for urgent treatment on account of her pregnancy and her need for detention on the basis of her mental disorder alone.

The cumulative statutory requirements are commonly understood to mean that compulsory admission should be in some sense a last resort: beneficence may only trump autonomy when there is no alternative. Or, as Lord Steyn observed, "Parliament was not content in this complex and sensitive area to proceed on the paternalistic basis that the doctor is always right".[12] An issue which illustrates as well as any the friction between beneficence and liberty concerns the stage at which it is legally permissible to invoke compulsion when a patient is suffering from a deteriorating illness. The Inquiry Report, *The Falling Shadow*, contended for the legality of early intervention, particularly where the "nature" of the illness raised fears for the safety of the public and was, by implication, critical of waiting for "psychotic symptoms to ripen before resorting to the powers in the Mental Health Act".[13] This view has not met with universal agreement,[14] and the suggestion that no deterioration is required post voluntary cessation of medication in order for a patient with a relapsing history to be immediately detained has been expressly challenged.[15] That it is still entirely possible to debate when intervention first becomes lawful in the course of a deteriorating illness is testimony to the difficulty of deriving any precise meaning or intent from the Act's criteria.

Even acknowledging the inherent difficulty of defining the appropriate threshold for compulsory admission, the existing formulations appear needlessly general and provide an inadequate guide to practitioners. Adequate protection for the patient from unjustified compulsion calls for much greater clarity of statutory expression.

The consensus of lay and medical opinion and the role of the nearest relative

In requiring a consensus of lay and medical opinion before compulsory admission can be sought the Act seeks to protect patients from over-enthusiastic medical intervention. Under the present structure the non-medical element can be provided by either the nearest relative or an ASW. In 1957 the Percy Commission favoured the family, rather than the medical welfare officer, taking the initiative.[16] However, if the non-medical input is to provide any significant balance to the medical view it is likely to be afforded more weight when it is offered by a professionally qualified person subject to a statutory mandate. While the Act imposes a sequence of statutory criteria and procedural requirements on an ASW's application, a nearest relative operates free from any equivalent requirements. The nearest relative has only to assert that he has seen the patient sufficiently recently and that the required medical recommendations are

---

[12] R. v. *Bournewood Community and Mental Health NHS Trust, ex parte L* [1998] at 305.
[13] Blom-Cooper *et al.* (1995).
[14] Jones (1996), 31.
[15] The view expressed in Mental Health Act Commission (1998).
[16] Royal Commission (1957), para. 403.

in place. Moreover, whereas the untrained nearest relative can veto the trained ASW's desire to admit for treatment, the ASW has no veto on an application sought by a nearest relative. This asymmetry exposes patients to at least the theoretical risk of an admission at the behest of a nearest relative which would not have taken place if the responsibility had been left to an ASW operating under statutory criteria.

The Percy Commission regarded a sufficient consensus of medical and non-medical opinion as provided by a relative or mental welfare officer with two supporting medical recommendations.[17] Whether the requirement that there be such a consensus is protective of patients' rights depends in some part on the interaction between psychiatrists, other recommending doctors and ASWs, or, in the minority of cases sought by them, nearest relatives. Bean's research, based on observing 325 domiciliary visits between 1975 and 1977, drew largely pessimistic conclusions.[18] He found the psychiatrist to be the dominant member, with the second doctor – often a GP – frequently failing to provide a corrective. Social workers, he reported, "have no expertise which qualifies them to do anything but the most simple and basic tasks in the compulsory admission procedure. They know less about the patient than the relative and less about psychiatry than the psychiatrists".[19] In terms of providing patients with protection from psychiatric dominance these are bleak conclusions and are echoed in more recent research published in 1990: "one concern arising from our analysis of our research findings is that social services staff themselves have a tendency to defer to psychiatric explanations and responses".[20] This would appear to provide a clear example of the difficulties which can arise in any attempt to seek dialogue between professional cultures. The Act tries to impose a brake on psychiatry by demanding the involvement of a non-medical opinion, but in practice this brake proves ineffective. Social work, it seems, is unable to provide sufficient challenge to the professional hegemony of psychiatry; the communication is unequal.

DISCHARGE FROM HOSPITAL

Each section of detention has its own period of duration and, where appropriate, renewal. In respect of each there are also mechanisms for discharge from hospital. For non-restricted patients these include the nearest relative, the Responsible Medical Officer (RMO), the hospital managers and the mental health review tribunal.[21] In the case of restricted patients authority to discharge lies with the Secretary of State and the tribunal only. The following discussion will concentrate on the role of the tribunal.

[17] *Ibid.*, para 438.
[18] Bean (1980).
[19] *Ibid.*, 215.
[20] Barnes, Bowl and Fisher (1990), 184.
[21] Hoggett (1996); Eldergill (1997).

Mental health review tribunals possess the power to discharge a patient from detention even in the face of opposition from the RMO and, in the case of restricted patients, the Home Office. Tribunals thus protect the patient's right to be free from detention and compulsory treatment where such is not justified under the Act. This role as 'rights protector' is clearly illustrated by the history of section 73, which gives tribunals the power to discharge restricted patients. The inclusion of this power was forced on a reluctant government by the European Court of Human Rights in order to provide protection for the right to liberty guaranteed by Article 5 of the Human Rights Convention.[22] In order to assess the record of the tribunal as a rights protector we will consider four distinct issues: delays, the criteria for discharge, the nature of the hearing and the powers of the tribunal.

Delays

Neither the 1983 Act nor the Mental Health Review Tribunal Rules[23] stipulate any maximum period of time within which a tribunal must decide an application made by a patient detained under section 3 or 37. For these categories of patients delays have been a major cause of concern, and the most recent figures available indicate that in the last quarter of 1996 only 35 per cent of nonrestricted cases were being heard in under eight weeks, while 22 per cent had to wait over 12 weeks. For restricted cases the figures are worse, 1 per cent of cases in special hospitals and 7 per cent in other hospitals were heard in under eight weeks, while the figures for those waiting over 20 weeks are 63 per cent and 49 per cent respectively.[24] These are serious delays which can cause the unnecessary, and hence unjustifiable, detention of patients. While we appreciate that the tribunal administration is trying hard to deal with the problem with desperately limited resources, the current waiting times significantly reduce the efficacy of the tribunal as a protector of rights. The position under the ECHR is discussed below.

Criteria for discharge

In the case of all patients detained for treatment the tribunal must discharge if it is satisfied about any *one* of three states of affairs:

---

[22] *X* v. *United Kingdom* [1981]. See below for further discussion of Art. 5.

[23] 1983 S.I. 942. A hearing in the case of a s. 2 patient must take place within 7 days of the receipt of the application.

[24] The figures are taken from Mental Health Review Tribunal (1997). For early criticism of the delays see Council on Tribunals (1989) and (1990). In response, independent research was commissioned: Blumenthal and Wessely (1994).

1) that the patient is *not* suffering from either of the four specified forms of mental disorder;
2) that the patient is *not* suffering from that disorder to a nature or degree making it appropriate for him to be detained in hospital for medical treatment, or
3) that it is *not* necessary for the patient's health or safety or for the protection of others that he should receive such treatment.[25]

All three states of affairs are expressed in the negative, which effectively creates a presumption against discharge. The alternative, positive, formulation would require the tribunal to discharge unless, for example, it was satisfied that the patient *was* suffering, and would place the presumption the other way, against continued detention. Under the existing formulation there is no obligation on the tribunal to discharge unless it is satisfied of the absence of one of the three features. In practice, in the absence of an actively inquisitorial tribunal, the patient must satisfy the panel either that he is not suffering or that he is not in need of treatment in hospital, or that he is not a danger to himself or others. Thus on the strength of the statutory words alone doubts are raised about the efficacy of the tribunal as a protector of the patient's right to liberty.[26]

In addition to the creation of a presumption against discharge the negative formulation may encourage caution on the part of tribunals. In cases of doubt it is easy not to be satisfied of the absence of illness, need or danger, and there is no indication of what level of doubt is necessary properly to achieve a failure to be satisfied. However, the negative formulation is not the only source of uncertainty in the wording of the statutory criteria. Several of the phrases contained within section 72(1)(b) are open to wide interpretation. When, for example, is a disorder such as to make it appropriate for the patient to be detained in hospital? Does the answer depend solely on the disorder or should thought be given to the level of care available outside hospital? When is detention necessary for the protection of others? Is the phrase "nature or degree" conjunctive or disjunctive? And what is the difference between nature and degree? What is psychopathic disorder and what amounts to "abnormally aggressive or seriously irresponsible conduct"?[27] As we have pointed out, very similar uncertainties confront the ASW and psychiatrist at the time of admission.

Since mental health review tribunals are subject to judicial review it would, in theory, be possible to seek clarification of the criteria from the High Court. However, with one notable exception, very few of the decided cases have considered the interpretation of the criteria themselves. The exception is provided

---

[25] These criteria are found in s. 72(1)(b). In the case of non-restricted patients the tribunal also possesses a discretion to discharge: s.72(2). The discharge criteria for patients detained for assessment are found in s.72(1)(a).

[26] Peay (1989), 85. It is interesting to note that the powers of release given to the discretionary lifer panels are worded in a similar fashion: Criminal Justice Act 1991, s 34(4)(b). For discussion see Richardson (1993). The position under the ECHR is discussed below.

[27] The phrase is taken from s 1(2), the statutory definition of psychopathy.

by *R. v. Cannons Park Mental Health Review Tribunal, ex parte A.*[28] Here the court had to consider the relevance of treatability to the discharge of patients suffering from psychopathic disorder. The Court of Appeal held that a tribunal does not have to direct discharge merely because the medical treatment is not likely to alleviate or prevent a deterioration in the patient's condition. To the extent that it has provided definitive guidance, the Court of Appeal's decision has reduced uncertainty. However, in overruling the High Court the Court of Appeal selected an interpretation which favoured continued detention, and whatever the legal merits of the decision it has done nothing to enhance the role of the tribunal as a protector of patients' rights, certainly as regards the negative rights of those suffering from psychopathic disorder.

Thus the statutory criteria for discharge are full of uncertainties, and little attempt has yet been made to seek clarification from the High Court. Some might argue that, given the subject matter, these uncertainties are inevitable and are best left to be resolved on a case-by-case basis by a three-person panel which can draw on a wide range of expertise. According to this view the principles of certainty and predictability customarily required by law in the protection of individual liberty must cede to the requirements of beneficence and public safety. However, whatever the merits of such an approach, there is a very real danger that the breadth of discretion contained within the criteria, coupled to their negative formulation, serves merely to encourage an understandable pre-disposition towards caution and a consequential diminution of the tribunal's strength as a protector of the patient's right to liberty.[29] An appreciation of the difficulties surrounding discharge decisions should not lead to the wholesale reduction of customary legal safeguards.

Constitution and procedures

Tribunal members are appointed by the Lord Chancellor.[30] Each individual panel is comprised of three members: a medical member, a lay member and a lawyer as president. Although administered and resourced via the Department of Health, the mental health review tribunal is independent of central government and each individual panel is independent of the detaining authority.[31] While the tribunals are empowered to take binding decisions, their procedures are essentially inquisitorial rather than adversarial.[32] General rules dealing with

---

[28] [1994]. However, see now also *R. (A Patient) v. Secretary of State for Scotland* [1998]. The meaning of treatability has been further considered in *R. v. MHRT, ex p Macdonald* [1998]. Further, in a recent application for judicial review the phrase "nature or degree" has been held to be disjunctive: *R v. MHRT for S. Thames ex parte Smith* [1998].

[29] See Peay (1989) for evidence of the tribunal's tendency merely to endorse the recommendations of the RMO.

[30] 1983 Act, Sched. 2.

[31] The independence of the tribunal is a requirement of compliance with the X judgment.

[32] See *W v. Egdell* [1989].

procedures and preliminary matters are provided by delegated legislation, but each president is responsible for the precise procedures adopted at the hearing.[33] Legal aid is available and in the vast majority of cases the patient is represented.

In considering how far their procedures promote the role of the tribunal as a protector of the patient's rights three issues need to be examined: the nature of the evidence and the inquisitorial capacity of the tribunal, the role of the medical member and the duty to give reasons. It can be argued that the inquisitorial model is the preferred model of decision-making in the circumstance facing a mental health review tribunal, particularly in view of the wording of the discharge criteria.[34] Only a tribunal which is truly inquisitorial can provide adequate protection for the patient's right to liberty against the conflicting demands of beneficence and social protection.

Under the procedural rules the tribunal must receive certain reports and may call for further information on its own initiative and adjourn for that purpose.[35] In practice the statutory reports are often delivered late, giving little time for preparation and, although tribunals will occasionally use their powers to call for further evidence, there is a reluctance to cause any further delay than is absolutely necessary. At the hearing oral evidence will typically be given by the RMO, a social worker and possibly a nurse. Research suggests that the RMO's evidence is likely to be the most influential and is likely to be accorded more weight than that of any independent psychiatrist commissioned by the patient.[36] While this preference for the evidence of the RMO does not on its own indicate a lack of rigour, it is essential that the evidence be adequately challenged. The doctor who appears before the tribunal may have a relatively limited knowledge of the patient and may not even be the author of the report.[37]

In relation to restricted patients the Home Secretary must be informed of any tribunal applications, provided with all reports and given notice of the hearing. The object is clearly to enable the Home Secretary to make representations to the tribunal and to oppose the discharge if he so wishes; as the House of Lords has stated; the Home Secretary is "the only party capable of representing any interest the public may have in opposing an application for discharge".[38] In theory the effective and open presentation of the public safety arguments against discharge should only improve the quality of tribunal decisions: if the patient's right to liberty is to be trumped by the interests of public safety those interests should be specifically stated and open to challenge. In practice, however, the Home Secretary's participation falls far short of this ideal. Typically it

---

[33] See Eldergill (1997).

[34] For an interesting discussion of the merits of an inquisitorial model see Bayles (1987); Bayles (1990). For a specific application of the arguments to the MHRT see Richardson (1993).

[35] Rr. 6, 15(1) and 16(1).

[36] Peay (1989).

[37] See, e.g., the criticism of the medical care provided at one special hospital: *Report of the Committee of Inquiry into Complaints about Ashworth Hospital* (1992), XVII. And see Mental Health Act Commission (1991), 21.

[38] *R v. Oxford Regional MHRT, ex parte Secretary of State for the Home Dept.* [1987] at 10.

is limited to the provision of a written statement and the occasional appointment of counsel to cross-examine witnesses advocating discharge. Again, in theory, an actively inquisitorial tribunal should demand the opportunity directly to question the evidence contained within the Home Office statement, particularly in so far as it bears on the "safety of others". However, the preliminary findings of research currently underway suggest that this rarely, if ever, occurs.[39] Tribunals tend to regard the Home Office contribution as a formality, predictable and unenlightening, and see little to be gained from further investigation of it.

Finally on the question of inquisitorial rigour, allegations of misconduct entered in the patient's records may influence attitudes towards his diagnosis and/or dangerousness. In such circumstances if the patient wishes to challenge the accuracy of the allegations the tribunal is under a duty to allow the necessary questioning,[40] and no doubt some tribunals will take the necessary initiative themselves. Realistically, however, definitive proof one way or the other may never be available and the tribunal must then be relied upon to discount the challenged evidence.[41]

In practice it seems full inquisitorial rigour is hard to achieve, however desirable it may be. Working within existing resource constraints tribunals are rarely in a position to initiate the provision of further evidence, and at the hearing the extent to which the evidence of the RMO is challenged and the accuracy of the medical records is questioned will ultimately depend on the personality of the tribunal members or the determination of the patient's representative. The same is true of the weight which is attached to the views of the Home Office. So, if the inquisitorial model is to be relied upon, tribunals must be adequately resourced and trained. An inadequate inquisitorial forum provides proper protection for neither the patient nor the public.

The presence on the tribunal of a medical member might be offered as a partial answer to any charge of lack of inquisitorial rigour. The medical member is obliged to examine the patient prior to the hearing in order to form an opinion on the patient's mental condition.[42] He or she has access to the patient's medical records and may also speak to members of the clinical team. The medical member is also typically invited to lead the questioning by the tribunal of the RMO. Thus the tribunal has an expert within its own membership who has had the opportunity to make his or her own clinical assessment of the patient. The

---

[39] Research, funded by the ESRC, to study the impact of judicial review on the decision-making of mental health review tribunals is currently in progress under the direction of one of the present authors, Richardson.

[40] *R. v. MHRT for Merseyside, ex parte Kelly* [1997].

[41] This is perhaps a particularly good example of the core conflict between 'legal' and 'clinical' models. The conflict arises where a clinician uses factual information, determined to his or her own 'standard' of proof, towards making clinical decisions, but where a tribunal might properly be invited to test the same evidence against a different standard and in a different way, a way never intended by the clinician.

[42] R. 11.

tribunal has, to that extent, acquired its own evidence. However, this situation produces its own problems. In the first place, given the natural concerns of psychiatry as a discipline, the presence of a doctor on the panel may incline the tribunal towards beneficence rather than autonomy, towards therapy and away from rights. Taken in isolation this may not be a cause for concern: if the cultures of law and psychiatry are to inform one another then a structure which represents both may be appropriate. However, given the minimal protection afforded to the patient's autonomy by the statutory criteria any further emphasis on beneficence may be a step too far. Secondly the presence of the medical member creates a potential source of unfairness to the patient.[43] On examining the patient the medical member may adopt a firm view on the advisability or otherwise of discharge which he or she reveals to the other members prior to the hearing, or may take a different view of the patient's mental state from that taken by the RMO and reveal this to the other tribunal members only in the deliberations after the hearing. In either event the patient will have no opportunity to challenge the doctor's view. While the legal position is relatively clear, namely that failure to reveal to all parties any evidence on which a tribunal intends to rely will amount to a breach of natural justice,[44] the preliminary findings of research currently under way suggest that the care with which tribunals deal with the 'evidence' from their own doctor differs widely.[45]

Finally, the tribunal is under a duty to provide written reasons for its decision. Among the many purposes which can be attributed to the giving of reasons are several which relate directly to the protection of the patient's rights. The giving of reasons will indicate to the patient what needs to be achieved in order to improve the chance of future success. Proper reasons should also reveal whether or not there has been an error in the tribunal's decision and thus whether there are grounds for judicial review. Moreover, the obligation to give reasons may itself impose a discipline on the tribunal which will encourage more rational decision-making.[46]

In the early days of the Act a number of tribunal decisions were challenged on the grounds of the alleged inadequacy of their reasons. It is now clear that adequate reasons cannot merely recite the words of the Act and that it must be possible to determine from the reasons whether they refer to the presence of mental disorder under section 72(1)(b)(i) or to the presence of risk under section 72(1)(b)(ii).[47] In certain circumstances it may also be necessary, in cases where there is a conflict of medical evidence, to indicate why the evidence of one

---

[43] See the reservation expressed by the Council on Tribunals (1983), para. 3.22.

[44] *Mahon* v. *Air New Zealand* [1984] and *R.* v. *MHRT ex parte Clatworthy* [1985].

[45] The research is mentioned above.

[46] The literature on the duty to give reasons is now extensive. For recent judicial views on the purposes of reason giving see: *Doody* v. *Secretary of State for the Home Department* [1994], *R.* v. *HEFCE, ex parte Inst. of Dental Surgery* [1994] and *R.* v. *Ministry of Defence, ex parte Murray* [1997].

[47] *Bone* v. *MHRT* [1985] and *R.* v. *MHRT, ex parte Pickering* [1986].

witness was preferred to that of another.[48] While it is unclear how far these requirements are complied with, there is at least anecdotal evidence that there has been an improvement in the standard of written reasons in recent years and certainly the decision form itself has been redrafted.[49] However, it is worth noting that tribunals do not as a matter of course refer to the reasoning given in any earlier tribunal relating to the patient. Thus, by meeting the concerns of the first tribunal the patient cannot assume he will satisfy the second.

We have argued here that the essential constitution and structure of the mental health review tribunal is appropriate to the protection of the rights of patients. It is formally independent of the executive and the detaining authorities and is designed to adopt an inquisitorial model of decision-making. However closer scrutiny reveals significant problems relating in particular to the lack of inquisitorial capacity and the role of the medical member which, in combination with the reservations already expressed concerning the nature of the discharge criteria, give rise to serious doubts about the tribunal's ability to protect the rights of patients.

The powers of the tribunal

The core powers of the tribunal as they relate to non-restricted and restricted patients are contained in sections 72 and 73 respectively. These powers are severely limited and have been much criticised on the grounds that they provide the tribunal with insufficient flexibility and thus inhibit its ability to facilitate the patient's return to the community.[50]

In the case of restricted patients there are two particularly significant limitations to the tribunal's powers. The first relates to the transfer of patients between hospitals. The tribunal does have the power to direct a conditional discharge and there is evidence to suggest that the availability of this power encourages discharge.[51] However, for many restricted patients in high-security accommodation discharge directly into the community is regarded as inappropriate. Patients usually spend a period of time in a regional secure unit before discharge. This approach is almost invariably advocated by RMOs and widely accepted by tribunals. But tribunals are impotent to compel transfers; only the Home Secretary can consent to the transfer of a restricted patient.[52] Thus

---

[48] *R. v. S.W. Thames MHRT, ex parte Demitri* [1997].

[49] The research referred to above is examining the process of reason-giving by tribunals: how easy the legal requirements are to understand and apply and the extent to which the obligation to give reasons affects the decision-making itself.

[50] Peay (1989) and Richardson (1993). See Eldergill (1997) for a full account of the powers.

[51] Dell and Robertson (1988).

[52] S. 42. The minister has agreed that informal recommendations by the tribunal concerning transfer will be considered: Hansard HC vol. 121, cols. 261, 262, 28 Oct. 1987. However, the minister is under no obligation to follow those recommendations and may refer the case to the Advisory Board: *R. v. Sec of State for Home Dept, ex parte Harry* [1998]. And see *R. v. MHRT, ex parte Booth* [1998] for the frustrations caused by the absence of a power to direct transfer.

despite the decision in *X* v. *UK* the executive retains this most significant power to control the usual progression of restricted patients to ultimate discharge.[53] The second major limitation relates to the tribunal's power to ensure adequate after-care. Although the tribunal may defer a conditional discharge until the necessary arrangements are made, there is little it can do in the face of inaction. Rule 14 gives tribunals a power of subpoena, and so a representative of a social services department, or even a director, could be compelled to appear to explain why hostel provision, for example, has not been made, but in the last resort a tribunal lacks any power to compel resource provision.[54] This lacuna in tribunal powers contributed directly to the European Court's decision in the *Johnson* case which we discuss below.

In the case of non-restricted patients different but arguably equally severe limitations apply. In the first place the tribunal has no power to order a conditional discharge and, when the choice is between absolute discharge or continued detention, a cautious tribunal may be understandably reluctant to discharge. In an attempt to fill this gap the Mental Health (Patients in the Community) Act 1995 introduced 'supervised discharge'.[55] If placed under supervised discharge the patient may be required to live at a specified address and to attend at a specified place for medical treatment, occupation, education or training, and may be taken to those specified places. Although the tribunal cannot order a supervised discharge, it can recommend that the RMO consider doing so. However, a supervised discharge which relies for its ultimate enforcement on the application of a fresh section is not equivalent to a conditional discharge, under which the patient can swiftly be recalled, and thus, whatever its other limitations, supervised discharge does not constitute a significant extension to the options available to a tribunal. Secondly, as is the case with restricted patients, a tribunal cannot order adequate after-care; it can only recommend and reconvene.[56] Again supervised discharge provides no solution here since it provides no additional rights to aftercare enforceable by the tribunal.[57]

These gaps in the powers of the tribunal severely limit its efficacy as a rights protector. The tribunal is entrusted with the protection of the patient's right to liberty. However, its ability to offer adequate protection to this traditional, negative right is grossly compromised. In the first place the nature of the negative right itself poses a problem, particularly in restricted cases. The right to liberty

---

[53] S. 42 of the 1983 Act. This represents a different type of example of the core conflict referred to above, in that a legal model would infer the right to transfer whereas a clinical model might, in particular circumstances, be at variance with this (e.g., because of a risk of physical harm or therapeutic disadvantage to others arising from a particular patient mix in the receiving hospital unit)

[54] See the case of *Fox* discussed above. There would ultimately be a challenge to the providing authorities if they remained in default, but, as mentioned above, the court stopped short of mandating the authority to provide.

[55] Formally known as 'after-care under supervision' (ACUS).

[56] S. 72(3)(a). Unlike the case in relation to restricted patients, under this section the tribunal may reconsider its original decision and may decide to discharge: *R.* v. *MHRT for N. Thames Region, ex parte Pierce* [1996].

[57] For an interesting discussion of supervised discharged see Exworthy (1995); Eastman (1995).

recognised by the Act is the right to be free from *all hospital detention*, whereas in practice what is required is the right to be free from *all unjustified security*, which should then be enforceable by means of a power to direct transfer.[58] Secondly, the negative right to liberty becomes difficult to protect in the absence of any positive right to after-care enforceable by the tribunal. With no power to order after-care a tribunal may be reluctant to discharge a patient into inadequate community provision, only to see the patient relapse and return to detention.

COMPULSORY TREATMENT

As a general rule capable adults have the right to refuse medical treatment. Treatment cannot be imposed on a capable adult in the absence of his or her consent. In relation to treatment for mental disorder this general rule has been modified by statute for patients detained under the 1983 Act. Part IV deals with consent to treatment and identifies three categories of non urgent medical treatment for mental disorder: treatment requiring consent and second opinion (section 57), treatment requiring consent or second opinion (section 58) and treatment requiring neither consent nor second opinion (section 63). For reasons of space we concentrate on the second category, since the creation of a structure to allow for the compulsory administration of core treatments lies at the heart of the treatment provisions within the Act. Under section 58 a detained patient may be given drugs or electro-convulsive therapy (ECT) in the absence of consent provided a second opinion appointed doctor certifies that, despite absence of consent, "having regard to the likelihood of its alleviating or preventing a deterioration of [the patient's] condition, the treatment should be given".[59]

Although Part IV has been described by Unsworth as "the high-water mark of legalism in the Act",[60] it effectively represents an uneasy compromise between the views of the psychiatric profession, as previously represented by the Royal College, on one side and the advocates of stricter controls over professional discretion on the other.[61] Section 58 overrides the patient's right to refuse treatment: beneficence and, in certain cases, social protection are given precedence over autonomy. Given the provision of a power to detain for medical treatment it is hard to see how it could have been otherwise, but the power to treat is not absolute and an important question remains concerning the adequacy of the safeguards provided by the law. In addressing this question three important issues emerge: the notion of consent under the Act, the role of the RMO and the nature of the independent oversight.

---

[58] See further, below, for discussion of the position under the ECHR.
[59] S. 58(3)(b).
[60] Unsworth (1987), 324.
[61] For the history of the provisions see Fennell (1986), (1996), and Unsworth (1987).

Consent under section 58

Under section 58 no ECT at all and no medication after three months may be given unless the RMO certifies that the patient consents, or an appointed doctor certifies either that the patient consents or that the treatment should be given anyway. Thus, the importance of consent is recognised but its absence may be overruled with the agreement of an independent doctor. In his discussion of consent to psychiatric treatment Bean identifies four features of consent: awareness, information, specificity and the absence of coercion.[62] For a patient's consent to be valid under section 58 either the RMO or an appointed doctor must certify that the patient "is capable of understanding the nature, purpose and likely effect" of the treatment and has consented to it, and it may be revealing to consider how far the scheme recognises the essential aspects of consent implied by Bean's four features.

Awareness refers to capacity and is expressly included as a requirement of section 58(3)(a).[63] In this context a valid consent apparently implies both "the ability, given an explanation in simple terms to understand the nature, purpose and effect of the proposed treatment"[64] and the ability to understand the consequences of not receiving the treatment,[65] but it is not necessary that the patient understand "the precise physiological process involved".[66] Although section 58 makes no express reference to information the emphasis on capacity must assume the provision of information. Indeed the case law reflects such an assumption, and the Code of Practice recognises the relationship between capacity and information and specifies that the explanation of the treatment should be appropriate to the patient's ability.[67]

In theory, the question of specificity is dealt with by sections 59 and 60. In recognition of the need to respond to a patient's reaction to particular drugs and dosages section 59 allows the certified consent to refer to a treatment plan containing some flexibility. However, a patient may subsequently withdraw consent from either a specific treatment or a plan of treatment. Thus an attempt is made to retain specificity for the patient while at the same time avoiding the need to re-certify consent prior to every slight alteration.

The statutory notion of consent, as interpreted by case law and official guidance, appears therefore to reflect the essential elements of awareness, information and specificity. The extent to which those elements are respected in practice, however, remains uncertain, as does the attitude of the courts to any breach of the formal requirements. Remembering that the whole focus of sec-

---

[62] Bean (1986).

[63] See also Bynoe and Holland (this vol.) for a discussion of the common law definition of the capacity to consent to (any) medical treatment.

[64] The words are taken from DHSS (1976), para. 6.23. See also DoH (1993).

[65] *Re R.* [1991] at 187 and DoH (1993).

[66] R. v. *Mental Health Act Commission, ex parte X* (1988) at 87.

[67] *Ibid.*, 86, and see DoH (1993), 15.

tion 58 is to provide for treatment in the absence of consent, the courts are unlikely to regard too severely any alleged invalidity in the original consent.

Similar reservations may be voiced in relation to Bean's final element, the absence of coercion, but here perhaps the reservations are more systemic in nature. To be valid a consent must be voluntary, it cannot be coerced: in legal terms, "an apparent consent will not be a true consent if it has been obtained by fraud, misrepresentation, duress or fundamental mistake".[68] However, within conditions of indeterminate detention where crucial decisions concerning leave of absence and discharge are made either by the RMO or with reference to a report from the RMO, it may be hard to acquire truly voluntary consent.[69] Many detained patients will feel considerable pressure to co-operate with any treatment proposed by their doctor and, while such pressure may not amount to duress in the legal sense, it must severely compromise the true voluntariness of any consent given.

The role of the RMO

Whatever reservations may attach to the notion of consent contained in section 58 it is, as implied above, somewhat artificial to consider consent in isolation from the rest of the statutory scheme. Since the main thrust of section 58 is to provide for a system to enable treatment to be given in the absence of consent, the role played by consent is significantly reduced. Consent is not included within section 58 in order to guarantee patient autonomy but rather to trigger access to the safeguards provided by external peer review. In the absence of consent peer review is required, but if the RMO certifies that the patient is capable and is consenting there need be no peer review. The RMO is gatekeeper to the statutory safeguards. Whatever the formal requirements of the law, it is the RMO's operational interpretation of capacity and consent that is crucial. But, as figures from Broadmoor immediately following the introduction of the Act indicate, the exercise of that role is plainly open to abuse.[70] If the RMO is to be retained as gatekeeper routine monitoring by an independent body is essential. At present there is little external scrutiny. While commissioners from the Mental Health Act Commission check the consent status of all detained patients interviewed during their routine visits to hospitals there can be little confidence in this as an adequate safeguard.[71]

---

[68] *R v. MHAC ex parte X* [1988], 85.

[69] See, by analogy, the position of a prisoner receiving treatment where it was held that the coercive nature of the institution (together with the RMO's powers to decide on release) may prevent consent being freely given, but each case would turn on its own facts: *Freeman* v. *Home Office (No 2)* [1984].

[70] See the figures published in Mental Health Act Commission (1985).

[71] The MHAC is established by s. 121. See Richardson (1993), chap. 10 and the references therein for its role in relation to consent.

Independent oversight

At the heart of section 58 lies peer review. In the course of the negotiations leading up to the reforms of 1982–3 the idea of multidisciplinary panels was abandoned in favour of external peer review.[72] However, an element of the multidisciplinary model survives in the form of section 58(4), which requires the appointed doctor to "consult two other persons who have been professionally concerned with the patient's medical treatment"; one must be a nurse and the other neither a nurse nor a doctor. Even this modest requirement to involve another professional was unacceptable to some psychiatrists at the time of its introduction[73] and it has continued to pose practical difficulties. In his study of the work of appointed doctors Fennell reported a few instances of clear non-compliance with the duty to consult a second professional, but a far greater number of cases where the consultee was either unqualified or only remotely concerned with the treatment of the patient. Fennell concludes that the "duty to consult the other professional is becoming seen as a tiresome formality, and if the other professionals consulted are too junior or too unfamiliar with the patient to express a valid view, the decision will effectively be left to doctors".[74]

Thus the uneasy compromise represented by the duty to consult is demonstrably ineffective. At present it is regarded as a sterile formality, as legalism at its worst. There should, in theory, be nothing anti-therapeutic in an emphasis on the multi-disciplinary nature of the treatment of the mentally disordered, and decision-making structures which facilitate communication between disciplines must be achievable.[75] In a fully resourced system the second opinion should be sought from an appropriately multi-disciplinary body. However, if psychiatric peer review is retained the formal requirements must be structured in such a way as to recognise the contribution of other disciplines without alienating psychiatry. At present the inequality of influence is similar to that encountered by ASWs at the admission stage.

Before certifying that treatment should be given to a non-consenting patient the appointed doctor must have regard to the likelihood of that treatment alleviating or preventing a deterioration in the patient's condition. The Act does not require that the proposed treatment be the same as that which the appointed doctor would have chosen herself, and the published guidance states "doctors vary in their therapeutic approach and appointed doctors should feel able to support a consultant proposing a programme which others would regard as one that should be followed".[76] As Fennell explains this effectively amounts to the

---

[72] Unsworth (1987) and Fennell (1996).

[73] See letter from two doctors at Broadmoor quoted in Bean (1986) and Parl Debs., Special Standing Committee, 22nd sitting, 29 June 1982, col. 812.

[74] Fennell (1996), 208.

[75] This suggestion implies that it should, at least in some circumstances, be possible to achieve resolution of the conflict between the 'legal' and 'clinical' models.

[76] DHSS (1984), para. 17.

best interest test as enunciated in *Bolam*, where the patient's best interests are to be interpreted in accordance with a responsible body of medical opinion.[77] Admittedly the Code of Practice does require due weight to be given to the patient's reasons for withholding consent when the patient is capable, but this simple requirement cannot be equated with a system of proxy decision-making where the substitute decision maker must reflect the views of the patient.[78] The test employed under section 58 is reflective of beneficence with little if any concession to autonomy.

Given the nature of the test, a high level of agreement between appointed doctors and RMOs is perhaps to be expected. Nevertheless, considering that the "purpose of the second opinion is to protect the patient's rights",[79] the rates of agreement actually recorded are startling and raise real concerns about the nature of the protection provided. The Mental Health Act Commission reports a 94 per cent to 96 per cent rate of agreement between appointed doctors and RMOs, and this rate is confirmed by Fennell's study.[80]

Of course, it may be that the high rates of concordance are only achieved because the RMO agrees to incorporate significant amendments to the treatment plan following discussion with the appointed doctor. However, out of approximately 1,000 certifications studied Fennell found only seven cases of significant changes to the treatment plan.[81] Another possible explanation may be found in the suggestion that the very existence of the second opinion process encourages the adoption of conservative treatment plans. While this might to some extent be true, Fennell nonetheless found that polypharmacy was "extensively practised"; in 12 per cent of the second opinion certifications for medicine, doses above the British National Formulary (BNF) limits were authorised. In one case this involved oral antipsychotics up to six times BNF, depot antipsychotics up to four times BNF and anxiolytics at up to three times the limit.[82] In the absence of an alternative explanation, therefore, the levels of agreement between appointed doctors and RMOs must be taken at face value: the vast majority of appointed doctors are happy to endorse the treatment proposed by their professional colleagues.

On this evidence certification by an appointed doctor is remarkably unimpressive as a protector of patients' rights. In reality, whatever the original intentions of Parliament, the only protection provided to a non-consenting patient by section 58 is protection from treatment which no reasonable body of psychiatric opinion would regard as in the patient's interests. This is surely to weight the scales too heavily in favour of beneficence and social protection and against patient

---

[77] See *Bolam* v. *Friern Hospital Management Committee* [1957]; Fennell (1996), 204.

[78] See DoH (1993), para. 16.39 and Law Commission (1997).

[79] DHSS (1984), para. 16.

[80] Fennell (1996), chap. 12 where he discusses the MHAC rates and those revealed by his own research.

[81] *Ibid.*, 210.

[82] *Ibid.*, 202-15. See also Caldicott, Conlan and Zigmond (this vol.) for a discussion of the effects of such overprescribing on patient compliance.

autonomy. If the safeguard is to be worth anything the treating doctor's opinion must be open to effective challenge. The reviewing body must be properly multi-disciplinary, the application of the *Bolam* test must be modified and the duty to consider the views of the patient, whether directly or by proxy, must be incorporated.

EUROPEAN CONVENTION ON HUMAN RIGHTS

Against the foregoing background, is incorporation of the European Convention on Human Rights (ECHR) likely to be a source of improved rights protection for the mentally disordered in UK law? The rights set out in the ECHR are drafted in broad declaratory form,[83] but their practical application to mental health has now become reasonably clear following decisions of the European Court and Commission in a sequence of cases from the UK and elsewhere. We have already seen the impact of the Convention on the powers of the tribunal with regard to the discharge of restricted patients. With the advent of incorporation by way of the Human Rights Act patients will in some instances be able to secure enforcement before the UK courts within meaningful time-scales, though for breaches grounded in statute the most that domestic courts will be able to deliver will be declarations of incompatibility. The discussion here will concentrate on the implications of Article 5 for the law in England and Wales.[84]

Most of the rights safeguarded by the ECHR are essentially negative in character, in that they guarantee freedom from state interference. Article 5 sets out the basic guarantee of liberty and security of person and then allows "lawful detention of persons of unsound mind" as one of the permitted exceptions. Thus detention on grounds of mental disorder is permitted provided certain safeguards are met. However, these safeguards are material and have already proved significantly more demanding than those required by UK law, as the introduction of the tribunal's power to discharge restricted patients testifies. The Article can also be used to ensure objective medical evidence is present to justify detention,[85] to ensure that patients are not deprived of access to a tribunal by reason of the particular power used to redetain[86] and to ensure that applications to tribunals are resolved speedily. In 1994 the European Court upheld a Norwegian application where a newly detained patient only received a decision 55 days after lodging his request for review.[87] The court held that it was insufficiently speedy under Article 5(4). While the Norwegian case involved a newly detained patient the court considered the position for longer-term patients in *Koendjbiharie* v. *Netherlands* and held a four-month delay to be

[83] See Heginbotham and Elson (this vol.).
[84] For a more general discussion see Thorold (1996).
[85] *K* v. *United Kingdom* [1994].
[86] *Roux* v. *United Kingdom* [1997].
[87] *E* v. *Norway* [1994].

excessive.[88] These decisions have set standards of speed which the UK system regularly fails to meet and may prove extremely useful in forcing a reluctant government properly to fund the tribunal service.

According to the *Winterwerp* case Article 5 implies that compulsion must end when the patient ceases to meet the threshold test of unsoundness of mind warranting confinement.[89] Here again UK law may fall short, since there is no explicit statutory duty to discharge a patient who no longer meets the statutory criteria for admission. Further the power of future discharge for non-restricted patients under section 72(3) could constitute a breach if the delay were lengthy, possibly more than a couple of weeks. Indeed, the UK has already been held to be in violation in the case of restricted patients and deferred conditional discharges under section 73(7) where the delays can be very lengthy indeed.[90] In Mr Johnson's case the delay amounted to three years and seven months. The Court acknowledged that a state has a "margin of appreciation" permitting a period of delay even after a decision to discharge has been made by a "court", for purposes such as securing effective post-discharge rehabilitation facilities, but it did not specify a maximum length. However, in the immediate case this did not absolve the government of an Article 5(1)(e) breach throughout the period from the tribunal's decision onwards, due, it would appear, to their recognition that a tribunal lacks appropriate powers to compel provision. The case is therefore highly significant because it is likely to force the government to fill the crucial gap in tribunal powers. In the meantime there is a strong argument that, when a tribunal has deferred a conditional discharge pending the making of arrangements, a patient ought at the very least to be allowed unescorted leave of absence from the hospital in which he is currently detained.

Finally, under Article 5 there is a potential challenge to the discharge criteria themselves. At present, as described above, the Act mandates discharge only when the tribunal is satisfied that the admission criteria are not met. Doubt is therefore resolved against the patient. There is certainly an argument that the *Winterwerp* decision interprets Article 5 so as to place the burden of proof on those detaining.

CONCLUSIONS

We have argued that most of the rights protected by the 1983 Act are negative in form; the right not to be compulsorily detained without justification, for example, and the right not to be treated in the absence of the requirements laid down by section 58. Such rights carry with them secondary rights to safeguards such as access to a tribunal and review by an appointed doctor. In addition, the Act does impose duties on various actors, the section 117 duty to provide

[88] (1990).
[89] *Winterwerp* v. *The Netherlands* [1979].
[90] *Stanley Johnson* v. *UK* [1997].

after-care and the duty of the ASW to make an application for admission, but these have not yet been recognised as creating a correlative positive right to facilities enforceable by the patient in private law.[91]

It is not our intention to deny the benefit of traditional negative rights and safeguards. They are essential to any system of mental health care which authorises the use of compulsion, as was powerfully stated by Lord Steyn in the recent House of Lords decision in *Bournewood*,[92] and we welcome the opportunities which have been opened up by incorporation of the ECHR to strengthen our domestic safeguards further. However, it is important to be aware of the limitations of legal regulation and therefore to devise structures which are sufficiently sensitive to the cultures in which they operate to encourage them to attract more than token compliance. It may also be necessary to strengthen the extra-judicial mechanisms available to monitor the efficacy of the safeguards we already have. The Mental Health Act Commission cannot, on its routine visits alone, provide adequate independent oversight of both admission practices and the operation of section 58.

In reality, however, what many people who suffer from mental disorder desperately need is access to treatment or facilities in one form or another, not compulsion, and here the 1983 Act provides few answers. Indeed, as we have suggested above, there are grounds to suspect that, in the absence of any alternatives, compulsory admission is now being used by clinicians (and perhaps, even patients) as a device to force the provision of facilities.[93] While it may be impractical to think in terms of Parliament creating directly enforceable individual rights to treatment, there are other mechanisms available through which to strengthen the patient's position. As regards the provision of services generally there is certainly scope for central government to impose specific standards of provision on local health authorities by issuing directions and circulars which the courts can then enforce indirectly by way of judicial review.[94] In the case of individual patients we have already stressed the need to extend the powers of tribunals. Tribunals must be given the power to order a transfer. They must also

---

[91] See the discussion of *Fox* above. It is of interest to note that the action brought by Christopher Clunis to claim damages in negligence against the Health Authority for its failure properly to assess and treat him was struck out on the narrow public policy grounds that he retained some responsibility for his own criminal conduct and because no cause of action was thought to arise from the defendant's failure to carry out its functions under s.117 of the 1983 Act: *Clunis v. Camden and Islington HA* [1998]. See also Peay (1999).

[92] *R. v. Bournewood Community and Mental Health NHS Trust, ex parte L* (HL); and discussion thereof Eastman and Peay (1998a).

[93] See Caldicott, Conlan and Zigmond (this vol.). The DoH advice published in the aftermath of the *Bournewood* case (above) notably draws attention to the fact that under s.117, after-care duties apply when a patient leaves hospital following a period of detention under s.3, whether or not discharge from hospital takes place immediately after the patient is discharged from detention under the Act. Thus, s.117 after-care entitlement applies to all patients who have been detained under s.3, *no matter how briefly*: DoH (1998); *R. v. Bournewood* [1998].

[94] The Beta-Interferon case, *R. v. N.Derbyshire HA, ex parte Fisher* [1998] provides an example of the courts enforcing policy contained in a circular by way of judicial review.

be given greater powers to force the provision of after-care arrangements, ultimately a power to direct. While the proper protection of patients' traditional civil rights is essential, it cannot stand alone. People who suffer from mental disorder must have the ability to gain access to treatment and facilities and the law must be there to support them.

8

The Citizen Mental Patient

PETER BARHAM and MARIAN BARNES

Political and academic interest in the concept of citizenship is enjoying a renaissance. Debates about the nature of citizenship and the identity of citizens are being conducted in a number of contexts. One such contested area concerns the services individuals can expect to receive as social rights of citizenship, and whether or not rights to welfare have to be earned.[1] Concern about a democratic deficit in the governance of public services, and about the low level of participation of people within democratic processes, is also contributing to a re-analysis of the relationship between individuals and public policy-making.[2] An analysis of citizenship as constituting a set of responsibilities as well as rights suggests that citizenship not only has an inter-generational, but also an ecological, dimension – one which connects individuals to the physical as well as socio-political world.[3] Feminist analysis has demonstrated the gendered nature of classical theories of citizenship and has suggested that the concept is one which should relate to private as well as public lives.[4] But it is not only amongst academic and political analysts that the notion of citizenship is being re-examined. Practical action amongst community groups is demonstrating ways in which 'the practice of citizenship' might be developed and renewed.[5] This includes action being taken by groups of people who are or have been users of mental health services and who, together, constitute a part of a growing 'user movement' in the UK and elsewhere.[6]

A discussion of the significance of citizenship in the context of a book about mental health law needs to range wider than the explicit constraints represented by detention under the 1983 Act. It needs to take in broader questions concerning the inclusion or exclusion of people experiencing mental illness from the status or category of 'citizen'.[7] In order to do so we need to draw on both political and sociological conceptions of citizenship, and also suggest some of the moral

---

[1] Plant (1992).

[2] Burton and Duncan (1996).

[3] Roche (1992).

[4] Lister (1995), 1–36; Pateman (1992).

[5] Prior, Stewart and Walsh (1995).

[6] Barham (1997); Barnes and Shardlow (1996a), 275–86.

[7] And arguably, the equal jeopardy faced by those with psychopathic disorder or pædophilia in the context of serious personality disorder; see also Heginbotham and Elson, this vol., on discrimination.

connotations that the concept has come to attract. We are thus concerned with weighty issues: those of social justice, social exclusion and the moral responsibilities considered to attach to full membership of a political community. Needless to say, in what follows we do not claim to do more than map out what we believe are some of the key questions and dilemmas.

We also need to acknowledge the discomfort some people feel about the 'foreign' concept of citizenship. Whilst the discourse of citizenship is a familiar one in certain academic and political circles, we are not brought up to think of ourselves as citizens (indeed formally we are not citizens but subjects of the crown) and the language of citizenship is not generally part of lay discourse. In a state without a written constitution we cannot point to a statement of the inalienable rights of citizens and in a nation unsure of its identity we do not readily think of ourselves in terms of our relationship with the nation-state.[8] On the other hand, notions of fair treatment, of social justice and somewhat vague notions of 'our rights' do comprise part of the discourse of 'ordinary people' and come into play in any consideration of the responsibilities of the state towards those regarded as in some way 'in need' of help and support. In recognition of the more ready appeal to notions of citizens and citizenship elsewhere, we start with an example from another time and another place.

INEFFICIENT CITIZENS

Along with other categories of the sick, the mentally ill were beneficiaries of the medical reforms of the French Revolution. As Dora Weiner has described, the incurably mad were transformed into mental patients, madness became "mental alienation", and the task of the therapist was to restore patients to society and motivate them to become "citizen-patients". The Revolutionaries sought to instil a new compact between government and the sick in which, instead of being "Christians who meekly accepted pain and suffering", patients were to be transformed "into citizens aware of rights and duties when they were sick". For their part, the Revolutionaries recognised the obligations of government towards sick persons and understood that they "are neither 'free' nor equal to healthy persons if they are unable to earn a living".[9]

Even today the idea of the "citizen-patient" possesses a provocative continental resonance, and it was really only at the turn of the present century, especially in the aftermath of the First World War, with the heroic celebration of a citizen army and citizens in uniform, that a discourse about citizenship began to receive forceful and popular expression in Britain. "Citizenship is public health: public health is citizenship", wrote Dr Charles Porter in 1917 in an article on "Citizenship & Health Questions in War-Time".[10] The treatment of the men-

---

[8] See also the Human Rights Act 1998 incorporating the ECHR.
[9] Weiner (1993), 247, 8, 3.
[10] Porter (1917) 300.

tally ill was scarcely transformed, but for a time at least mental distress was seen in a less condemnatory light.[11] Servicemen suffering from what became known as 'shell shock' had, after all, broken down in the course of fighting for their country. Writing in the mid-1920s, J. R. Lord, a prominent psychiatrist who became Secretary of the National Council for Mental Hygiene, expressed the new mood:

> "In these pages I have tried to put in words some small things achieved – . . . or on the way to being achieved – which are designed to improve the lot of the mentally afflicted person, to soften the attitude of the 'group mind', commonly called 'the public', toward him, to find for him a place *within* the community during his necessary segregation as we do those sick in body, and not one *outside* of it, or on the fringe of it, estranged from the world as though he were a pariah or outlaw . . .; and, finally, at his recovery to welcome him back to full citizenship, and to find him suitable work so that he may live and thrive – which is the birthright of all men."[12]

Lord's inclusionary discourse has a decidedly contemporary shine – even in its gendered assumptions – but then a few pages later we read:

> "There is a tendency nowadays to forget, in the enthusiasm for the hospital treatment of early and curable cases, that one wholesome function of the Lunacy and Mental Deficiency Acts is the segregation from the public of those who, by reason of mental disorder or defect, impair the social machine by their inefficiency as citizens, and that the more thoroughly this is done the better for the home and for the nation . . . We thus reduce the intensity of many other costly social problems. In the majority of cases, the private care of the chronic lunatic is but a poor substitute for institution [*sic*] care . . . the proper place for such a person is undoubtedly a mental institution."[13]

On Lord's estimate about 50–70 per cent of the asylum population were chronic lunatics, so the birthright of all turns out to be the privilege of a few, and for all the talk about bringing the mentally afflicted back into society, it is apparent that the terms of welcome are somewhat conditional. A confusion between moral and diagnostic categories illustrates the uncertainties and dilemmas associated with identifying particular individuals as mad or bad, and thus whether their behaviour should attract condemnation or understanding. Practical social policy has always been involved with the development of policies and practices to ensure appropriate support for those in need and appropriate punishment for those who have transgressed, as well as developing systems to separate out the 'normal' from the abnormal or deviant in order to reduce the danger of moral pollution. In all these respects J. R. Lord typifies the debates in the inter-war period in which citizenship was a profoundly contested and ambivalent concept, pulling in several directions at once. A vision of society committed to the abolition of notions of ineligible citizens and of personally merited disease, and to the

---

[11] Contrasting with the more recent ambivalent response to those with PTSD; see *Alcock* [1992] and *Page* v. *Smith* [1996].
[12] Lord (1927), 2.
[13] *Ibid.*, 24.

eradication of "inequality before the best ascertained laws of health",[14] is at the same time accompanied by mistrust of the democratic potential of the "masses" and of the capacity of the "average sensual man", in Beatrice Webb's words, to exercise control over his own affairs, not least his own nature.[15] Though notions of giving people an opportunity to fulfil themselves as citizens (J. R. Lord's "birthright of all men") are certainly visible, they are accompanied by a sharp sense of stipulation, notably by forceful reminders that to qualify as efficient citizens individuals must be willing and able to fend for themselves in the market place.

EQUAL CITIZENS

Supposedly the qualms about the entitlements of mental patients to join the club were ironed out with the arrival of the National Health Service and its commitment to a welfare universalism. With the shortage of labour during the Second World War the disabled man became a potential asset and the *Lancet* was able to aver in 1942 that:

> "It seems inconceivable now that we should revert after the war to a system that left the disabled man derelict & demoralised to eke out his miserable years on public assistance."[16]

The highly gendered nature of the Beveridgean welfare settlement is once more explicit in this appeal. The apparent universalism of a system intended to ensure that citizens did not live in want was in fact based on assumptions of the male breadwinner contributing to the system through national insurance and taxation. Women as citizens were invisible to the architects of the welfare state, who assumed that married women would be financially dependent on their husbands. The invisibility of such assumptions indicates the indissolubility of conceptions of citizenship from the social context and social structure in which they are embedded. If women were implicitly only 'indirect' citizens, accessing welfare only via their husbands' public contributions (whilst at the same time being expected to provide private welfare directly in their roles as mothers and carers), what other implicit exclusions remained?

Conditional hesitation before equality of citizenship was apparently eradicated in the early 1950s when T. H. Marshall claimed that the social and economic rights of citizenship comprised the contribution of the twentieth century to the struggle for citizens' rights.[17] In fact, there was still substantial scope for disagreement about who could be considered to be included within the category of citizen, and, indeed, whether citizenship is a right of birth or a status to be

---

[14] Titmuss (1959), 299–318.
[15] Himmelfarb (1991), 374.
[16] Beach (1996).
[17] Marshall (1950).

earned. Though civil and political rights had been gradually won since the seventeenth century, the idea that rights were to be seen also as rights to welfare and resources (for the relief from poverty or illness, for example) originated only in the modern period.[18] The "basic human equality of membership", Marshall believed, had been "enriched with new substance and invested with a formidable array of rights".[19]

With the benefit of hindsight, we are obliged to be rather less sanguine and to recognise that behind the patina of egalitarian rhetoric there were long-standing divisions and patterns of inequality waiting to be rediscovered. Mathew Thomson has recently highlighted the impoverished role of mental health services, and the low status of the chronic mentally ill and the mentally handicapped, in the National Health Service of the 1950s.[20] Demographic changes, globalisation and patterns of migration have highlighted the possibility and the reality of new exclusions which would not even have occurred to those celebrating the enlightenment of the post war settlement. Optimistic assumptions about the capacity of economic growth to ensure adequate resources to provide for all those in need have been shown to be hollow and the conditional nature of access to welfare has been revealed. Notions of the 'deserving' and the 'undeserving' have not been relegated to history.[21]

THE WELFARE STATE AND THE DISEMPOWERED

A sceptical cast on the post-war welfare state in Britain was given in an essay by Michael Ignatieff in the late 1980s in which he claimed that:

> "the citizenship ideal of post-war liberals and social democrats stressed the passive quality of entitlements at the expense of the active quality of participation. The entitled were never empowered, because empowerment would have infringed the prerogatives of the managers of the welfare state."

Ignatieff went on to argue that welfare is about rights, not caring. Notions of the 'caring society' evoked for him the "image of a nanny state in which the care we get depends on what the 'caring professions' think it fit for us to receive". "Only someone who has not actually been on the receiving end of the welfare state", he continued, "would dare to call it an instance of civic altruism at work". The critical issue, he claimed, is not to "tie us all in the leading strings of therapeutic good intentions", but the "struggle to make freedom real" through the shared foundation of a "citizenship of entitlement".[22]

This analysis is one which is shared by many of those who are recipients of welfare services, although not all would agree that simply ensuring entitlements

---

[18] Plant (1992).
[19] Marshall (1950), 36.
[20] Thomson (1998).
[21] Langan (1998).
[22] Ignatieff (1989), 63–74.

to welfare services is a sufficient means of empowering those who use them. The relationship between people with mental illness, welfare services and citizenship is more complex than a question of rights and entitlements. It concerns the way in which problems are defined, who defines them and what scope there is for building civil society, as well as state systems, through which people can shape and control their world as well as have rights in respect to it.

This becomes clear when we look at the objectives and activities of self organ-ised groups of mental health service users:

"One of the most fundamental objectives of user groups is to claim the right to self def-inition for people whose identity and 'problems' have been defined by professionals. Reclaiming the right to define themselves and their problems is a prerequisite for attaining other objectives. Participation within such movements can demonstrate that those formerly viewed as passive and dependent recipients of welfare can be actors capable not only of controlling their own lives, but also of contributing to shaping the nature of welfare services and of achieving broader social objectives. Participation can itself contribute to a surer sense of identity."[23]

Experiences of injustice and social exclusion affect the capacity of people with mental health problems to engage as active citizens within the lives of their communities. It can be argued that a large proportion of people with severe mental illness in contemporary Britain form part of what post-industrial theo-rists have termed the 'new poor', a social group which is no longer nested within the classic lumpenproletariat or residuum, to be brought back into the labour market at times of high employment, but instead is permanently displaced and survives on welfare benefits.[24] The notable thing about the 'new poor' is that they are not empowered; they have no stake in society. As Ralf Dahrendorf has expressed it: "In a very serious sense, society does not need them. Many in the majority class wish that they would simply go away . . .". [25] Yet they *are* here to stay, it has been claimed, and the state may be forced to take repressive measures to keep the 'losers' in their place, through the increase of policing and surveil-lance and the erosion of citizen rights.[26]

Though the stances which people with a history of mental illness adopt within social life are as varied as those of any other population group, and there are wide variations in perception and belief, some recent studies have shown that there are a number of common themes and concerns which typify the per-spectives and circumstances of the 'new' mental patients of the 1980s and early 1990s, notably: the pauperisation of lives; the cruel effects of stigma and the 'taint' of mental illness; the barriers to equality with other people; the experi-ence of being made to feel less of a person or an inferior person; experiences of powerlessness in their efforts to exert some control over their lives, not least in their dealings with the medical profession; and the demoralisation produced by

---

[23] Barnes and Shardlow (1996b), 114.
[24] Bradley (1996).
[25] Dahrendorf (1988), 161.
[26] Bradley (1996), 69.

a health and welfare system that treats them as secondary sorts of people or as children.[27]

Here is an example of a contemporary 'citizen-mental patient'. Henry is an unemployed man in his late thirties with a long history of schizophrenic illness. He lives in a ground-floor council flat on a rundown estate on the edge of a town. Shame over his social situation now bothers him more than his illness:

> "The voices haven't come back. I'm pretty stable there because of the Modecate, but you feel ashamed at being unemployed so that when people ask me am I working, I don't like to tell the truth. I just walk away because I'm ashamed. . . . With schizophrenia you are not living, you are just existing. . . . I am labelled for the rest of my life . . . I think schizophrenia will always make me a second class citizen. I go for an interview for a job and the anxiety builds up . . . I haven't got a future. It's just a matter of waiting for old age and death."

In Henry's usage, 'schizophrenia' is not so much the name for an illness as for a social predicament to which the experience of illness has given rise. Henry illustrates not the *natural* consequences of mental illness, but the social consequences of becoming mentally ill as they enter into the person's most intimate sense of who he or she now is.[28]

Users of mental health services not infrequently exemplify Michael Ignatieff's sentiments on being at the receiving end of the welfare state. To be part of the welfare system, Simon remarks:

> "is a bit demoralising. . . . You're sort of tied to the strings of the hospital, the apron strings of the hospital I suppose you could say, you're being treated like a child really, and you prefer to think, well I'd like to be independent and this is OK temporarily, but I want to move on eventually and break away from all this."

In the experience of a young woman called Sarah:

> "the hospital encourages you to take on the tag, to go to groups and to live the life according to schizophrenia . . . it's a way of controlling you, where you are. I suppose it's a way of helping you in a way but it doesn't really help you and I have been institutionalised in that way and I want to break out of that mould now. . . . It creates half the schizophrenic's problems by doing that, by forcing them into a certain role or a certain mould or a certain way of life. . . . They hate you doing something stressful in your life, . . . and they just expect you to be a dummy and sit in groups and drink coffee all day."[29]

---

[27] Barham and Hayward (1995); Barham (1997); Barnes and Shardlow (1996); Read and Baker (1996).

[28] Barham and Hayward (1995), 77.

[29] Sarah appears to describe 'disabilities' induced by long-term institutionalisation. Whilst accepting such effects, the 'medical model' would probably describe many of her disabilities as arising directly from negative symptoms of the disease (e.g. social withdrawal and lack of motivation). This naturally leads on to questions whether behaviour patterns represent symptoms or choices. The former endow the person with welfare rights (albeit 'sub-citizen' restricted welfare rights—see Heginbotham and Elson) whilst the latter increasingly in the UK exclude the person from many welfare rights.

Ben provides a slightly different angle on the challenge to welfare paternalism when he says "I like to show that even though I have the illness, I can function as a person". He is anxious to ensure that by acknowledging an 'I have' illness, he is not surreptitiously transformed into an 'I am' condition. As he puts it:

"If I had a broken leg, I wouldn't say 'I am a broken leg'. In the same way, we shouldn't say 'I am a schizophrenic' . . . I might limp or something, but it shouldn't define your life.[30] . . . If people like me are to become part of the community . . . we need to be there as people in our own right with skills and failings, not as the local schizophrenic. I don't want to be a schizophrenic 'doing well': 'Isn't he good even though he's had a mental illness?' I just want my illness to be forgotten about. I'm not proud of it, it's a bloody nuisance. I hate being called a schizophrenic."[31]

AGENCY AND CITIZENSHIP

People who have used mental health services and work together to achieve social change are motivated as much by the need to challenge social exclusion deriving from poverty as from stigmatised identities, so as to ensure entitlements and create more sympathetic and responsive health and social care services. Brian Davey's work with the Nottingham Advocacy Group has led him to believe that action within the mental health system will be insufficient to enable people who have experienced mental illness to participate as citizens within their communities. He describes a strategy based in a recognition of the inter-locking problems faced by powerless people:

"Powerlessness has economic, environmental, social, interpersonal, health, emotional and cognitive dimensions. Powerless people live in limiting physical surroundings; they are spatially and socially separated from the people and places who decide about their destiny, they are not 'well connected', they have lower purchasing power as con-sumers; no purchasing power for entrepreneurial and investment roles and they are often emotionally and cognitively crippled by powerlessness – either not motivated to try to pull themselves out of a sea of troubles or driven by frustration to destructive or self destructive behaviour."[32]

The strategy he proposes includes the development of local projects to meet local needs in a way which brings together work and welfare. It is a strategy being developed elsewhere amongst those involved in community economic development.[33] Social and economic regeneration is seen as necessitating com-munity participation – it is not something which can be left to either state or market. The same is true of action to reduce health inequalities. This is why col-lective action amongst mental health service users (which may be understood as communities of identity) is a key part of a strategy to transform the mental

[30] See Matthews (this vol.).
[31] Barham and Hayward (1998).
[32] Davey (1998).
[33] West (1997).

patient into the citizen.[34] Participation within user groups contributes to a process which Ranson *et al.* describe as necessary to the existence of civil society, which recognises and includes difference, and in which the defining quality of citizenship is agency: "citizens are makers and creators as well as members of the worlds in which they live".[35] Research which has explored the objectives and strategies of user groups has demonstrated that this can happen in a number of ways.[36] The following quotations come from interviews with user activists undertaken as part of that research.

At an individual level, user groups support people receiving mental health services in making complaints about poor treatment, in asserting their right to receive information to enable them to choose their preferred mode of treatment, and in appealing against detention under the 1983 Act. People often need support to exercise their procedural rights:

> "One strand of the advocacy group [is] . . . trying to get access to information and guiding people in knowing the system and knowing how to get the best out of the health services, how to appeal against sections of the Mental Health Act and all those sorts of things where perhaps ordinarily people would advocate for themselves, but in a period of crisis they need that bit extra support."

User groups also exhibit broader concerns with issues of social justice and seek ways of reducing the experience of discrimination outside the mental health system as well as within it. For some, the motivation to become involved in user groups has come from personal experiences of injustice or poor treatment, or of having observed the experiences of others both in hospital and outside. Whilst advocacy is used to seek individual rights to services and to ensure fair treatment under mental health legislation, public awareness raising is also seen to be important in overcoming stigma and discrimination. Some groups have regular targeted campaigns which aim to overcome public fear by emphasising the normality of mental distress.

In other arenas user groups can become part of the accountability process between public services and their citizen users. Prior, Stewart and Walsh consider that "participation in the governance of the collectivity" is the "defining activity of citizenship".[37] They argue that the practice of citizenship:

---

[34] Interesting questions arise about the locus in which one's citizenship is to be grounded. What is, e.g., the responsibility of the mentally ill person to their family? Indeed, the relevance of this conceptualisation is expressed in alternative advocacy (or pressure) groups representing carers. Such carers often take a very different view of the person's needs, whilst complaining that their own rights are both restricted to being the nearest relative under the 1983 Act and by way of not being professional carers with a 'need to know' important clinical information, which has a bearing upon their own position. Hence, this juxtaposes the rights of one citizen against another. Ironically in this context the medical model, via rules of professional confidentiality, serves to protect the rights of the patient against those of the carer with conflicting interests.

[35] Ranson, Martin, McKeown, Nixon and Mitchell (1995).

[36] Barnes and Shardlow (1996).

[37] Prior, Stewart and Walsh (1995), 19.

"is one which locates citizens as active participants in this relationship [between individual, state and civil society] and which entitles and empowers citizens to be fully engaged in the process of its renegotiation and redefinition."[38]

The contribution user groups can make to the accountability of mental health services and, in becoming 'co-producers' through involvement in planning and decision-making fora, can be considered in this context. One described the process as follows:

"I think it is very easy for professionals to write a really glowing document saying this is what we are providing, but if the end result is that it is not what is really happening, then they have to be made accountable for that particular statement and so one of the roles I think we play is to actually challenge the quality assurance issues, for instance, laid down in the contract between the mental health unit and the purchasing group of the health authority. And if they don't meet that then we will actually raise it both with the purchaser and say, you know, what are you going to do about this?"

Giving account to and being held to account by users can be uncomfortable experiences for mental health professionals. Professional defensiveness has been evident in initiatives which have sought to empower mental health service users and users who speak out put themselves at considerable risk.[39] Thus the support of peers is critical if users are to engage in potentially critical dialogue with those who, in other circumstances, can exercise control over their treatment and their liberty.

In different ways user groups provide 'safe environments' in which sometimes fragile identities can be supported, and confidence and skills can be developed. The groups themselves provide a location in which new roles can be taken on, and for some that may be a stepping-stone to other things:

"In some ways it turned out to be a positive step for me. It changed my life around from something that was killing me, virtually, to something that I finally got some kind of reward in."

The capacity to demonstrate competence to participate in decision-making is a particularly important aspect of the contribution of organised groups of users:

"One of the major roles that we can play is actually to say, we are users, we can participate at this level, we can articulate, we can challenge, we can negotiate, we can write papers, we can do this, instead of [being] some bumbling idiot that doesn't know what they are doing."[40]

---

[38] Prior, Stewart and Walsh (1995), 21.

[39] Barnes and Wistow (1994), 525–40.

[40] This discussion touches upon the conflicting roles that user groups and their advocates occupy. The gap between such groups as the NSF and MIND is considerable; see also Heginbotham and Elson chap. 4, this vol.

CITIZEN MENTAL PATIENTS?

Are the identities of 'mental patient' and 'citizen' compatible? What role does legislation have to play in ensuring that they are? Formally, the term "lunatic" was abolished in 1930, when the stigma of pauperism was at least moderated, and the pauper lunatic became a "rate-aided person". "Madness" disappeared with the Mental Health Act 1959 in which the "person of unsound mind" was replaced by the softer attribute of "mental disorder". In the contemporary idiom, the former mental patient or sufferer from mental illness is likely to be reconstructed as a 'person with mental health problems'. This remains very different from the self-designation adopted by some people who describe themselves as 'survivors' of mental illness or of oppressive mental health services. Still, despite this progressive distancing from their origins, contemporary mental patients in the community for the most part display a recognisable kinship with the poor lunatics of the last century and beyond: they have not succeeded in breaking the ancient association between poverty and lunacy.

A report by the Rowntree Foundation published in 1995 showed that since 1977 the very poor in Britain have in fact become poorer, both relatively and absolutely.[41] Not only absolute poverty but also inequality *per se* is associated with poor health and the evidence is that expected improvements in the nation's health have been slowing down as material inequality has increased.[42] Inclusionary counter-visions of mental health policy are bent upon redressing the inequalities which restrict the entitlements of citizenship, but it is apparent that in the case of this (and of course other) disadvantaged groups the hour of the citizen has once again been postponed. A survey conducted by MIND revealed the extent to which stigmatising attitudes and discriminatory practices serve to compound the exclusionary effects of poverty and the debilitating impact of mental illness itself.[43] Release from the stigmatising discourse of psychiatry may not entail much more than the freedom to be picked up in the stigmatising discourse of poverty.

Though people with mental health problems possess certain civil rights, we must agree with Ralf Dahrendorf in arguing that "until traditional entitlement structures are broken, and elements of a civil society created", we cannot properly say that they have arrived as citizens. Instead, "they have merely gained a new vantage point in the struggle for more life chances".[44] One could, of course, present a more sanguine account of the fortunes of mentally ill people in Britain in the twentieth century that focused more exclusively on the great oak trees of legislative reform that line the historical avenue. But to do so would be to ignore or gloss over the continuing constraints on the life chances of people with mental health problems that legislative reform by itself has been powerless to affect.

[41] Rowntree Foundation (1995).
[42] Wilkinson (1996).
[43] Read and Baker (1996).
[44] Dahrendorf (1988), 161.

The options for identity formation and negotiation may have expanded, but the identities of former mental patients in the community are insecurely grounded, and so is the whole idea of the person with a history of mental illness as a trustworthy human being, capable of controlling his own nature. Though class antagonisms in British society may have abated, and Britain may be characterised as an increasingly classless society in which collective sources of membership are less and less significant, the reality for a large proportion of people with long-term mental illness is a class identity (that of a second class citizen) as a spoiled identity.[45]

A more optimistic view is that, like other social movements for which identities organised around class have been replaced by cultural identities based in ethnicity, sexuality or gender, users of mental health services and other disabled people have started to reclaim the right of self-definition and, by their actions, to challenge a perception of incompetence and dependency. Partial success in arguing that disability is a civil rights issue has been achieved with the passage of the Disability Discrimination Act 1995. But neither action by such groups nor anti-discrimination legislation in the absence of a genuine commitment and strategy for the reduction of inequality can resolve the structural exclusions which consign mental patients to the category of marginal citizens. In any case, the advantage of identifying mental distress as a 'disability' as a means to secure civil rights in concert with other disabled groups is hotly contested within the mental health user movement.[46] By the light of the inclusive rhetoric of patients' charters and so forth, it is of course easy to scoff at J. R. Lord's discriminatory judgements; but on the other hand if we look at what is actually happening – at what former mental patients like Henry are actually saying – it becomes apparent that Lord's doubts about the social membership of chronic lunatics, far from being consigned to the rubbish bin of history, find renewed expression in the social fabric.

Law and its associated regulations and procedures do have a role to play. It is to be welcomed that the Mental Health Act Commission now includes user commissioners – not only for the inclusion of patient experience within a statutory body which oversees the implementation of the law, but also symbolically in placing citizen mental patients alongside other groups represented within the Commission. But, as has been argued throughout this book, the law has only a marginal role to play. Its significance is not just a symbolic one – the law itself is part of the overall public policy discourse which places people as insiders or as 'others'. The law can define the explicit exclusions from citizenship which attach to the use of compulsion or to an assessment of incapacity, that is, it can define the circumstances in which action to limit the autonomy of citizens can be legitimated, and the procedural rights available to citizens to challenge such limitations, but it cannot require action to enable the *practice* of citizenship – it cannot directly achieve social inclusion.

[45] Barham and Hayward (1995); Bradley (1996).
[46] Sayce (1998).

'Citizenship' continues to be a contested arena for the reason that it is inextricably implicated in conflicting political and ethical agendas. Contemporary mental health policies set out to affirm "the humanity and worth of people with severe mental illness, and their rights as citizens".[47] But the translation of such prescriptions into significant action would presuppose the existence of a community with a substantive commitment to righting the disadvantages suffered by groups such as the mentally ill, and such a commitment is inevitably difficult to secure in a society, and a corresponding practice of medicine, that has largely been formed by an ethos of freedom.[48]

Recent discussions of citizenship have forefronted dimensions of the concept such as 'duties or obligations', hidden from view in the immediate post-war decades in the preoccupation with 'rights'. Yet as we have seen, over the course of the century calls to participate in the charmed circle have generally been accompanied by stipulations or conditions, even if these have not always been made explicit. Indeed, the very notion of the 'active citizen' may be read as a moral discouragement to more privatised or idiosyncratic life styles. For example, Jeffrey reports that whenever he sees his psychiatrist the question is always, "How are you filling your time, Jeffrey?" According to Jeffrey, the psychiatrist wants him to:

> "go to this centre which is another workplace . . . Well, I've said to him that I'm far better off doing what I'm doing, just going for a drink – all right, I'm a loner – going for a drink, having an occasional bet and filling my time either going swimming or walking."[49]

The question remains whether citizenship is a truly inclusive status or whether it has to be earned, and if so how it can be earned. The current preoccupation with work as the only route into social inclusion is bound to leave many people who experience long-term mental illness stranded without any means of gaining entry.

Similarly, recent trends such as the idea that the pursuit of good health is the responsibility of good citizens would have been wholly familiar to doctors and health educators in the opening decades of the twentieth century in which there was a new emphasis on civic duty and individual responsibility for the development and regulation of body and mind. "It is the individual which counts", as Dr Charles Porter put it in 1917.[50] Peterson and Lupton make explicit the link between citizenship, health and the social roles through which citizenship can be demonstrated: "[a] useful citizen engages in work, participates in social relationships and reproduces, he or she even goes to war to defend the country if prevailed upon to do so. Good health is deemed vital to achieving these activities."[51]

[47] Mental Health Foundation (1994), 17.
[48] Hauerwas (1986).
[49] Barham and Hayward (1995), 45.
[50] Porter (1917).
[51] Peterson and Lupton (1996), 61.

Implicit in this emphasis on self-regulation is a notion of 'responsible patient-hood', but it is obvious that today there is little consensus over what this is to mean in relation to people with mental health problems. As recently as the early 1960s, social scientists were urging the inmates of psychiatric hospitals to come to terms with mental patienthood by exhorting them to acquiesce in a conception of self which gave meaning to the fact that the mental patient was, "in an unavoidable, public sense, a 'mentally ill' person".[52] Today, one aspect of the discourse of responsible patienthood is that health services should only be accessed in genuine need. For those experiencing mental health problems the reality is more likely to be that attempts to behave responsibly and to access services before crisis point is reached are frustrated because of lack of resources. This is contributing to the increased proportion of psychiatric hospital admissions which take place under the 1983 Act.

The whole idea of education for citizenship is very much *au courant*. Perhaps the time will shortly arrive when there will be a ready market for lessons in how to be a good citizen mental patient. And one could plausibly argue here for a conception of 'responsible patienthood' that adopts a highly critical stance on orthodox medical perspectives and on the social straitjacketing of mental patient lives. For example, the responsible citizen mental patient recognises that she has a duty to return to work. So what does she say to the doctor who instructs her that she must be 'content to be on the sick and cope and manage as best' she can?[53] From this angle, 'responsible patienthood' is the site on which the 'citizen' and the 'mental patient' encounter each other, and recognise the enormous gap between what has so far been achieved and the race that is still to be run.

---

[52] Pine and Levinson (1961).
[53] Barham and Hayward (1995), chap. 2.

9

Auditing the Effectiveness of Mental Health Law

NICK BOSANQUET

The role of law in mental health services in England and Wales has vastly increased: from 1986 to 1997 the number of patients formally admitted to NHS facilities and registered mental nursing homes in England alone rose from 14,780 to 24,191[1]; the number of hearings before mental health tribunals has also risen very significantly, with 2,972 hearings held in 1986 and 7,575 in 1996,[2] as have official inquiries.[3] These changes could be taken as the inevitable result of a more open system and as indicators of success. Alternatively, they could also be seen as the result of service pathology – of extreme problems faced by staff in trying to manage services in ways which can inspire confidence. The aim of this chapter is to point to a management and service development process which could reverse the tide of resorting to the law, litigation and inquiry. It also points to an agenda for more constructive use of legal principles. It asks, what would be the role of law in an effectively managed process of care?

Increased use of legal process is usually seen as a sign of failure in an organisation serving customers or clients, while for most organisations law is a matter of a few key principles which they apply during their daily work. This primary level of law sets targets and aims in areas such as employment rights and duties, and health and safety. There are many people, including housing managers, human resource managers and health and safety officers, who administer such key principles. Beyond this primary level of law there are then the secondary levels involving recourse to solicitors and the lower courts; and beyond even this lie the tertiary peaks of law in the higher courts which are scaled only by the very rich, the very poor (through Legal Aid) or the very determined. Unhappy is the organisation which has to make extensive use of the higher reaches of the law. In fact, apart from a few specialised areas, such as patent law, it is hard to think of any section of society which routinely makes so much use of legal process

---

[1] DoH (1998).

[2] DoH (1997a), App. 5.

[3] The marked increase in official inquiries is attributable to the circulation of NHS Executive Guidance HSG(94)27, in May 1994, which made it mandatory to hold an independent inquiry in cases of homicide by people who had had contact with the mental health services. See, generally, Peay (1996); Sheppard (1996).

beyond the primary stage as do the mental health services and their clients. Apart from the frequency of sectioning and of tribunal hearings, at the secondary level, annual expenditure on inquiries over the last two years can be estimated to have cost at least £10–15 million a year, which is about 10 per cent of total spending by social services on mental health and considerably more annually than the amount being spent on assertive outreach teams.[4]

There are, of course, some special and obvious reasons for legal involvement when there can be consideration of compulsory detention or treatment. There has always been a special framework of law covering compulsory detention, and this will continue to be needed, as will a procedure for appeal; but the developing role of law in mental health goes far beyond this inescapable aspect. The recent search for new law may have been used as a substitute for achieving a consensus about policy and as a way of dealing with perceived problems in providing care. The law is also used as a way of examining, and even auditing, the process of care (again through the rising number of inquiries and through negligence litigation[5]). Law is seen therefore as a remedy for failure in the system. However, at worst, law could represent a displacement activity which creates the impression that something is being done, while in fact key management issues are not being addressed in a critical and constructive way. So, although some law is inevitable and necessary, its role needs to be reviewed in the light of its possible costs, as well as any gains in clarity and direction arising from its use. There could, for example, be moves towards evidence-based law which would be formulated on a more explicit assessment of the costs of law, arising through delay[6] and through reducing voluntary compliance.[7] Law cannot be a substitute for an effective process for managing services.

This chapter aims therefore to address three main issues. First, what should be the balance between law and management process? Secondly, how could we develop a more appropriate balance in the future between legal involvement and other kinds of initiative? Thirdly, what would be the research agenda if law were to be evidence based? The chapter ends by posing some more general questions about auditing the operation of mental health law.

THE MANAGEMENT PROCESS

The use of law has to be seen against a background of policy and care development. There has been great public concern about services for people with severe

---

[4] Bosanquet (1995).

[5] Eastman (1996b).

[6] Richardson and Thorold (this vol.) describe and comment upon the example of delays in holding MHRTs; a cost analysis would include the costs of unnecessary detention in hospital, some imputed cost arising out of the unjustified period of detention and the cost of the administrative process which lies behind the delay. Some of these costs also arise where tribunals have to be adjourned because of the absence of information or key witnesses.

[7] See Caldicott, Conlan and Zigmond (this vol.).

mental illness, with one of the main themes being the unreliability of services in containing patients who are likely to be violent. This concern is very different from those which gave rise to the 1983 Act, which related largely to the view that law was likely to be over-restrictive in curtailing the freedom of those who were under treatment. Government reacted, first by setting a series of aspirations for better care programmes and then by funding a series of projects for better services at the local level.

Clearly, any new programme should aim at reducing the costs imposed on the individual and society by mental illness. Total costs were recently estimated at £32.1 billion for the UK.[8] For schizophrenia alone, the annual 'burden of disease' in 1996 in England was £4.1 billion, covering treatment costs, social security support and indirect costs of lost output (Table 1). Lifetime costs for patients with the most severe illnesses could be as great as £750,000. New evidence from OPCS shows that the quality of life effects are even greater than was previously realised. People with long-term mental illness have a lack of independence and choice in society which must rank them as one of the most deprived of social groups.[9] Even for patients in hospital, social contacts are limited. The recent census by the Mental Health Act Commission and the Sainsbury Foundation showed just how poor were the day-to-day environment and living conditions for many such patients; 45 per cent of hospital residents felt close to no-one in the establishment, exposing the myth of an idealised world of hospital care.[10] There are also heavy direct economic costs, since 70–80 per cent of people with long-term mental illness are out of the workforce and

Table 1: Costs of Schizophrenia—
England 1996

	£M
Hospital Care	953
Primary Care	11
Social Services	141
Voluntary Services	39
Law and Order	56
Social Security support	800
Total Direct Costs	2000
Indirect Costs	2100
TOTAL	£4.1Bn

Source: Bosanquet (1998).

[8] Patel and Knapp (1998).
[9] OPCS Report No. 6 (1996).
[10] Mental Health Act Commission/ Sainsbury Centre (1997).

likely to remain unemployed long-term; indeed, they are one of the groups under retirement age who are most likely to be out of the workforce long-term.

There are opportunities, however, to minimise costs: longer-term follow-up suggests that the results for patients in terms of recovery are good compared with those for many kinds of severe physical illness, with a third or more of patients making a good recovery and even more doing so with the use of modern anti-psychotic drugs.[11] Such drug therapies now hold out the promise of much more effective treatment, reducing negative symptoms and increasing the potential for effective care outside hospital.[12]

The challenge to local managers and clinicians therefore is to put together a programme which will provide security during the first stage of illness and increase opportunities for social rehabilitation and quality of life. This will involve the development of organisations which will be able to meet the challenge of providing continuous and effective care, through using contributions from different teams, the setting of clear aims and the use of resources in effective ways to meet targets. Such a discipline of general management was well set out for the NHS by the Griffiths Report.[13] This suggested that the job of general managers was to lead the organisation towards better performance through setting clear aims and targets.

The managers in an effective organisation will face different challenges at different periods of time. These will vary with the local culture and the changing environment. However, there is a major challenge in developing effective supported care programmes which require in-patient care in the first phase, together with use of new drug therapies. There needs then to be intensive support after discharge and assertive outreach to ensure continuing contact and support. After this should come a stage of rehabilitation, employment support and improved access to housing. Such a programme has been costed at £13,000 per patient for a cohort of 100 patients.[14] This includes an initial investment, in that it will rarely be easy to reduce costs of old services in a way that is exactly synchronised with the rise in the costs of the new. The programme also needs effective management in order to establish credibility with patients, funders and the local community.

Managers of mental health services therefore face a new agenda which can be defined as containing five main areas. First, there is a need to improve the care process for patients so as to make use of new therapies and to provide more consistent support. For England there will soon be new standards set out in a National Service Framework. There is also already more regular auditing and benchmarking of care. Concern about quality and standards of care has led to top-down initiatives. At the same time Trusts in the Inner City Initiative Group are investing in benchmarking in order to provide more evidence about their

---

[11] Warner (1985).
[12] Guest, Hart, Cookson and Lindstrom (1996), 59–67.
[13] DoH Report (1983).
[14] Bosanquet (1995).

own performance. However, improvement in the care process will often run up against funding constraints, especially in the use of new drug therapies. Only about 15 per cent of patients have atypical anti-psychotics prescribed for them; yet there are at least 30 per cent of patients who are described as treatment resistant. Survey evidence shows there is currently severe rationing of access to newer therapies.[15]

Secondly, there must be improvement of rehabilitation and reduction of social exclusion. The public image of patients is that of the minority of young male patients who are a threat to themselves and others. Yet there are many other patients for whom the main problem is their declining contact with society. There are also many women patients for whom conditions in care are poor and opportunities limited. Such conditions fail markedly to meet those set out in the Patients' Charter. For example, the Charter states, under the heading of "single sex wards", "[i]n all cases, you can *expect* single sex washing and toilet facilities"[16]; yet the Mental Health Commission/Sainsbury survey of acute hospital wards showed that, for at least a third of women patients, there were no single-sex washing and toilet facilities.[17] The agenda for managers is to develop effective services for all these groups.

Thirdly, there must be support programmes for carers. The contribution of carers within mental health services is recognised to be very large, yet even communication remains poor between carers and service providers,[18] a shortcoming repeatedly emphasised by the inquiries which have followed homicides by patients who have had recent contact with the mental health services.[19] In fact, the latter represents an example of a conflict between service reality (and its economic evaluation) and the ethical and legal models that are applied within services. Hence, in reality many carers are part of the 'caring team' and, therefore, in terms of efficiency, should share information from the professional carers on a 'need to know' basis. However, professional carers are bound by ethical and legal rules of confidentiality which define the 'need to know' solely in terms of intra- and inter-professional relationships. Although the basis of these rules is that there may be a conflict of interest between the patient and their family, in many circumstances this is not the case and, unless the patient consents to disclosure, the result is likely to be service (and economic) inefficiency. This sets service efficiency and law in direct opposition to one another.

Fourthly, there is the challenge of developing cultural pluralism. Many patients with the most severe problems tend to be from ethnic minorities and African and Caribbean patients are, in particular, more likely to be detained in hospital under section. The law, therefore, is applied in an uneven way, which

[15] NSF Report (1996).
[16] Emphasis in original—DoH (1996).
[17] Mental Health Commission/Sainsbury Centre (1997).
[18] Rogers, Pilgrim and Lacey (1993).
[19] Peay (1996).

may arise from cultural stereotypes; use of the law can, in turn, reinforce such stereotypes.[20]

Fifthly, there is a need to win the community's confidence. There is often strong local resistance to any community projects; and the degree and intensity of NIMBYism has increased greatly over the past five years. So, public concern about the existing programme has had side effects which have then made it more difficult to introduce new services.

In response to these challenges a new generation of managers is now beginning to show how there can be constructive local initiatives. The task for managers is to create a sense of confidence in a different future. This agenda can be broken down into a series of tasks or problems facing managers. They include tasks relating to management time, funding, staffing and outside alliances.

Management time

Any diversion of time from short-term operational problems could be seen as dangerous, even frivolous. All the short-term pressures on Trusts are to concentrate on the crises, inquiries (including the fear of them) and information requests from above; but, unless the chief executive, chairman and board show their belief in 'the future' then no-one else will.

Funding

Each Trust has to establish how its own funding and that of mental health services in the area have changed. Programme budget data for England show that nationally spending in real terms for mental health services within the NHS actually fell from 1991/2 – 1995/6, a fall of 2.5 per cent.[21] Spending by social services remains at a very low level. Total spending by social services on residential and day-care services was £238.6 million in 1995–6. This contrasts with spending of £917 million on clients with learning disabilities.[22] Many Trusts are being coerced by falling funding and the rising costs of hospital services.[23] This blocks out any margin available for investment in new services and expenditure on new drug therapies. A realistic assessment of the funding base is an essential first step towards local negotiation about investment.

[20] African and Caribbean People's Movement (1998).
[21] Health Committee Public Expenditure on Health and Personal Social Services (1997).
[22] *Ibid.*
[23] *Ibid.*

Defining an investment strategy

This is needed as a focus for developing services and bidding for funding. A full programme would cover in-patient care, intensive home support, rehabilitation, employment schemes and access to housing. Costing of an investment programme for one Trust in an inner city area showed the spending needed to provide this kind of service for a district with a cohort of 50 patients (suffering from schizophrenia) in the first year and 100 in the second as £1.3 million or £13,000 per patient[24] (see Table 2). The strategy includes some continued use of in-patient beds, but it is realistic to assume that this could be less than under the present system. Any investment strategy also has to include greater use of new drug therapies, in order both to reduce the effects of long term medication with drugs which have pronounced negative effects and to promote earlier rehabilitation.

Table 2: Investment programme for schizophrenia treat-ment/care

	Cost (£)
Community Team	225,000
Day treatment/care	186,000
Respite housing/care	20,000
Family doctor/primary care support	4,250
Staff training in psycho-educational support	20,000
Continuing care/community support	291,000
Carer/peer support counselling	54,000
Drug treatment/prescribing	37,000
Work programme	54,000
In-patient support (10 beds)	400,000
TOTAL	£1,291,000

Source: Bosanquet (1995).

Re-skilling of staff

At present there are many unusual aspects of the staffing situation in mental health services. It is an area in which desperate staff shortages are often claimed, but with little evidence about working patterns or of clear aims being set for staff. It is also an area of social merit but low morale; one in which communication is vital, yet, as the Mental Health Act Commission/Sainsbury Centre

[24] Bosanquet (1995).

showed, there is very little contact between patients and staff.[25] Further, it is an area with many training needs but with control over both training and job structures highly fragmented in the interest of professional baronies. Since there are 80,000 staff working in these services, and there may be 1,500–2,500 working for a single local Trust, the investment required is substantial.

The way forward

Yet the manager has some potential resources; first the talent, energy and commitment of staff working in the service at present, plus the scope for in-service training, using local resources in higher education. Managers cannot afford to wait for a whole new generation with multidisciplinary training; they have to 'make it happen' using local resources. A recent Sainsbury Report on future staff roles and training has defined the whole agenda in a very useful way[26]; the challenge for local managers is to define and fund what can be done at the local level. Managers can also broaden out the staff team and ensure that use is made of psychologists and of new skills from a variety of other disciplines.

Winning new allies

At present attitudes to people with schizophrenia are regressing, with a rising tide of NIMBYism. There therefore has to be a sustained attempt to identify possible allies and to win them over. There *are* some opinion allies in groups of concerned local citizens. There are also some resource allies in housing and employment. Managers have to win a share of spending on special housing schemes and on employment rehabilitation. Health managers have to use their own health funding effectively: but they can go further in expanding the funding by winning support from others. In fact, since their job is to win for people the chance of a normal life in the community, it is essential to win allies and to arouse interest among those who are prepared to share the vision and the challenge of improving opportunities for one of the most deprived groups in society. Family doctors also have an important opinion and resource role. Indeed, some evidence suggests that they may, in fact, be more trusted by patients than are psychiatrists.[27]

New partnership with the private sector

In the past the private sector has been used as a branch line for shunting problem patients; the level of suspicion between the NHS and the private sector is

[25] Mental Health Act Commission/Sainsbury Centre (1997).
[26] Sainsbury Centre (1997).
[27] Rogers, Pilgrim and Lacey (1993).

both mutual and high. Yet there is scope for a much more creative partnership. The private sector can offer new advantages in terms of access to capital and speed of innovation. There could also be new relationships with the voluntary sector so that Trusts might use options other than direct public employment for providing services. As things have been, there has been inefficiency through confusion of commissioning by health authorities between the NHS and private sectors (branch line shunting). It is also probably the case that the economic perspective applied by commissioners to their funding of the private sector has been limited to simple tariff comparisons of the NHS with the private sector, thus emphasising a highly 'partial' approach. A more comprehensive approach would address not only direct and immediate costs (by way of tariffs) but also attempt to put values on differential benefits arising from utilising, or not, the private sector within the overall commissioning programme.

Support to carers

Any move towards community-based care is likely to imply increased roles for carers compared with the old custodial system, and one positive change in the 1990s has been the move towards greater involvement of both clients and carers in planning services. There is likely then to be an increase both in time and cost for carers once patients are spending more time outside hospitals.

Managers face a major task, therefore, in making progress on this agenda, as well as keeping the existing system going and dealing with day-to-day crises. The task will be greatest in inner city areas, which experience a combination of increased need with reduced funding. The closure programmes for some hospitals, for example Friern Hospital, have made some special funding available for patients who were there, but they did not provide for the loss of admission spaces where patients would otherwise have been treated. It is also in the inner cities that there are the greatest problems of communication with patients from ethnic minorities and the highest obstacles to developing voluntary services that patients will actually seek to use. The alternative to the inviting carrot is the coercive stick, relying heavily on sectioning of patients. This brings us, at last, more substantively to the law.

A CONSTRUCTIVE NOT PATHOLOGICAL RELATIONSHIP

What would be the interface between law and the management process if it represented a constructive rather than a pathological relationship? Clearly, the law could contribute to service improvement, rather than its use becoming an almost ritualistic expression of unease at the major problems of managing services. There would be clear definition of primary principles in law which staff could themselves use in order to work on developing and improving services.

Mental health law would be seen as setting positive principles of good service and care which would help to give some sense of direction to the care process.[28] Principles defining patient interest would also help to focus on the issues of funding and rationing, issues which are often concealed and yet which are vital to patients. At present there is no clear duty on professionals to put the patient's best interests first in decision-making. Rather, the first consideration is that of local funding pressures bearing down on patients. These pressures may mean that drugs are prescribed which have serious short- and long-term side effects. Inevitably there will be resource choices to be made and resources will be limited; but at present there is nothing to counterbalance the impact of funding pressures. This may mean there is little improvement in care to this group even over a period when general funding to the NHS increases. Thus, as we have seen, funding of mental health services fell by 2.5 per cent over a period when real terms funding rose to the health service as a whole. Law cannot create a utopia of infinite resource availability: but it *can* reduce the role of secretive decisions on rationing and increase the sense of duty towards a relatively weak group in the struggle for resources.[29] Empowering the ward sister, the ward staff, the day centre staff, care workers and care managers with a sense that they are the guardians of some important legal principles and legal duties could help to shape the law 'bottom-up' rather than 'top-down'. The effectiveness of 'bottom-up' law, an example of which is the Health and Safety at Work Act 1974, derives from an individual awareness that people 'own' these long-term responsibilities; they do not always need lawyers to remind them. Indeed, it seems more likely that staff will 'own', and therefore seek to implement, law which encourages resourcing than law which is restrictive of patients' civil rights, albeit also protective of those rights.

A well-managed system should also be able to carry out investigation and reviews relatively quickly, so that the results can be available within weeks rather than years. At present, when there are serious incidents the main method of inquiry is through special inquiries, some of which have reported as much as four years after the event. There would be no reason for such delay in discovering important information if there were to be better organised care programme and audit systems, including much more information on patient and carer perspectives. Such better organisation of information would, therefore, make it

[28] E.g., the Patients' Charter (see above) is couched primarily in terms of expectations rather than rights. It contrasts markedly with, e.g., the Tenant's Charter, which clearly sets out the rights and responsibilities of tenants at a local level; see, e.g. Scottish Office (1991). An alternative approach might be through the health oath approach, setting out the duties of professionals, see Hurwitz and Richardson (1997).

[29] In relation to general medical treatment see *R. v. Cambridge DHA, ex parte B* [1995], where although it was held that the health authority had acted lawfully in deciding to refuse further specialist treatment to a child with leukaemia, because it was advised by its own doctors that it such treatment was not clinically indicated, the effect of the case was to make transparent (and more public through the media) the decision processes through which the health authority had gone in making what amounted strictly to a rationing decision in the face of opposition from the father.

possible to achieve a preliminary report within days and a full report within weeks. The results of any such investigations would then be available to help with improving services rapidly. There would still sometimes have to be special inquiries where unusual problems arose, even if they were seen to arise much less often than at present. However, even these could be serviced much more easily by improved information sources, which would also be available much more quickly. The development of better management and audit information could therefore assist the quasi-legal process. In particular, the process would be able to draw on the results of effective management information systems, which would provide a much more reliable base for such inquiries. In summary the law could provide a lever to help staff with the day-to-day problems of improving services rather than having an occasional presence related to severe crises and possible discredit. [30]

RESEARCH AGENDA FOR EVIDENCE-BASED LAW

A new agenda for evidence-based law points towards the need for careful and objective assessment of the costs and benefits of using the legal route towards improved national mental health. The costs include the direct costs of the legal process, but they may also include the costs which arise from any effect of the law in reducing the ability of local managers to take effective decisions. If managers are able to use law and to respect its principles at the primary level of law, this should reduce service involvement with its higher and more problematic levels.

Prospective additions to law could be investigated much more explicitly through scenario or impact planning. Public discussion of laws usually concentrates on the first round effects and the later effects usually get little attention: yet these may well involve much more serious costs. Clearly, the varying impacts of the law concern not just immediate costs but also longer-term effects on decision-making.[31] The savings or reductions in disbenefit which may result from the initial use of law may well be offset, or even (as in the case of legislation on rent control) completely dwarfed, by later impacts arising from private decisions. Thus, in the case of the mental health services our current law may have had the effect of reducing the drive towards improving process at the local level. So, we need more research on the continuing and reactive effects of the law, as an incentive, on decisions made in its shadow.

Laws could also be designed so as to minimise costs and to maximise the role of voluntary action. For example, the use of law in treating patients on a com-

---

[30] See Eastman (1996a). It can be argued that service improvement is better addressed by continuous audit (utilising the 'audit cycle') than by *ad hoc* inquiries, even if they go beyond inquiring into a single event and address the whole service in which the event occurred. The advantage of audit is that it can be fitted into the 'process' of mental health care.

[31] See Bartlett and Phillips (this vol.).

pulsory basis may solve one short-term problem but it may well also lead to another longer-term problem through reducing overall compliance with treatment.[32] Law *could* be used as a last resort to encourage and reinforce voluntary action. So there may be important opportunity costs to the use of the law in reducing voluntary action and innovation. The research agenda should investigate these opportunity costs.

Use of the law represents a complex process involving referrals to different levels. The primary level involves lower cost but often less assurance of due process and sometimes less defined standards and professional expertise. The secondary and tertiary levels involve more cost but also more assurance of procedural safeguards. Decisions at the primary level are available quickly, while those at the higher levels take much longer. In some areas of activity professional self-regulation (for example, by the General Medical Council) goes alongside the primary level of law, through delegated authority. Future development needs to be through a partnership between law and voluntary action to secure effective results. The alternative is an increasing amount of law, as more and more of it is passed in order to make up for defects in voluntary action and self-regulation.

Although it has been argued that audit can be used to regulate the provision and allocation of tangible resources in a cost-effective manner (an example being evaluation of the effectiveness of new treatments for leg ulcers) and that legal audit might be used to set and raise standards, the role of clinical and service audit in respect of psychiatric care generally, and specifically in respect of the effectiveness of coerced care, is much more problematic. Whether, and what, audit might tell us about the relative effectiveness – both in the short and longer term – of coerced, as opposed to voluntary, care is much less clear. How, for example, might one begin to think about costs associated with the loss of liberty when the use of compulsion is justified?[33] Similarly, how might one think about the costs to the community's well-being arising out of a failure to use compulsion in circumstances where, again, it would be justified? Fear of crime is sufficiently problematic; fear of crime committed by the mentally disordered is an phenomenon about which we know almost nothing[34]; costing it, even in non-monetary terms, is likely to be complex and challenging. Weighing the costs of using fewer 'dirty drugs' against more draconian mental health law may create an equation that is soluble in its first element, but devilishly slippery in regard to the effects of more draconian law on civil liberties generally.

[32] See Caldicott, Conlan and Zigmond (this vol.).
[33] See Afterword for a detailed analysis of this point.
[34] See Pearson (this vol.).

10

Madness and Moral Panics

GEOFFREY PEARSON

Mental illness is no longer the neglected 'Cinderella' of the health service when it can command a bold front-page headline – "U-TURN OVER MENTALLY ILL" – such as that in the *Daily Mail*.[1] "The controversial care in the community policy is to be altered", the news story announced, "in an attempt to end the tragic toll of killings by freed mental patients". This has by no means been the only headline of its kind, linking the policies of hospital closure and community care to violence and homicide. In one of the most sensational, following the publication of the report of the Boyd Inquiry into homicides and suicides by mentally ill people, the *Sun*[2] headlined the news "Free to Kill", while the *Daily Mail*[3] on that occasion responded with "Sick and Dangerous".

The aim of this chapter is to set these controversies in context. I will not attempt to assess the scale of the difficulty, nor will I discuss policy implications. It has been clear for some years that there were significant areas of linkage between mental disorder and the criminal justice system, with some estimates suggesting that as many as one-third of men serving prison sentences, and one-half of women, suffer from some identifiable mental health difficulty.[4] Quite apart from homicides linked to mental illness, the 'mentally disordered offender' has become a preoccupying focus in a more general sense, with some justifiable reason to believe that mentally ill people are coming into increasing contact with the police and courts as a direct result of the failure of community care policies. In one local study which looked at a diversion scheme for mentally disordered offenders in a busy inner London Magistrates Court in Islington, although it was only a thin trickle, as many as 100 seriously disturbed defendants were identified each year.[5] These were overwhelmingly men, and one-third had been charged with some form of personal violence, compared with an average of 5 per cent of all notifiable offences. Black people were also disproportionately represented in this group, with one-third of Afro-Caribbean descent, and in a related study of probation officer reports more than one-half of offenders identified as having mental health problems did not have

---

[1] *Daily Mail*, 17 Jan. 1998.
[2] *Sun*, 18 Aug. 1994.
[3] *Daily Mail*, 18 Aug. 1994.
[4] Gunn *et al*. (1991); see also Singleton *et al* (1998).
[5] Burney and Pearson (1995); Burney (1996).

permanent accommodation, and were three times more likely to have no fixed abode. One-half of them were also assessed as having problems with either drugs or alcohol.[6]

While it is not possible to generalise from a small-scale initiative such as the Islington Mentally Disordered Offenders Project – either in terms of the links between homelessness and mental illness, the pattern of violent offences, the prominence of alcohol and drugs or the vexed question of the over-representation of people of Afro-Caribbean descent among those with a diagnosis of schizophrenia – this kind of evidence does nevertheless point to local pockets of serious and inter-linked difficulty. To be blunt: is community care failing, and are the sensational news headlines justified? Or are we going through some kind of moral panic? First, it will help to clarify what a 'moral panic' is.

THE NATURE OF MORAL PANICS

It is sometimes assumed that to allege that the mass media are generating a 'moral panic' is to imply that problems are being 'invented' and that the press are 'making up' stories. This is, however, a crude misrepresentation of the notion of a moral panic.

The term was first employed by Stanley Cohen in his book, *Folk Devils and Moral Panics*, which was concerned with the Mod–Rocker disturbances at seaside towns in southern England in the mid-1960s. Cohen's point was that while these clashes between rival groups of youths were very real, albeit spasmodic, they came to be falsely represented in the news media in a variety of ways. For example, the disturbances were often understood as a consequence of post-war affluence, although the majority of those convicted of offences were in low-paid jobs; the violence was linked to young people riding motor-bikes and scooters, although the vast majority had travelled to the seaside by coach or train; the trouble was seen as orchestrated by organised gangs, although "the groups were loose collectivities or crowds".[7]

In these ways, a moral panic does not 'invent' news, but places an emphasis on some aspects of events while diminishing others. One can also see in the case of the Mods and Rockers that these kinds of distortions were not random, but tended to reflect other deeply held preoccupations, such as the supposedly demoralising effect of post-war freedom and 'affluence' on Britain's youth. Something similar was found in the late 1980s when social concerns focused on the so-called 'lager louts' who were projected in the media as products of the 'loads-of-money' Thatcher years, but who, in an authoritative Home Office study of the phenomenon, emerged as young men who were either in low-paid, unskilled jobs or unemployed.[8] Indeed, where young people are concerned there is a deeply rooted historical tradition in Britain to identify the problems of today

[6] Burney and Pearson (1995), 300-2.
[7] Cohen (1972), 34-5.
[8] Tuck (1989).

as entirely new and unprecedented, and to contrast them uninvitingly against a lovingly remembered but hopelessly falsified past of peace and tranquillity.[9]

Where mental illness is concerned, we are perhaps in danger of lapsing into a similar state of dreamy nostalgia for the 'good old days' of the asylum, forgetting that madness has probably always been an emotionally charged subject. One need only think of the vast social energies put into the building of the Victorian asylum, and the care devoted to the design of its 'moral architecture', to sense what forces were imagined necessary to tame these unruly passions.[10] Madness and criminality have their own linked history as well, as is testified to by the far from untroubled history of the emergence of the 'insanity plea', where lay perceptions, medical testimony and legal principle tussled over thorny moral questions of free will, responsibility, and compulsion.[11]

Renewed controversy is entirely to be expected, therefore, when we begin to tear down these vast Victorian edifices which are such a part of the landscape – both physical and cultural. Complaint has come from some quarters, however, that media controversy is misrepresenting mental illness and stigmatising the mentally ill. Such complaints have been voiced by members of the Royal College of Psychiatrists[12] and others with a specialist interest in the matter such as MIND. From another quarter, however, special interest groups have made deliberate attempts to dramatise the dangerousness of the mentally ill supposedly in order to mobilise support for improved institutional care. Thus, a poster campaign launched in the late 1980s by the charity SANE (Schizophrenia: A National Emergency) depicted the mentally ill in the following terms, with a far from subtle dig against professional expertise:

"HE THINKS HE'S JESUS
YOU THINK HE'S A KILLER
THEY THINK HE'S FINE"[13]

This is clearly an area in which much emotional energy is invested, a far cry from rational policy considerations. If one area of concern is whether 'moral panics' inspired by mass media coverage (or other interest groups) might undermine public confidence in hospital closure programmes and community care strategies, a preliminary consideration must be what we know about public attitudes towards mental illness.

POPULAR FOLKLORE AND MENTAL ILLNESS: PREJUDICE AND TOLERANCE

In his book, *Mystical Bedlam*, which offers an extraordinary illumination into how mental health issues were understood in seventeenth-century England,

[9] Pearson (1983).
[10] Scull (1989).
[11] Eigen (1995).
[12] Philo (1996), 113.
[13] Barham (1997), 152.

Michael MacDonald offers the neat observation that "[e]ver since antiquity, mental illness has been defined by experts but discovered by laymen".[14] It is in fact an insight that was already available to sociologists working in the field of social psychiatry in the 1950s, namely that – whether in terms of pathways to treatment and care, or subsequent rehabilitation – the career of the mental patient was significantly determined by the perceptions or actions of immediate family, friends, neighbours, workmates and others in his or her environment[15]; and that these perceptions and actions were themselves not simply a function of widely-held social beliefs about mental illness and madness, and could often be in opposition to rejecting and discriminatory belief systems about mental illness and the mentally ill.

This 'folklore' of madness is nevertheless one which remains stubbornly intact to what specialists and experts might have to say – whether doctors, lawyers, social workers or forensic scientists – although this folklore is subject to shifts and changes, its own internal momentum governed and interacting with wider sets of social preoccupations. Broad-based surveys of public attitudes, which have been usefully summarised by Wolff,[16] offer a mixed-bag of results – suggesting a complex and little-understood blend of prejudice and tolerance. The findings of surveys of this kind are also by their very nature somewhat distant and fail to capture subtle movements in people's attitudes and responses when actually confronted by mental illness. It might therefore be more helpful to use the small-scale sociological studies of the 1950s to think through how the more immediate and intimate environment governs the fate of mental patients.

If, to follow MacDonald, mental illness is first 'discovered' by lay people, it is equally true that this discovery can lead to different forms of action. Equally, lay perceptions and responses are not always what we think they are. One possibility which emerges from this earlier tradition of social research is, rather obviously in view of the stereotypes which encircle madness, social rejection; although another influential study found that feelings of stigma were felt and expressed by relatives towards former mental patients in only a minority of families.[17] Indeed, a common response was to ignore the oddities of behaviour and conduct, or to 'normalise' these and to place them within a common-sense framework of understanding.[18]

In two separate studies from this period of spouses' reactions to the onset of mental disorder in their husbands or wives, a common response was to see changes in behaviours as a result of stress at work or other humdrum aspects of everyday life.[19] People might typically say, "[h]e's run down", "[s]he's not

[14] MacDonald (1981), 113.
[15] Clausen and Yarrow (1955); Goffman (1959) and (1968); Spitzer and Denzin (1968); Scheff (1967).
[16] Wolff (1997).
[17] Freeman and Simmons (1961).
[18] Scheff (1966).
[19] Yarrow *et al.* (1955); Schwartz (1957); Sampson *et al.* (1962).

herself at the moment", "[h]e's a bit under the weather" and so on without defining the family member in any way as 'sick' – and these 'normalised' judgements would even extend to what others (including psychiatrists) would see as quite bizarre and frankly psychotic behaviour.

It was work of this kind which informed much of Erving Goffman's essay on "The Moral Career of the Mental Patient", which was originally published in 1959, subsequently forming part of the collection of essays known as *Asylums,* and which came to be deeply influential in the critique of the institutionalisation effects of the mental hospital. In reference to the family studies, Goffman summed these up as showing "the extraordinary amount of trouble a person may cause for himself and others before anyone begins to think about him psychiatrically, let alone taking psychiatric action against him".[20] Elsewhere, a different gloss was put on this body of work as one which documented "the monumental capacity of family members, before hospitalisation, to overlook, minimise, and explain away evidence of profound disturbance in an intimate".[21]

One should also say that these research studies indicated not only a profound capacity for tolerance in many, although not all, of the families studied; but also a painful struggle in terms of living with mental illness, not knowing what, if anything, to do about it, and later the equally painful struggle of living with and relating to someone labelled as a 'mental patient'. The labelling by professionals, together with the admission of the wife or husband into hospital, would often lead family members to accept medical definitions and to 'realise' that what they were confronted with was mental illness. But this was not true in every case, and while some people clung to their 'common-sense' framework, for others there was an uneasy truce between lay definitions and professional definitions, involving ambivalent and sporadic movements back and forth. In other words, these responses by married partners towards spouses who sometimes demonstrated quite bizarre distortions of thought and feeling was not a question of indifference; rather it was a manifestation of solidarity.

The point we can take from this kind of research, which now lies often neglected on dusty library shelves, is that madness is inextricably a question of lay definitions. It would seem that no amount of campaigning and education can displace folklore and substitute the 'true' understanding of expertise. On the one hand, this is a stronghold of prejudice and stigma – witness the extraordinary range of derogatory terms and phrases used in common parlance to describe mental illness and the mentally ill.[22] It should also be remembered, of course, that expertise can itself embody a bastion of dogma, prejudice and stigma which has historically assisted in the social exclusion of the mentally ill.[23] It is equally true, however, that this research reveals that people have a capacity for tolerance of quite extraordinary dimensions towards the symptoms of

---

[20] Goffman (1968), 120, n. 3.
[21] Sampson *et al.* (1962) 88.
[22] Philo (1996), 119-21.
[23] Barham (1984).

mental illness in close relatives and friends. The field of lay perceptions, in other words, is a complex blend of sympathy and solidarity, discrimination and exclusion, banishment and belonging.

Finally, what should not go unrecognised is that this mid-1950s North American research was informed not only by a social scientific scepticism towards the exclusive domination of medical expertise in the field of mental health. It was also informed by a set of concerns to understand the meaning of mental illness in people's lives, as a way to improve their access to treatment and other forms of professional help. It was feared not only that delays in seeking help could worsen both the patient's mental condition and the quality of life for other family members, but also that an improved understanding of the meaning and impact of mental illness within the family and wider community could assist in devising more appropriate systems of after-care following hospitalisation.

Now of course with the closing of the asylum and the advent of 'community care', the ground has shifted appreciably. Not only is sustained after-care an unimaginable luxury, but family obligations and the labours of love of carers are cashed in by the state and exploited as an uncosted element in the policy of 'care in the community'. This is by no means solely a question which affects the field of mental health, of course, and the de-institutionalisation of psychiatry is only one part of a wider strategy to shift the costs of care away from state provision. Research on the meaning of 'community care' to informal carers has largely been concerned with the elderly and general health care, and the disproportionate burden which this places on women.[24] As Janet Finch[25] indicated in her book, *Family Obligations and Social Change*, taking the care of the elderly as her focus, the financial implications of the shift were potentially massive:

> "the unpaid support given to frail and elderly . . . has saved the Treasury very large sums of money . . . this unpaid support for elderly people is at least equivalent in financial terms to the total expenditure on health and social service for the over 75-year-olds".

Where the mental health field is concerned, however, this fiscal squeeze has come to be associated not with the 'invisible welfare state' of family obligations, but with a newly demonised vision of unchecked madness rampaging in the streets.

FEARS OF MADNESS I: THE UNIVERSAL 'OTHER'

If people's attitudes towards mental illness, at least where family members are concerned, are much more tolerant than one might suppose, how can we account for the widespread anxiety and fear which the subject seems to evoke?

[24] Finch and Groves (1980); Graham (1984); Ungerson (1987).
[25] Finch (1989), 125.

One common line of thinking is to regard madness and the mentally ill as a manifestation of unruly and ungovernable passions, the irrational 'other'. It is certainly an unavoidable aspect of madness (or what is thought of as madness) that it involves a deeply experienced transgression against what is taken for granted, 'commonsense', the 'obviousness' of perceptual reality and rationality. As recently portrayed by Jackson and Williams[26] in a sensitive and yet disturbing study, these are the "unimaginable storms" of psychosis. Although having said that, it is equally true that a dominant aspect of twentieth-century culture, following the first romantic and modernist artistic experiments of the nineteenth century, has involved transgressions of these same 'obvious' dimensions of space, time and thought: the perceptual distortions of cubism; the disruptive nature of atonal music; the 'stream of consciousness' and floating temporality of the novels of Virginia Woolf and James Joyce; the autistic ramblings of Samuel Beckett's characters; the subversive qualities of surrealism and dadaism; the 'cut-up' novel of William Burroughs; the dramatic perceptual and temporal dislocations of photomontage in film and television, and now, of course, the 'virtual' realities of the computer-age and the post-modern turn.[27] In other words, twentieth-century culture has involved a playful attitude towards the 'real' and the 'rational', to such an extent that we live in an environment which is decisively shaped by the same transgressions which we find objectionable or incomprehensible in madness.

There is something quite wrong and unconvincing about an absolutist view which sees prejudice and fear towards the mentally ill as a primeval response to the 'other', as if to shut off the mentally ill against fellow citizens as a totally oppositional entity. It is a point of view often attributed to Foucault's work: "[a]s Foucault has argued, we live with an ingrained predisposition to view madness as essentially 'other'".[28] And yet, the central thrust of Foucault's history of madness – right or wrong – was to show how the responses of utter rejection, denigration and confinement were themselves historical processes associated with the Enlightenment and the rise of scientific reason.[29]

If the fear of madness cannot be attributed to the fear of a universal 'other', it can nevertheless be a terrifying visitation, damaging the lives not only of the mentally ill themselves, but also their friends, families and sometimes neighbours. Indeed, the material of madness would neither hurt nor offend so much if it were not such an intimate a part of human experience – in the way that HIV/AIDS has become such a universally preoccupying illness, charged with intense emotional energy, whether in the form of solidarity or denial and revulsion – because it potentially touches each and every one of us through the fundamentally human exchange of sexuality, whereas a broken leg (unlike a broken heart) is merely a dull fact of biology. At other times and places, other illnesses

---

[26] Jackson and Williams (1994).
[27] Pearson (1995).
[28] Pilgrim and Rogers (1993), 59.
[29] Foucault (1967) and (1972); Still and Velody (1992).

have been charged with similar emotional contents – cholera and consumption for different reasons in the nineteenth century; cancer in the mid-to-late twentieth century; anorexia and bulimia as cultural symbols of a supreme cost paid in homage to a version of femininity portrayed in the late twentieth century. Whereas madness – although always with us – has found itself inter-locked with a shifting terrain of associated cultural images and preoccupations: an object of curiosity and mockery in the ceremonies of Bedlam; as the final downfall of intemperant habits in Hogarth's *Rake's Progress*; as the "madwoman in the attic" who, as Elaine Showalter[30] has said, "haunts the margins" of nineteenth-century women novelists' texts; as the worm-within of a degenerate "submerged tenth" or "residuum" so deeply feared in the late nineteenth century, to be excised by eugenics and confinement[31]; and now as the sign of a rampant and racially tinged violent masculinity.

FEARS OF MADNESS II: THE 'MEDIA' AND THE 'FEAR OF CRIME'

As both Foucault and Showalter have shown in their different ways, it was the poet, novelist, and artist who gave expression to popular imaginings of madness and helped to shape them in earlier times. Today it is the mass media, and one key issue in terms of how social scientists have described the nature of 'moral panics' is in terms of media effects, and more recently in terms of how these might influence the so-called 'fear of crime'.[32] In order to assess the role of the mass media in relation to public perceptions of mental illness and the mentally ill, it will first be helpful to look at the debate on representations of crime and criminality since this area is more advanced in terms of media studies.[33]

Public debates on mass media influences invariably tend to 'blame' the media for one thing or another. A deeply traditional form of grievance – which I have shown in my book, *Hooligan*, can be traced back to accusations against the early Victorian Music Halls and beyond[34] – is that portrayals of crime and violence encourage imitative 'copy cat' behaviour. At different times such accusations have been brought against children's comics, the cinema, television, video-nasties and the radio.[35] In the latter respect, in 1948 the Chief Constable of Gloucestershire even went so far as condemn the radio serial, *Dick Barton, Special Agent*, as "crime propaganda".[36] The controversy is seemingly never-

[30] Showalter (1987), 4.

[31] Pick (1989).

[32] Sparks (1992); Kidd-Hewitt and Osborne (1995).

[33] We also have the benefit of considerable research on the 'fear of crime', including several sweeps of the British Crime Survey (cf. Hough (1995)). While leaving any number of riddles about the 'fear of crime' phenomenon, much has been clarified. By comparison, we know very little of substance about the 'fear of madness'.

[34] Pearson (1983).

[35] Pearson (1984); Barker (1984); Kidd-Hewitt (1995).

[36] Chibnall (1977), 55.

ending, with one side defending the freedom of expression and the other calling for the censorship, with over-statement always possible on either side.

More directly related to our concerns are the ways in which the mass media are also often accused of over-dramatising and sensationalising public issues. This can sometimes be a naïve response, as when 'news' is taken to be (in an ideal world) nothing more than neutral facts. What constitutes 'news' in the sense that something is newsworthy, and the way in which 'news' is produced, is however far from being a neutral process. As Stuart Hall[37] described it in his introduction to *Paper Voices*, a study which compared the *Daily Express* and the *Daily Mirror* in the post-war years:

> "Our starting-point was the assumption that at all times, but especially in periods of rapid social change, the press performs a significant role as a social educator. By its consistent reporting and comment about people and events, the press reflects changing patterns of life in a society. More significantly, by its selectivity, emphasis, treatment and presentation, the press interprets that process of social change."

Hall went on to describe how these processes of selectivity and interpretation were combined with the need for the paper to appear "fresh every day, giving dramatic coverage to urgent events", struggling with its competitors on being "first in the field, with the 'fullest' possible coverage", always searching for a "new angle":

> "Yesterday's news is stale. . . . Even the best news stories have only a brief half-life in the daily press. The emphasis, then, is on immediacy, topicality, the dramatic . . . News stories break and disappear with indecent speed."

It is therefore in the very nature of the news media that they depend upon these processes of selectivity, emphasis and interpretation. It is equally true that the readers of newspapers and the viewers of television are not mere passive receptacles and that there is an active interplay between 'message' and 'receiver'.

In what is undoubtedly the most sophisticated recent attempt to unravel these relationships, Richard Sparks in *Television and the Drama of Crime* examines the debate on media portrayals of crime and how these may relate to those social anxieties summed up as the 'fear of crime'. The position adopted by Sparks is that those who claim a direct transmission or cultivation of fear as a result of television viewing[38] are both "simplistic and over-stated" and "very difficult to defend empirically".[39] One particular difficulty is why people actively choose to watch crime fictions which they know will be 'scary', and in a subtle argument Sparks suggests that crime fictions offer to viewers "moral tales" which are not merely entertaining but which may also provide certain kinds of reassurance to their audience. Just as news stories are not merely factual depictions, fictions

---

[37] Hall (1975), 11.

[38] E.g. Gerbner and Gross (1976).

[39] Sparks (1992), 3, 7.

maintain lines of connection to the 'real world'. The blurring is of course complete when fact and fictional representation collide, as in *Crimewatch UK* where actors play out 'real life' re-constructions of real crimes.[40] By way of conclusion, while admitting that it would be folly to claim any finality in these tortured debates, Sparks writes that:

> "It seems to me inescapable that one has to take in earnest the expressive and emotive character of the themes of crime and punishment. . . . The fact that expressiveness and emotiveness seem inherent does not however mean that certain of their manifestations may not be damaging – distracting, excessively simplified, anachronistic, illiberal. The question is thus not whether people have emotional responses to crime and punishment, but rather whether the uses made of the emotiveness of the topic are exploitative, ulterior, sectional, and in this sense ideological. Yet the notion of a rational response to crime, purged of social sentiment, is equally a distraction."[41]

MENTAL ILLNESS IN THE MEDIA: A MORAL PANIC?

How do attempts such as these to develop what is both a critical and sympathetic understanding of how mass media images are produced and consumed relate to mental illness? In their recent book, *Media and Mental Illness*, Greg Philo and his colleagues in the Glasgow University Media Group document the ways in which mental illness is commonly portrayed.[42] Particularly useful is a study by Lesley Henderson[43] of how TV producers for 'soap operas' such as *Coronation Street*, *Brookside* and *Casualty* constructed story-lines concerning mental health issues – illuminating complex processes of negotiation and decision-making, resulting in different kinds of images. Generally speaking, however, the authors emphasise the wholly negative ways in which mental illness and the mentally ill are represented in the mass media – a view shared in another recent review of the subject which appeals for a "balanced view".[44] What I wish to ask is what is meant by a 'negative' image, and what might a 'balanced' image of madness look like?

In a detailed analysis of British media content in April 1993, the Glasgow Media Group demonstrated that stories concerning mental illness were heavily slanted towards violence and harm to others, as against other categories such as harm to self, prescriptive advice, or 'comic' representations. In all, two-thirds of stories mentioning mental illness involved harm to others.[45] However, there are serious methodological problems with this estimate. It should be noted for example that the survey was undertaken at the time of the Waco siege in Texas which resulted in almost 100 deaths of people belonging to a religious cult, and

---

[40] Ross and Cook (1987); Kidd-Hewitt (1995).
[41] Sparks (1992), 162.
[42] Philo (1996).
[43] Henderson (1996).
[44] Wolff (1997), 160.
[45] Philo (1996), 48.

one-third of the news stories analysed were generated from this source alone. So that, if these were removed from the analysis, the proportion of news stories focusing on violence would be reduced to one-half of the total concerning mental illness.

Even so, if one-half of media images concerning the mentally ill focuses on violence, this arguably remains a disproportionate emphasis. In terms of the details of these media stories provided by the research, however, it is hardly a matter for surprise that a student nursery teacher convicted of sexual assaults on 60 children in his care within a ten-month period (for example) should be described by the tabloid newspapers as a "sex fiend", "sex pervert", or "sex monster".[46] Or that the case of a nurse, Beverley Allitt, who faced 26 charges ranging from grievous bodily harm to murder of children in her care – where legal counsel agreed that she suffered from a personality disorder – should also figure prominently in news media reports.[47] These and other stories analysed by the researchers involved court cases and convictions for serious crimes, and it is therefore difficult to understand the Glasgow Media Group's argument – since what would a 'positive' news report of crimes of such enormity amount to? Quite apart from any other consideration, in objecting to such 'negative' portrayals of socially and personally destructive behaviour, the authors seem to have forgotten Emile Durkheim's elementary sociological observation that the very existence of crime and outrage fulfils a positive social function, by defining the limits of what is regarded as socially unacceptable conduct and thereby reinforcing social and communal solidarity.

One aspect of communal solidarity which these kinds of news stories reflect is the perceived obligation for the State to provide care for the vulnerable and protection for fellow citizens. This reflects, in part, a managerialist attitude towards what we call 'risk management' and towards the role of professional expertise in minimising 'risk'. As Nikolas Rose[48] has described it, particularly in the sphere of psychological expertise, "a new role is opened for experts". Whether in terms of condemnations of social workers in child abuse scandals, or accusations that mental patients have been 'freed to kill', experts are placed in the hot seat:

"that of identifying, recording, assessing risk factors in order to predict future pathology and take action to prevent it. Expertise can turn chance and happenstance into certainty and predictability; alternatively, others can demand that it does so and berate it when it fails to prevent delinquency, child abuse, and so forth . . . within the new logics of risk, professionals acquire the obligation to bring the future into the present and render it calculable."

Rose suggests that, while some 'evangelical' professionals might have sought to over-promote their powers of prediction and control, the elevated status

---

[46] Philo (1996), 54.
[47] *Ibid.*, 64-5.
[48] Rose (1996), 94-5.

afforded to expertise in these affairs reflects a more general public disdain for chance and risk. It is a post-Enlightenment mentality which, as a consequence of being more civilised, wishes that these kinds of things would not happen, but then finds itself haunted by the spectre of chance and hazard which, in an 'ideal' world, would be under control and predictable. It wishes the unpredictable rendered predictable, and it wants the genie put back in the bottle (or rather behind high asylum walls).

To state the issue in this way is to raise the discussion to a different level, in terms of what kinds of human beings we wish to be and what kind of society we wish to live in. The Enlightenment legacy is one of wishing and believing human subjects to be perfectable through various techniques of education, rehabilitation and treatment. This imagined perfectly ordered world was perfectly captured in the ordered architecture of the Benthamite Panopticon, the asylum, and the penitentiary.[49]

The closure of asylums and the return of mentally ill people into civil society thereby represent a major cultural shift, and it would be truly extraordinary if this were not accompanied by certain amounts of anxiety (even sometimes alarmist) in the news media and elsewhere. There is a historical symmetry in the 'moral panic' associated with this closure programme and the attendant risks (real or imagined) of a 'community care' programme which is at the same time novel, under-funded and seemingly fragile.

CONCLUSION: UNFINISHED BUSINESS

I have tried to sketch out some of the issues which should be taken into consideration in interpreting media responses to mental illness. Undoubtedly, the large proportion of news stories which focus on violence and harm to others found by the Glasgow Media Group research indicates one dominant feature of a 'moral panic': the tendency to emphasise one kind of event, and thereby to diminish the importance of others, leading to distortion. Earlier Canadian research found something similar, with news stories about the mentally ill heavily biased towards those with a diagnosis of schizophrenia and whose behaviour was troublesome.[50] If this much is clear, it must also be said that a response which attempts to rest its case on this basis risks the accusation of naïvety. 'News' is not a passive reflection of 'reality'; 'news' is not a balanced scientific analysis, and does not try to be; 'news' is not constructed out of mundane, humdrum, non-troublesome events.

A second point which I have tried to emphasise is that, if moral panics can distort and manipulate events, they also act as a crystallising focus for legitimate anxieties and discontents. Social change is not an even process, but one involving many detours, false leads, bumps-in-the-night, prolonged periods of stagna-

---

[49] Rothman (1990); Ignatieff (1978); Foucault (1977); Scull (1989).
[50] Day and Page (1986).

tion and sudden shifts of gear. Britain has been going through a massive change of policy towards the mentally ill in recent years, a huge social experiment which turns its back on the looming edifice of the Victorian asylum, an experiment still in its infancy and in which the outcome is by no means certain. As Peter Barham[51] has perceptively observed, it would be a mistake to think of community care as no more than "the substitution of one locus of care for another" – that is from hospital to community – in that it also invites "a drastic reshaping of the ways in which we think about, describe and, in particular, relate to people with a history of mental illness". The experiment involves, in a nutshell, attempting to make available to mentally ill people a relationship based on citizenship rather than the paternalistic arrangements of patienthood. It would again be naive to expect such a fundamental cultural shift not to be accompanied by moments of turbulence and public disquiet.

Finally, there is the question of resources. Concern has been expressed in a number of quarters about under-resourcing in terms of both community and hospital provision. In 1993, the Mental Health Act Commission's customarily unhurried prose described a "crisis" in inner city psychiatric facilities, with a rapid turnover of highly disturbed patients, some patients fearing for their own safety, others sleeping in corridors.[52] Four years later, these modern scenes from Bedlam were still to be found by Commission visitors, with more than one-half of all wards visited reporting problems with sexual harassment of women patients by male patients, with no staff observed to be in contact with patients on one-quarter of the wards visited, and with staff time in many wards absorbed by the continuous observation of small numbers of 'at risk' patients.[53] The resource difficulties of community care are equally notorious[54] and the plight of many former mental patients in the community nothing less than a national disgrace.

Media reports of violence associated with former mental patients are the tip of an iceberg. The tip is a highly visible and red-hot news story, albeit involving legitimate concerns about social protection and community safety. The submerged depths conceal the dull monotony of many more people's lives (and not only those of mental patients) within this unfinished story of a deteriorated welfare state.

---

[51] Barham (1997), 151.
[52] Mental Health Act Commission (MHAC) (1993), 17-18.
[53] MHAC (1997).
[54] Mental Health Foundation (1994), 65-6.

11

Decision Making and Mental Health Law

ANNIE BARTLETT and LAWRENCE PHILLIPS

It is taken for granted that the application of mental health law involves multi-disciplinary and often multi-agency work. The recognition of this, and the challenges it poses for professionals, have underpinned government advice to agencies particularly over recent years. One way to think about the issues relating to multidisciplinary and multi-agency working is to address the cultural differences which follow from the varying intellectual perspectives and professional outlooks of the professionals involved. Such differences are played out in day-to-day decision-making, including the use of mental health law. A further dimension of such decision-making is the perspective brought by those to whom, one way or another, mental health law is applied, that is, users of services and those upon whom it impacts, for example, patients' friends and families.

Any changes to mental health legislation would presumably have to be justified on the basis that there would be consequent benefits for users, their friends and families and the general public. However, such benefits could only follow from the decisions made with changed law by practitioners, by whom we mean both mental health practitioners and the wider group of professionals involved with mentally disordered offenders, e.g., probation, social services, judges, lawyers. We suggest, therefore, that improvements to the law must consider not only how decisions *should* be made but also how they *are* made currently in practice. This chapter considers both these aspects of decision-making, but it does not consider the *detail* of (current or new) legislation itself.

We note in passing that, for many practitioners and patients, mental health legislation is marginal to their main role and experience respectively. For others, again both practitioners and patients, it is central. Also, in contrast to what was true historically, most mental health work is undertaken without recourse to any legislation. However, multi-agency work not infrequently requires that mental health professionals work with professional groups which are explicitly concerned with the law in general rather than with mental health law in particular. Decision-making across disciplinary and agency boundaries sheds light on the values and belief systems of these different groups. Any attempt to introduce significant changes in mental health legislation would therefore need to take these values and beliefs into account.

In an effort to highlight some of these values and beliefs we have chosen to explore rational decision-making and how well, or otherwise, it fits with the application of mental health law in practice. This seems particularly pertinent since the law is explicitly intended to be rational. The structure of the chapter is therefore to consider briefly the notion of culture and how it applies to professional and non-professional groups involved in decision-making processes. Then we summarise decision theory, which highlights the elements of rational decision-making and provides a guide for how decisions should be taken in an uncertain world where objectives conflict. We then focus on empirical research, which shows how people actually make decisions. This leads us to propose a list of common errors in and of decision-making, which we illustrate with examples taken from the field of mental health. Finally, and in detail, we examine a complex case vignette. This was initially explored by the authors with a mixed group of professionals and users operating under time constraints[1]; it brought into focus the reality that conflict toleration within a hierarchical system may offer a better description of how mental health law operates than pure rationality. The way forward may be therefore to consider the balance of power between regular key players, as well as the principles of law itself.

THE CULTURE OF PROFESSIONAL GROUPS

An important first question to ask is what marks anyone out as belonging to a particular group of professionals. No doubt this could be answered in many ways. A starting place is to see culture simply as a summary of what a group of people does, says, believes and possesses. The group is defined by similarities rather than differences, although a given person can see themselves sharing more than one cultural identity. Whilst for many individuals their work is not a significant identity, for many professionals it is. It will focus their lives but equally circumscribe it. Young doctors will eat, breathe and, if they are lucky, sleep their work. Young pupil barristers adopt certain styles of speech and dress which enhance their chances of being taken on as a tenant. The coalescence of professional identity and self is that much more likely if the identity has a positive value and if it represents a lifelong career choice.

Intrinsic to the apprenticeship systems of most criminal justice and health care professionals is the adoption of professional standards, in terms of both personal and professional *behaviour*. Drunk judges make tabloid headlines precisely because, when stopped in their cars, they breach the internally and externally perceived codes of behaviour for judges. Underpinning the elements of professional practice are *ideological principles* embodied in terms such as the

---

[1] This occurred in the second stage of the project which underpinned this book.

'caring professions' or 'advocacy'. Both explicitly and implicitly the trainee professional becomes 'one of us'. She acquires exclusive and sometimes highly prized knowledge which is mystified by *technical language* specific to the social group and which may be translated only reluctantly. Accompanying that knowledge is an understanding of the *process* in which this knowledge is king; to anyone standing in the dock of a criminal court for the first time the process of the courtroom and its implications must be hard to follow.

Historically, the study of social organisation was carried out where social organisation embodied a single cultural group's way of doing things i.e. structures, strategies and underlying beliefs. However, the application of mental health law involves the analyst in a more complex social setting. There are multiple social arenas and multiple cultural groups; additional to the participating professionals is the service user and their family and friends. This description represents a subtly and importantly different perspective from earlier perspectives taken on the social world of mental health.[2] Perhaps accurately reflecting historical difference, it has tended to emphasise the practical isolation of mental health staff and patients from the rest of the world. However, community care has structurally changed mental health services, since they are now set against the backdrop of ordinary society in a way that was not true of an earlier era of secret asylums.

Thus the job of the social analyst of mental health law is difficult. Mental health law must operate not only in relation to its own principles and detail, against the background and scrutiny of wider society, but also within small social arenas of great complexity. These small social arenas can be seen as 'melting pots' of the different cultures involved. Curiously, when representatives of these different cultures meet it is often explicitly in order to share in a single social activity, that is, decision-making.

ELEMENTS OF RATIONAL DECISION-MAKING

Modern decision theory can be of use to a professional decision-maker on occasions when she wishes decisions to be coherent or internally consistent. Coherence is a relatively simple concept: with the presumption lying behind it that you would not wish to make decisions that are certain to lead to worse consequences than if you had not taken those decisions. The notion can be operationalised as a set of axioms of coherent preference. For example, you might easily make incoherent decisions if you did not have any feeling of preference for the outcomes of your decisions. Thus, one of the very axioms states that either you prefer outcome A to B, or you prefer B to A, or you are indifferent between outcomes. It disallows the relation "I don't know". Another axiom states that if you prefer A to B, and B to C, then you should prefer A to C. This is the

---

[2] Wing (1962); Goffman (1968).

principle of transitivity. A third axiom states that if all the possible consequences of decision A are at least as good as the consequences of decision B, and one or more of A's consequences is better, then decision A should be preferred. A final key principle states that any possible consequences that are common between decisions A and B should be ignored in forming a preference for one decision over the other.

The surprising logical result of these innocent-sounding axioms is that theorems can be proved. This is much like Euclidean geometry in which simple statements like "the shortest distance between two points is a straight line" combine with the laws of logic to yield non-obvious conclusions, such as the Pythagorean theorem describing the relationship between a triangle's hypotenuse and its two sides.

Three theorems result from decision theory's axioms, and they tell us what elements to pay attention to in any decision, and how the elements should combine to provide a guide to coherent decisions.[3] The first two theorems focus on the (multiple) consequences of our decisions, telling us to pay attention to *value* and *uncertainty*. That is, we should weigh up how much we value the consequence and then weigh up how likely it is to occur. The third theorem tells us to address these questions for each possible consequence, and then to weight the value of each consequence with its probability and to add together the weighted consequences. Mathematically, this gives the total 'utility' of a course of action; across a range of possible outcomes the decision to go for is the one with the highest utility.

In practice, every decision situation is characterised by a *context* and is framed according to the perspective of the decision maker. Various options are considered, and their possible consequences anticipated as best as can be achieved with the information available. The relative desirability of each consequence is considered, possibly based on multiple criteria, in which case the relative importance of the criteria has to be judged. The overall total utility of each consequence is then weighted with its probability of occurring. Those products are summed for each option, and the option with the highest overall score is chosen.

Even if you never make an expected utility calculation, this model of rational decision-making provides an agenda that will help you to work through a real decision problem. Here, stripped of the mathematics, are the ten steps constituting that agenda:

1. Consider the issues you face and examine them from different perspectives, being sensitive to context. Develop an appropriate frame for the problem.
2. Consider your goals and objectives, what it is you are trying to achieve and the value you wish to create. From these develop the criteria against which you will judge the possible consequences of your decision.

[3] Dawes (1988).

3. Generate the general options that may eventually achieve your goals and objectives.
4. Consider the uncertainties that characterise the future, making it impossible to predict with certainty what outcomes will occur.
5. Develop alternative scenarios about the future, leading from your options to the possible consequences. Describe each consequence on all the criteria.
6. Consider the relative desirability of the consequences, uninfluenced by how frequently the consequences are reported, or how memorable, or how recent.
7. Consider the likelihood that each consequence will occur, uninfluenced by how desirable the consequence is.
8. Balance the desirability of each consequence against its likelihood of occurrence.
9. Determine an overall ordering of your options on the basis of the relative desirability of their consequences, balanced by their probabilities of occurring.
10. Informed by this analysis, make your choice.

An experienced decision analyst would stress the importance, between steps 9 and 10, of sensitivity analysis: changing the input assessments of utility and probability in order to reflect the imprecision in assessing those numbers, or to examine differences of opinion when several people are involved in the decision.

BEHAVIOURAL DECISION THEORY AND MENTAL HEALTH PRACTICE

The above theory of how decisions should be made formed the basis for research from the late 1950s into how people actually form preferences, make judgements, consider uncertainty and take decisions. A substantial body of relevant literature now exists, much of it well presented in the books by Baron and Dawes.[4] A popular exposition of common flaws in making decisions is given by Russo and Schoemaker.[5] We now draw on that research, and Phillips' experience of applying decision analysis to real problems faced by individuals and groups in organisations, in order to suggest the following ways in which decision-making can go astray. The reader will note that these parallel the ten-step agenda given in the previous section. We illustrate each problematic area of decision-making with examples from the real world of mental health (some cases, some research findings) which illustrate conflict with our ideal world of rational decision-making.

---

[4] Baron (1994); Dawes (1988).
[5] Russo and Schoemaker (1989).

Frame constriction

The two most common problems are failure to consider the context of the decision, and adopting a single perspective which is too narrow. A classic mental health example was reported by Jewell,[6] in which an American Indian, a Navaho, was diagnosed as schizophrenic but was in fact not mentally ill at all. His behaviour was culturally derived and acceptable in his tribe, but was interpreted as abnormal in the white society of the USA.

In practice, decisions involving the use of mental health legislation are 'multi-authored', even though the final decision may be devolved to one person, for example, a responsible medical officer or a judge. This makes it important to consider the role of any given practitioner and the perspective they bring to any given decision.

One of the authors has experience of setting up a Court Diversion Scheme. Professionals both from the court and local mental health services were involved. The decision was made to take referrals to the scheme from any court user. As is usual with such schemes, expert medical evidence is given orally to the court after defendants are interviewed. In practice, some solicitors became concerned about the operation of the scheme; in particular, their advocacy roles at times conflicted with the expert role of the scheme psychiatrist. Further information on this role conflict was obtained in a court user audit. Information from 55 solicitors using the same south London Magistrates' Court suggested that the solicitor's role in relation to a defendant would be either to follow the client's instructions, even if the client had obvious mental health problems, or to act paternalistically with regard to the client (their 'best interests' perhaps being at odds with what they actually said), making them much more likely to take the advice of a scheme psychiatrist. It is evident therefore, that the perspective that solicitors and doctors bring to decision-making, which follow from their professional roles and duties, can give rise to considerable conflict. It is reasonable to argue that in such circumstances people do not, and perhaps should not, frame decisions in the same way.

Such role conflicts can have very interesting consequences. For example, in the same court scheme Ms A had stabbed a man and was facing serious charges. She had a long history of mental health problems into which she had little insight. Her solicitor accosted the duty psychiatrist and said there was no reason why his client should not have bail. The duty psychiatrist thought rather differently, not least because Ms A had recently discharged herself from hospital against medical advice. In this instance, the objective of our two decision makers may be very different; 'liberty at all costs' is balanced against 'the safety of the public'. Both objectives are legitimate but the conflict between them poses problems in terms of decision-making.

[6] Jewell (1952).

Value blindness

This involves focusing on a single objective, which may or may not be the most important, whereas most decisions involve several objectives. When objectives conflict, decision-makers often adopt simplifying strategies, such as accepting the option that is expected to lead to the best consequence on the immediately most important criterion. A slightly more complex approach would be to eliminate options by repeating the same process for the other criteria in order of their importance, until only one option is left. However, even this approach fails to consider the advantages and disadvantages of the consequences of all options on all the criteria.

It is useful to consider the value and significance of mental health law to different professional groups. Even within a wholly health service context, different mental health disciplines may approach decision-making in different ways. Consider the case of Ms B. Ms B was detained in hospital. She had asked for leave. There was no reason why she should not have local leave, but in fact she requested several weeks of leave to her family many miles from the unit. She had previously absconded from hospital. Her husband had, in a number of different ways, obstructed mental health services' attempts to return her, despite Ms B revealing homicidal thoughts about him at the time. The immediate consequence of this had been consideration of whether her husband should be prosecuted in relation to obstructing the Mental Health Act. The case discussion was complex and revealed sharp differences of opinion between nurses and doctors. Nurses thought the most important criterion by which the decision should be made about leave was the wishes of the patient. Doctors attached great importance to the avoidance of a further similar episode. Thus, very different values were attached by the different disciplines to the significance of the Act and to the woman's detained status in terms of the goal of allocating appropriate leave. It *may* be relevant that in this context nurses have relatively little legal training and forensic psychiatrists have rather more.

The 'single option' fallacy

Pressure of time often leads to another problem: the failure to develop several options. A common error is to analyse a single option by weighing up its advantages and disadvantages, then accepting the option if the advantages outweigh the disadvantages or rejecting it if they do not. But rejecting the option is the same as accepting the *status quo*, which is another option. Perhaps the disadvantages outweigh the advantages even more for the *status quo*, in which case rejecting the other option is like jumping from the frying pan into the fire. 'Look before you leap' applies to all options, not just to the single option that appears to be the only way forward.

It is a cultural characteristic that professionals are not observers of the social world, they are actors who do things. In fact, within mental health the obligation is to attempt to help people; there is a duty of care. Other professionals involved in mental health but with different agency allegiance, for example, probation services, may have different imperatives. None the less the pressure to do things on receipt of information is considerable. If the case notes of whatever agency show masterly inactivity for months on end then this is unlikely to be seen as confirmation of best practice. There is thus built into professional activity a bias against recognising the *status quo* as an option. Any other option, however badly developed, is better, particularly if the pressure to act comes from a crisis.

Avoiding uncertainty and 'best guess' planning

We do not like to admit that the future is uncertain, and this often leads us to consider that it is certain. We feel sure that, if we do this, then the predicted consequence will certainly follow; one option, one consequence. It is hard to resist the expert who 'knows', the guru who seems to have a special insight into the future. Similarly, when faced with the discomfort of an uncertain future, we often make a best guess about what will happen, and then take decisions based on that single scenario. By ignoring the lower probability possibilities, we are in danger of missing a seriously undesirable consequence. On the other hand, taking a decision solely in order to avoid that most undesirable consequence is also a mistake.

It is in the area of risk assessment and management that psychiatry most commonly has to deal with explicit uncertainty, but is still required to 'guess'. An issue, therefore, for those revising mental health law must be to what extent can or should recent piecemeal guidance and statute law be reconfigured; notably, recent innovations such as supervised discharge have received a less than rapturous welcome from many psychiatrists.

The case of Mr C illustrates how certainty and uncertainty are played out in practice. Mr C suffers from major mental illness. His most serious offence to date is 'actual bodily harm'. He is never compliant with care after discharge from hospital and has been repeatedly hospitalised after being picked up for minor offences. He presents well in medico-legal fora, for example, MHRTs and Managers' Hearings. A particular case discussion of Mr C revolved around the issue of continued detention at a time when Mr C appeared well. It focused on the detail of the Mental Health Act, illustrating how defensive psychiatry can become in that it was assumed that, were Mr C to become ill again, he would be highly dangerous if left at home. This was the 'best guess'. Other issues were relegated to second place, for example, quality of life. The decision made was to detain him further by using a notion of 'certain risk'. The team could therefore avoid tolerating any uncertainty when Mr C was at home. In fact he was discharged at his next Managers' Hearing. Perhaps the managers were better at acknowledging and living with uncertainty than the clinicians, who operate more obviously in a scapegoating culture.

Value biases

Judgements on the values of consequences are particularly prone to biases induced by "group think",[7] a tendency for cohesive groups, particularly those facing difficult situations under time constraint, to exert pressures on their members to conform and come quickly to a consensus view that is then held to be superior to competing views. Another value bias is a recency effect: if a recent decision led to an undesirable consequence, the negative value of that consequence is enhanced. Context can also affect value: purchasing new furniture at the same time you are buying a house may seem a minor additional expense, but if the furniture is purchased later it may seem to be an extravagance.

Both recency and "group think" are current issues in psychiatry. The net effect of the discernible anxiety in the media, politics and in the general public about 'failures' of community care has led to a change in mindset among clinical teams. Douglas[8] suggests that the "institutional filter" through which risks are assessed affects the understanding of probability. Our current filter is a climate of blame and the relative recency of so many psychiatric homicide inquiries is likely to prejudice clinical decisions. In policy terms, it has resulted in the wholesale introduction of untested measures designed to reduce risk.

Over-confidence

One of the most widespread research findings is that people are usually too sure of themselves when assessing probabilities. When people say they are 100 per cent sure, they are typically correct about 80 per cent of the time. Authoritarian people are even more susceptible to this bias; they say they are 100 per cent sure more frequently than the rest of us, and are more frequently wrong when they say it. This universal phenomenon is perhaps rooted in the discomfort we all feel from the anxiety that accompanies our experience of uncertainty. However, whatever the reasons, failure realistically to consider uncertainty about the future can lead to hasty and ill-considered decisions.

Although this is a criticism regularly levelled at all kinds of people, not least at doctors, lawyers and men, there is considerable evidence that it may be a real problem for those deciding the fate of mentally disordered offenders. For example, surveys of consultant psychiatrists and probation officers[9] revealed the

---

[7] Janis (1982); Janis and Mann (1977).
[8] Douglas (1985).
[9] Bartlett *et al.* (1994).

following. Many consultant psychiatrists did regular forensic work. Approximately one third had no training in forensic work. Slightly fewer than half the probation officers had no training in mental health. These findings indicate the dangers inherent in being called to give evidence to the courts in relation to mentally disordered offenders, since both professions are likely to lack crucial areas of knowledge and definitive statements from either group should be viewed with some caution. Nowhere in psychiatric training, for example, is information about crime rates or causes of crime taught. Its absence must be relevant to rational decision-making.

Errors in integrating information

Common errors in integrating information are both to take into account flawed information and to fail to revise judgements appropriately. Because the brain is limited in its ability to process information, bringing together separate pieces of information can be particularly troublesome. What, for example, is the overall impact of several diagnostic signs? Extensive research on this topic has shown that people do not revise their judgements sufficiently in light of fallible information. Another common error is ignoring base rates once diagnostic information is obtained. As an example, diagnosis of sexual abuse in a child admitted to hospital for other reasons should not ignore the fact that, of all children admitted to hospital, only a small proportion will have suffered sexual abuse. That small proportion should be combined with the appropriate likelihood derived from diagnostic testing in order to give a probability that the child has in fact been abused. The proper way to do this is to use Bayes' theorem, a consequence of the laws of probability.[10] Unfortunately most mental health practitioners are unaware of this approach, and the status of probabilistic evidence is problematical, at best, within the legal profession.[11]

The following example, describing the relationship between judges and psychiatrists, suggests that the forgoing may represent areas of important difficulty in relation to defendants facing serious criminal charges who come before the Crown Court. Material obtained from a series of interviews with members of the judiciary[12] indicated that frequent failings identified by judges in psychiatric evidence were first delays, secondly naïveté and thirdly treatment refusal. Although in the words of one judge, psychiatry was felt to be "increasingly respectable", and was certainly in this sample of opinion held in higher esteem than the Prison Medical Service, it was considered that the failure to obtain available and relevant information (such as depositions) led psychiatrists into over-optimistic assessments of defendants. "In a sense you could say that they are not cynical enough. Whatever is fed into them by the patient-client, they

[10] Von Wintenfeldt and Edwards (1986).
[11] Schum (1994).
[12] Bartlett *et al.* (1994).

tend to accept as the truth." It is perhaps against this background that the view of psychiatric evidence as only one of many sources of evidence available to the courts should be set. No judge in the study felt that psychiatric evidence, even where it suggested a positive psychiatric disposal, should be automatically followed.

Shooting from the hip

This relates to thinking you can keep in mind all the information relevant to a decision, and deal with it (all) intuitively, instead of using a systematic procedure. By contrast, the model of decision-making we have presented here is the rational weighing of all options in the light of all available information and value judgements.

For example, many patients amass huge case notes; looking through them in detail is sometimes not appealing. In clinical decision-making authoritative voices in the ward round can carry the day even when, despite long-term work with particular clients and patients, they can be factually wrong. One of the authors recently caught herself out imagining that she could remember the response of a patient to a particular drug some years ago. She was wrong, as was apparent when the pharmacist checked.

Ignoring your track record

How do we know if our decisions are good if we do not keep track of the results? We take credit for our successes and rationalise away our failures, but if every hand of bridge were treated in this way we would never learn to be better players of the game. In fact, a good decision can show poor results, and a bad decision may, through luck, give good results. So keeping track means not only looking at the outcomes and consequences, but also reviewing the very process of analysing the decision. Were several options considered? Was relevant information gathered? Were values carefully considered? Were the consequences anticipated? And so forth. Experience is not always the best teacher; very often it teaches us nothing at all unless we take the trouble to find out the results of our decisions.

There has been much greater attention paid to track records in psychiatric practice in the last ten years than previously. Audit projects can be useful and result in guided change in practice. However, as far as the authors know, this is not a feature of Managers' Hearings or, routinely, of the decisions of MHRTs. This is potentially a serious criticism of the legal arm of medico-legal work.[13]

---

[13] This criticism does not imply necessarily that the outcome measure of such hearings should be clinical; it might more properly be civil rights outcomes (see Afterword).

The examples we highlight above of 'faulty' decision-making do not lead us to suggest, at least in terms of our theoretical model, that either the process or outcome of decision-making in mental health and law is atypical. However, we suggest that these examples spread across the arena of multi-agency work using mental health legislation and indicate that decision-making is very unlikely to be entirely rational. It is debatable whether or not a degree of irrationality in decision-making is inevitable within multi-agency work, and equally debatable whether or not any attempt could or should be made to alter the *status quo*. However, it does seem pertinent to consider whether it is automatically a 'good' thing that the alternative discourse within the world of mental health, for example, care and common sense, should be drowned out by an increasingly legalistic psychiatry.

WHAT DO CLEVER PEOPLE DO REALLY?

As we have already indicated this chapter was originally the focus of a presentation to a group of concerned professionals and users reflecting on the utility of current mental health legislation. Part of that presentation was a role play, one version of proxy decision-making, based on an anonymised case vignette. To participate members of the group had to be 'something' other than themselves; and they were explicitly asked to explain the basis of their decision making. Edited highlights of that exercise follow.

Case vignette

A 50-year-old man was originally admitted to a secure hospital following a serious assault on his grandchild. Acquittal in court was on the grounds of lack of evidence. He left hospital without psychiatric follow-up, some years ago. After moving to a new area of the country he becomes unwell. He is hospitalised using section 3 of the Mental Health Act. Prior to coming into hospital the main problem at home had been extreme physical neglect; on admission he has bed sores. Although efforts had been made to work with the family before admission the relationship had broken down. The family remains willing but not necessarily able to care for this man. When out on leave his wife fails to return him to hospital. When retrieved he is more psychotic. It has become clear to staff involved that the man's wife has an alcohol problem. She continues to want to care for him at home. Nursing staff are divided; some think he ought to return permanently to the care of his wife even if he is neglected and some disagree. The family approach the Advocacy Service; the advocate puts forward the view of the wife, the man agrees. The view of the consultant is that the man is highly suggestible by virtue of his mental health problems and lacks the capacity necessary for self-determination. The family complain about the care of the man; they are abusive to the psychiatrist. *The solicitor acting for the man takes part in a Mental Health Review Tribunal; the decision of the Tribunal is that he be further detained. Placement of the man becomes an issue. It is not clear that the staff agree and the family are inconsistent with regard to long-term placement. The man is relatively well by now and the ward staff increasingly suspect that the family are interested in his considerable wealth. It is difficult to find a suitable placement in the borough and rapid placement would mean moving him away from his family; the alternative is to remain in hospital. The psychiatric team view is that prolonged hospitalisation is inappropriate. Guardianship is the preferred legal option but would require displacement of the man's wife as "nearest relative". Also, whatever its merits it takes time to put into place. What should happen at the next Managers' Hearing and why?*

The roles the participants were offered were to be one of the following: solicitor, (lay or legal) advocate, RMO, ASW, ward nurse, wife, the man, or child of the man. Although this already amounted to a substantial cast list, the group felt that more people needed to be involved since they would have valid viewpoints to represent. However, it was accepted that, in practice, it would be well nigh impossible for all to be included. Also, although it was not raised, such inclusiveness might be opposed by those already allocated a voice, for example, on the ground of confidentiality.

From the discussion conducted with this initial cast list it rapidly became obvious that it is possible for people to flavour professional identities with personal issues. Hence, the (role-playing hypothetical) solicitor could be paternalistic and follow the advice of the team in favour of guardianship. On the other hand together they could disagree with the consultant's assessment. One of the group's (real) solicitors did not like what the (hypothetical) solicitor advocate had done because she had not taken the trouble to identify the man's wishes separately from those of his family, thereby underlining the importance of advocacy issues to (real) advocates.

Within roles the various RMOs also took different views on priorities in the case. One thought dangerousness trumped everything else and should lead to further detention; she would do anything to avoid being castigated in the prevailing climate of blame. Another was less convinced about the diagnosis, favoured consensual working and was reluctant to give up on the family. A third thought the overarching issue was that of childcare and that social services should take a serious interest. One social worker reported that, unfortunately, all the social workers in the group were up to their eyes in other cases and would only reluctantly answer the telephone. Even when a second social worker did answer the telephone she felt it was not her responsibility but that of someone else. A third social worker expressed major reservations about the bureaucracy associated with guardianship and hinted darkly at a political perspective in the higher tiers of local social services. As decisions continued to be delayed by the processes identified by the group, the disgruntled nurses said, in no uncertain terms, that there was no point in them *having* a view, despite so much contact with the man, since no-one took any notice of them anyway. A ward nurse who did speak up said that the man was fine now but past events did seem a bit worrying.

Entering unsolicited into the debate, the family GP, who had known the man for years and was antipathetic to hospital care, said he could not see what all the fuss was about; this provoked irritation amongst the ward nurses. In startling contradiction of the confidence of the GP, the local police (who had somehow come to hear of the case) wanted to explore the original charges but did not think it was their job to obtain the relevant information. A local councillor, who was also a neighbour of this problematic family, thought that there was no reason to send the man home as it would cause nothing but problems for the neighbourhood and complaints to the council.

Several wives spoke. One took the line that it was entirely reasonable to benefit from her husband's money and that this was likely to last longer if he came home. Another was fed up with the way the hospital staff were behaving and was no longer prepared to co-operate. A third said that if the only way to get what she wanted was to appear to go along with the hospital's advice she would do that. However, other family members were not entirely in agreement with this wife, and one in particular was worried about the safety of her child. But the most surprising new information which came to light was from the grandchild, who was the alleged victim of the offence which was not proven. This person, now older, said that she had stolen money from her grandfather who, on discovering it, had meted out punishment in the form of a beating. Cross both at not having kept the money and at having been punished, the grandchild said she had elaborated the situation and that no-one had ever heard the first half of the story as the man's mental state had deteriorated because of the stress.

While all this was being clarified, the man's own complaint was that no-one was listening to him, and anyway to whom was he meant to talk? He was fed up and thought the staff had missed the point. The problems he had were, he said, basically physical and he needed to see a physical doctor. Also, everyone seemed obsessed with the unhappy times and to ignore all his good life experiences. They had got a bee in their bonnet about a time long ago when, in any event, his records had been confused with those of someone else with a similar name so that he had ended up being misdiagnosed, and no-one had been able to sort it out since. Lastly, although he knew he was meant to have an advocate, and did, it was not at all clear for whom she was really working.

There are several serious points easily demonstrated in the above role play. First, even in cases where important events have not occurred years in the past, it is common for crucial documentation to be missing, and decisions therefore need to take that into account if they are to be rational. However, if our group is right, some people will not identify the need to do this, as the GP did not. Secondly, the whole group was together in one room. As pointed out already this is unlikely ever to happen in reality, and it is not necessarily even desirable that it should do so. And yet the voice of those absent can be crucial in determining outcome; as, for example, in the case of a local council's willingness to offer accommodation. Similarly, at a Managers' Hearing, the focus of the decisions in the vignette, even the original cast list is unlikely to attend. Also, at such hearings, and in other medico-legal fora, the weights attached to the views of members of the group will not be as observed in the role play. Different voices carry different weight; indeed, this is enshrined in mental health law. It was therefore interesting that, in the role play, the group enthusiastically adopted the role of the man and his family members. Again, in being people other than themselves, the group revealed great diversity of approaches to decision-making, as well as total disagreement about the desirable outcome. However, they also (and this was for real rather than by proxy) illustrated, in their portrayals of other people, how they saw others. These views and related beliefs, evident in the above account, would not necessarily be conducive either to cordial working relations or to consensus decision-making. This said, perhaps what people believed should happen was an irrelevance. For example, in the group discussion a 'senior nurse' suggested that, whatever anyone thought should happen, the man would have to go somewhere quickly when his bed was needed!

DISCUSSION

We have demonstrated areas where rational decision-making according to our theoretical model is flawed; individual professional roles, perspectives, inadequate information and 'political' pressures on decision-makers can get in the way. However, such faults may not be evident in terms of ultimate outcomes (although mental health care services are not renowned for their rigorous assessment of outcome); rather they represent possible failures of process. Indeed, even though these errors may be *relevant* to decisions made by mental health practitioners and legal specialists, albeit not necessarily apparent in decision outcomes, it is not immediately clear how law reform might in any event improve matters. Whether the law *per se* can be of any help remains an open question.

We have also questioned the inherent desirability of applying the model of rational decision-making in the field of mental health and related law. Perhaps we would all like to be seen as operating rationally, or perhaps not. Also, although the law lends itself to being rational in its decision-making, it is less clear that, if made explicit, this would be the only valued way of deciding anything in mental health care. Real-time constraints on the average mental health professional may make the "Ten Point Plan"[14] look like an extravagance and resource constraints may make even the idea of 'options' genuinely redundant. For example, there is increasingly little place for informal admissions to

[14] DoH (1993).

hospital, because the lack of availability of hospital beds implies that the only way to get someone in is under section.

We have discussed issues of decision-making in relation to *current* multi-agency and multidisciplinary experience of operating mental health legislation. The value of our comparison of real-life situations with decision-making theory is that it illuminates aspects of this work and highlights cultural difference, as indicated by roles, behaviour, beliefs, values and relative power. We are not making a recommendation for a wholesale introduction of a potentially novel and unusually explicit method of decision-making. However, understanding how things work may stop further idiocies. The example that springs easily to mind is that of guardianship; a worthy piece of legislation in itself, but one that is seldom used. If something is not used, it cannot work.

Additionally, the particular preference of lawyers for rational decision-making, which is arguably a more pronounced explicit preference than is found in other professional groups, means that our comparison does have special relevance. Changes or expansion in mental health legislation (in its widest sense) will inevitably focus the multi-agency mind on the law rather than on the other day-to-day issues with which it is normally preoccupied. In so doing, cultural conflicts may be emphasised. The advent of 'managerialism' has led, amongst other things, to a loss of professional power within the NHS. The discourse of the power-brokers has changed and health care professionals were, and are, both anxious and caustic about these changes. Whether, within the more restricted arena of mental health and the law, hackles would similarly be raised or feathers preened is not yet clear. Were certain proposals to be pursued, or even adopted, for example, were the responsibility for compulsory hospitalisation to pass from doctors and social workers to other professional groups, such as psychologists or magistrates, then cultural values would undoubtedly be invoked in the ensuing power struggles. Were very radical proposals pursued, addressing the demonstrable inequality between lay people and professionals, then that would require a major shift in the status of certain kinds of knowledge; would being someone's friend or partner of 20 years begin to count the same as a couple of years of psychiatric training? Previous power struggles would pale by comparison.

12

Researching Law

BRAM OPPENHEIM

Research can only provide answers to problems if they are represented as clearly formulated questions. In the absence of clear agreement on what topics related to mental health legislation might benefit from empirical research it is difficult, if not impossible, to suggest appropriate research designs or techniques. However, this book, together with other initiatives, seeks to make a contribution to thinking about suitable research topics and methods, since it begins to delineate some of the problems faced. Where possible, we also need to consult any previous research into the operation of mental health legislation, though some of this has been piecemeal and unco-ordinated.

Any research planning will also need to confront a number of presuppositions.

One assumption is that we need to develop some kind of consensus or problem-setting agenda before we can give serious thought to research. But this begs a further question: who should set such an agenda? Is it the general public? Users and ex-users? Professionals in the field? The relevant government agencies? Academics? It is not at all clear who forms the constituency to whom research should be addressed, or who would benefit from the results. Indeed, this uncertainty about constituency reflects the problem of multifarious actors, value systems and agenda which threads through the entire book.

Another assumption is that such issues will be 'researchable'. But the answers to some of our questions may be found in ideologies, value systems, political doctrine, theology and morality, resource allocations, jurisprudence and so forth, and these are not amenable to social research. Such research cannot help us to decide whether a person or an action or a law is good or evil, whether or not a poem is beautiful, what should be included among human rights, whether rape is immoral or forced detention is virtuous. It might be possible to present some of these issues to a large sample of individuals to find out their opinions, but the questions themselves are not researchable because, essentially, they depend on value judgements.

A third assumption is that anyone wants to know and use the results of such research. It is, after all, quite common for innovations or interventions to be introduced without previous research. We often find changes in education systems, in the economy, in traffic control, in health legislation, in medical practice, in teaching curricula and in business enterprises being implemented without first doing, or reviewing, the relevant research. Indeed, in many fields there is a considerable gap between researchers and practitioners, even when the issues are researchable and have, perhaps, already been widely researched. Researchers are often treated as jokers at court, as the speakers of uncomfortable truths whose sayings can safely be ignored. Much social change is driven, or resisted, by other forces: by power struggles, by political imperatives, by bigotry and wilful ignorance, by false prophets or by the dead hand of tradition. The 'rational activist' cycle, encompassing problem-setting, followed by research, pilot studies, general implementation, monitoring and evaluation (such as we might find, say, in the introduction of a new pharmaceutical drug), is more often the exception than the rule – the more so when we view the process of law reform, which is more often driven by policy and politics than by research findings.

The field of mental health legislation is criss-crossed by values constraints. We may mention concerns about civil liberties, the protection of the public, the democratic legislative process, the professional codes of several groups of practitioners and the ideology of good administrative practice. Such constraints may affect both the nature of the research and its subsequent impact, if any, on legislation. In addition, researchers will find themselves further constrained by the problem of *research ethics*. However well-intentioned, researchers will often not be allowed to conduct even small-scale, controlled experiments with groups of patients or offenders unless certain safeguards are in place, safeguards which might negate the purpose of the intended research.

Do we know what research is needed?

While we are told that there is widespread dissatisfaction among practitioners and others with the 1983 Act or with its implementation, drawing up an agenda of researchable topics is no easy task. This is partly because we do not know who needs answers to what questions, but also because we do not have a full grasp of what is already known. This latter problem arises from the uncoordinated nature of the research that has been done or is at present in progress. For example, some methodologically sophisticated research is currently being undertaken into the legal, clinical, social, demographic and organisational factors influencing psychiatrists' decisions to detain patients under the 1983 Act. However, this research is locally funded and has not yet come to the attention of research planning at the national level. Elsewhere there is ongoing work which examines the influence of High Court judicial review on the decision-making practices of Mental Health Review Tribunals; this work has a particular focus on the intelligibility of the law to medical and lay members of such tribunals, and explores whether such members regard the law as counterproductive. Also, while recognising the difficulties associated with drawing lessons across different systems, we are remarkably ill-informed about international perspectives in this field. Many other jurisdictions have either recently reformed or considered reforming their own mental health legislation and have commissioned research which could well have a bearing on the dilemmas we face in this country. Similarly, incorporation of the European Convention on Human Rights (ECHR) means that there should be valuable lessons to be learnt from relevant case law.

It would seem, therefore, that some kind of preparatory research agenda is needed. The Department of Health appears to have come to the same conclusion, and has commissioned the College Research Unit of the Royal College of Psychiatrists to co-ordinate a programme of research about the use of the 1983 Mental Health Act.[1] The programme consists of two stages: the first stage is to identify the major concerns or issues about the Act; the second stage will carry out research investigations of the topics identified in the preliminary stage.

Researchers at the Unit have used systematic methods to obtain the views of professionals, service users, carers and their relevant organisations about the strengths and weaknesses of the Act in day-to-day practice. Using focus groups, in-depth telephone interviews and written responses, followed by a 'validation' meeting attended by representatives of national voluntary organisations, views have been collected on a wide range of topics. These were then subjected to a content analysis which yielded 11 key themes. These included inadequate informing of users and carers, inadequate professional knowledge about the Act, uncertainty about the application of legal terms and definitions, the operation of checks and balances, the effects of resource constraints on the use of the Act, the need to reconsider the role of the 'nearest relative', inadequate provision for treatment in the community and concern about *de facto* detention.

The main focus of the work will be on admission to hospital for assessment, admission for treatment, emergency admission for assessment and the search for and removal of a patient to a place of safety (Parts II and X of the Act). When this research has been completed, we hope to be in a much better position to suggest improvements both to the Act and to the ways in which it is being applied.

DIFFICULT BUT NOT IMPOSSIBLE

Let us now try to speculate more generally about some types of research that might be helpful. We shall ignore the difficult questions of sponsorship and funding, and of ultimate implementation, and we shall touch but lightly upon pertinent ethical dilemmas. We shall simply look at some of the issues that have emerged so far and which might be researchable, and consider some of the available methods.

It ought to be stressed that research of this kind should only be carried out by competent professional researchers, and not by people studying their own

---

[1] Dr. Paul Lelliot, personal communication.

organisations. The independence, comparative experience, technical sophistication, data processing and statistical competence required are generally beyond the range of those working in the field.

Factual information studies

Assuming the importance of obtaining factual, descriptive information about the working applications of the Act, some examples of researchable topics may include the frequency of use of the various provisions for detention under the several sections of the Act ; numbers over time of people held in secure accommodation of various kinds; length of detention before release; frequency of recalls and re-detentions; the representation of ethnic minorities; frequencies of recidivism, and many other factual variables, subdivided by region and by demographic attributes. Such information could be assembled by going systematically through the management records of a sample of hospitals and other agencies, assuming that confidential access can be obtained. However, critical attention should be given to the robustness, accuracy and completeness of such records.

Such factual information studies, where data on a number of variables are collected, can also provide the basis for exploring patterns of association between particular variables. However, it is important to distinguish between associations and causality. If it were shown, for example, that bed-availability was positively correlated with the decision to detain, or that under-provision of approved social workers reduced the probability of patients being presented for sectioning, this might lead researchers to explore the determinants of the admission process more closely, in an attempt to establish causes and their effects. This would require moving to a different research level, namely the study of operational decision-making.

Operational decision-making studies

The kind of descriptive research outlined above needs to be complemented by more analytic, operational studies among professionals, to find out *why* these patterns of application of the Act are happening. Such projects would require a considerably greater investment than factual studies and would need to be well focused on particular issues, particular professions or particular decision categories within the care framework, as well as within the context of particular types of clinical cases. For example, one could study the problem of *under-utilisation of existing provisions*, such as guardianship or the recently introduced orders of after-care under supervision, on the assumption that there is some kind of standard or expectation of their use, and that there is a shortfall. As a first step, that assumption needs to be verified. Initially this would require a 'paper' project, that is, going through the files of a sample of cases, using experts to identify those cases where such provisions might be appropriate under the Act and either have or have not been used, and then arriving at a proportional measure of shortfall. A demographic, diagnostic and geographical break-down of the data might throw some further light on the problem.

Such data might show the extent of the problem, but not why it is happening. If we want to know *why* such provisions are not used more often, or why they are used as they are, then it might be possible to conduct observational studies of case conferences and the like, followed by a sample survey, initially by interview and later by anonymised postal questionnaire, of professionals who have the choice to use or not to use these provisions. Such surveys might be possible, but they will always be difficult to conduct, because the respondents will often be sophisticated and may be particularly defensive; moreover, variations may be due to factors of which the respondents are not themselves aware. Alternatively, it might be sufficient to conduct focus groups, using fictional case studies, to throw further light on the subject. Later, assuming that the use of these provisions increased, we might wish to know something about their effects or outcomes.[2]

Operational research of this kind by non-judgemental 'outsiders' is difficult, very time-consuming and depends on the creation of trust; there are also difficult problems of ethics and confidentiality to be resolved. However, the rewards would be a much better insight into the way in which elements of the Act 'work' in day-to-day practice.

Attitudinal studies

Much of the work under the Act is guided by the attitudes, beliefs, perceptions and expectations of the relevant practitioner, often formed by training and experience. It would therefore be valuable to develop or adapt attitude scales covering such relevant topics as civil liberties, protection of the public, violence, the police, mental illness, community care, social workers, confidentiality, dementia, self-harming behaviour, sectioning, gender differences, treatment without consent and ethnic minorities. Such scales could be used to explore attitude differences between professionals and other groups, for example carers, or hospital managers. They could also throw light on the determinants of decision patterns (see above) and on the way the Act is applied (for example, in the so-called risk-aversive culture); they could show the need for better information and training or re-training; they could measure the effects of training courses; they could show divergences between the attitudes of different professionals, and between professionals and the general public, or those of service users; and they could also address other issues, such as the impact of the media on attitudes to 'dangerousness' and the mentally ill.

---

[2] See under *Evaluation Studies*, below.

Evaluation studies

From asking questions about how the system works, we now go on to ask: what are some of its effects? It is axiomatic that any intervention, or any change in intervention, should be accompanied by evaluation studies – drug treatment trials are an obvious example. Ideally such studies should initially be conducted as small pilot studies accompanied by control groups; these would also help to 'fine tune' the intervention. If it is decided to introduce the intervention nationwide, then it is essential that changes be regularly monitored from a measured baseline, over a considerable period, and using objective measures of outcome. It is equally important to ensure that such changes are 'attributable', that is, to be able to show that any observed changes have happened *because* of our intervention and are not due to other concurrent influences. We would therefore need also to monitor groups of randomly allocated control cases, who are either treated by traditional methods, or receive no intervention. The ethical and practical problems which would have to be overcome are all too evident. By contrast, government departments sometimes use existing 'indicators', such as mortality rates from different diseases, suicide rates, alcohol sales or prevalence rates as outcome markers, but these are often inappropriate and not causally attributable to any specific intervention.

There is now a considerable literature on programme evaluation in many social, medical, legal and other fields, and elaborate methodologies are available. Such studies are demanding and time-consuming, but they enable us to introduce changes that are 'evidence-based'. Local pilot studies can be particularly helpful. Evaluation studies would be especially relevant, for example, in the study of the effectiveness of care in the community and of psychiatric after-care. They would also have the important advantage that they involve users, carers and the general public, whose views are not always taken into account.

Prediction research

Some of the provisions of the Act require assessments or predictions to be made, for example, about 'dangerousness', about 'likely harm to others or to self', about likely compliance with self-medication, about likely re-offending, and so forth. We should recognise that most health professionals are neither trained nor equipped to make these kinds of predictions. Doctors, ASWs, psychiatrists and psychiatric nurses, among others, might therefore benefit from the development of appropriate predictor measures, such as those constructed by psychologists, for example, to predict the likelihood of violent re-offending. However, such measures should not be used in isolation, they would best be used as an integral part of clinical predictions and assessments.

If these prediction issues were tackled seriously (as they have been, for example, in heart disease and in dental studies, as well as in criminology), they would require a considerable investment over time by skilled research psychologists, among others, using multivariate predictor technology.

Psychological techniques could also be used, or developed, for the assessment of mental impairment, mental illness and psychopathic disorder, which is also required prior to 'sectioning' or detention under the Act. Such diagnostic psychometric measures might, however, be based on constructs which are different both from the existing legal definitions and from their clinical 'cousins'. They should not, therefore, be expected to stand alone but should be used chiefly as aids to good clinical practice. They could also be used towards beginning to resolve the divergencies between the psychological, legal and clinical constructs and standards, a problem that can best be addressed by further research.

BETTER LAW, OR BETTER IMPLEMENTATION?

There is an inevitable gulf between 'law as a passive presence, and human agency as an active interpreter of the law'. This is likely to imply a general problem, since it arises as much in magistrates' courts as in tax offices, among the Health and Safety Inspectorate, the Customs and Excise officials or in the allocation of welfare support. In short, wherever there are rules, these rules will be bent or broken or applied in unintended ways. Words, the 'letter of the law', are simply inadequate to capture the 'spirit' or intent of the lawgiver (much as musical notation can never fully capture the composer's imagined sonorities) and, even if they are adequate to their task, words and rules can always be perceived and used by others in different ways and from their own points of view.

'Better law' can therefore never be enough. Social scientists have shown in many domains that unintended variations occur in even the most highly regulated human systems (for example, in air crew, the military, road traffic, and compliance with medical instructions), sometimes causing hazards to safety. But these deviations can themselves become researchable questions, as we have indicated, and the results can then be taken into account when the law is redrawn. 'Human agency as an active interpreter of the law' *can* be studied, so that lessons may be learnt leading to better information, better guidelines, better training and better evaluation.

13

Afterword: Integrating Mental Health and Justice

NIGEL EASTMAN and JILL PEAY

This book is timed to be timely. It arose against a background of increasing public and governmental concern about mental health care and related law, and of growing professional concern that both service and legal resources were inadequate, leaving professionals at risk of holding substantial responsibility in combination with inadequate power. Equally, user and carer groups have been variously vocal in their complaints about the level and allocation of resources between types of services and the extent to which there should be coercive treatment in the community. It is published also as the government sets in train a fundamental review of mental health care services and law. Perhaps not this century has the debate about mental health law been so suffused with conflict, both between parties and between principles. If this book fails to inform about the issues which underlie current debate and conflict then it will have failed. If it at least enlightens that debate a little, by clarifying the field of the debate, as well as pointing towards a short menu of general solutions, then it may be able to claim modest success.

This 'Afterword' strives to summarise briefly some of the themes and problems which have emerged in the book, whilst outlining in skeleton form one of the more radical routes that might be taken towards reformulating the legal provisions relating to those suffering from mental disorder. We address below issues bearing on economics and law; ethics and law; mental sciences and law; practitioners and law; and research and law. Finally, we question whether current law is so anachronistic that it requires not mere pruning and grafting but root-and-branch reform. We start, however, with a somewhat crude review of the relationship between mental health and justice, since even a basic analysis of this begins to illustrate and detail the complexities and challenges of attempting their integration.

The aim of any reform ought to be the creation of a body of law which effectively finesses the twin objectives of mental health and justice. However, the pursuit of these two objectives may variously infer conflict or harmony between them depending upon the framing and application of the two concepts. Thus, mental health can be defined objectively (by professionals) or subjectively (by the patient). Justice might be broadly conceived in terms of 'being dealt with equitably and/or in accordance with the law'.[1] It can relate to the substantive law, as well as to its procedural application, and can be distinguished between the individual taken alone and the individual in relation to others. However, to what does it amount specifically in respect of the receipt of medical treatment? For, whilst the 'right to refuse treatment' is a well-grounded jurisprudential concept, the more recently argued 'right' to receive treatment (whose importance is emphasised by a parallel shift from hospital based to community based care) is altogether more problematic.[2]

Some examples of conflict or harmony being implied by different ways of framing and applying mental health and justice may assist. Hence, the patient who has to be coerced towards improved mental health suffers an individual injustice; she is denied her liberty (and perhaps the right to her psychosis) in the pursuit of objective mental health and there is disharmony between health and justice (of course, she may even experience improved subjective mental health, although this may be counterbalanced by the experience of injustice in terms of her overall subjective well being). By contrast, for the person who is not coerced, accepts treatment and experiences improved mental health, there is (very positive) harmony between health and justice. The person who is not coerced and wants adequate treatment but is denied it (because of inadequate resources) experiences disharmony, but a different sort of disharmony from the first patient, in that she retains her liberty (achieves justice) but does not get better. However, this patient also experiences (a very negative type of) harmony between health and justice, in that she neither gets better nor is she justly treated in terms of resources. Finally, the person who is coerced, receives inadequate resources and gains little or no mental health improvement again experiences profoundly negative harmony between mental health and justice, losing her liberty, having no right to resources and failing to get better (where the condition is inherently untreatable then, even if resources *are* applied, there is still negative harmony).

If justice is defined not solely for the individual but taking into account the benefit of others in society then the pattern of harmonies and disharmonies is different. Hence, justice and the pursuit of an individual's mental health are in harmony if the patient is 'justly coerced' by virtue of properly (and justly) balancing her right to liberty with the right of others to protection *and* she can get better. Similarly, if society justly allocates resources between individuals then there is harmony for the patient who is justly coerced and whose mental health is pursued with those (albeit restricted) resources. As a final example, for the patient who is justly (or unjustly) detained (depending on whether there is a real risk rather than an attributed risk of harm to others) but cannot get better (whether because of inadequate resources or an untreatable condition) there is

---

[1] See also the broader concept of social justice discussed by Barham and Barnes (this vol.) and Plant (1992).

[2] See, e.g., *R. v. Cambridge DHA, ex parte B* [1995] and the conflict between general and specific rights to care under the NHS Act.

disharmony (or profoundly negative harmony); this amounts to the *Baxtrom*[3] situation which a US court held amounted to unlawful detention.

These examples are not argued at all tightly, but they make clear one important point. Namely, the common juxtaposing of mental health and justice as arising where the patient is coerced and gets better (or could get better) is only one case illustration of the possible combinations of the two objectives being in disharmony and/or harmony with one another. The law and services must respond to all the combinations we have described, and more.

ECONOMICS AND LAW

The secondary title of this book started life by posing the question "what is (or can be) the 'marginal' contribution of law to mental health?", thus concentrating on just one of the twin objectives pursued. The question does not assume by use of the word 'marginal' that the contribution is trivial. Rather, it is posed from the perspective of the economist, to whom the word implies the notion of some additional (positive or negative) effect on outcome which can be directly attributed to the particular resource or intervention considered, in this case the law. Illustration that law, and even one piece of law, can be either positive or negative in its effect on health is provided by the example of 'confidentiality' being seen potentially as a clinical tool (as described below).

Clearly, the economic perspective on both mental illness *per se* and its care and treatment needs to be cast on a broader canvass in order to compare its perspective, and implied prescriptions, with other perspectives from which the contribution or role of law in mental health care can (and should) be viewed. However, economics offers helpful models for considering social choices, in relation both to the policy objectives pursued and the means chosen, which include, but go well beyond, economic factors in their implications. These models offer more theoretical detail on some of the 'costs of law' points made by Bosanquet in Chapter 9.

The model of 'cost-effectiveness' poses questions of the type "how can a given (measurable) outcome be achieved with least resource cost?" This offers nothing towards choices between objectives, either between or within individuals. However, it might be possible to show within it, for example, that a given mental health outcome improvement is achievable in patients with schizophrenia more cheaply by the introduction of a coercive community treatment order (CTO) than through the alternative of more widespread use of (highly-resourced) community outreach teams. In cost-effective terms the required choice is clear. However, introducing any possible detrimental effects of a CTO on the acceptance of involvement in the mental health care services of other ('non-CTO eligible') patients, arising from their observation of the risk of being

---

[3] See Steadman and Cocozza (1974).

subjected to a CTO,[4] would clearly alter the calculus such that the aggregate effect would not be equivalent to the sum of the individual CTO patient effects; albeit that this analysis would require the complexity of introducing interpersonal comparison, including by way of potential discounting for time differences of the effects, it could still be consistent with the cost-effective model (in aggregate mode). However, introducing the effects on the 'civil rights well being' of patients to whom the CTO was applied would take the calculation outside the model, since this would bring in an entirely different outcome variable towards which services and law were aimed. To illustrate, a research project funded by the DoH which was aimed at establishing the outcome (or 'effects') of MHRTs was refused site access by the chairman of one MHRT region because, according to his view, it was measuring the wrong outcome.[5] In choosing to measure essentially 'clinical' outcomes (including the sometimes detrimental effects on members of the public) of patient discharge it was, he argued, entirely misdirected. Rather, any such study should measure the 'effectiveness' of tribunals in delivering legally correct civil rights decisions. In a related vein, as Bosanquet describes, there may be direct conflict between the efficient pursuit of mental health *and* holding to ethical and legal principles such as patient confidentiality. It is important, however, to distinguish between the 'disbenefit' experienced by someone which directly arises from breach of their privacy *per se* (in absolutist ethical terms) and the effect, either positive or negative, of breaching confidence particularly on their mental health. The effect on mental health can clearly go either way since, for example, knowledge that breach may occur, or the experience of breach itself, may dissuade the patient from care which would improve their health *or* breach may improve their health by, for example, improving their care through open co-operation between professional family carers (as Bosanquet implies would be efficient).

These latter examples nicely describe the point from the economist's perspective. Measuring only one outcome is usually inadequate. However, even within the strict confines of 'health' objectives, it is problematic to do otherwise since there is then a need to compare unlike outcomes. Indeed, this takes the economist into a different model, that of 'cost-utility'. Here, there is not one outcome and the aim of achieving it by the resource cheapest route, but two or more outcomes which have to be variously 'valued' (at least in relative terms, either ordinal or cardinal) and between which a choice has to be made; the choice being made in conjunction with decisions about how to achieve the chosen portfolio of outcomes most cheaply in resource terms. Leaving aside the possible problem that the chosen outcome portfolio and the cheapest resource routes may not be independent of one another, the core difficulty lies in deciding how to weight the different outcomes, in terms of their relative desirability, and, where appropriate, how to weight the various outcomes in different

---

[4] See Caldicott, Conlan and Zigmond, this vol.
[5] Palmer, personal communication.

people. Difficult as these issues may be to resolve where the outcomes are health variables and are inherently measurable (for example, via validated and reliable mental health outcome scales), where one or more of the 'competing' outcomes is not a health variable at all and (in one sense) is inherently abstract, for example liberty or justice, the difficulties of utilising the model seem almost insurmountable. It amounts not to comparing apples with oranges but with, for example, love (or some other concept which has physical aspects or correlates of it but which is, ultimately, abstract in character). Indeed, this is not a problem just for the welfare economist but for anyone comparing and choosing between objectives whose natures are highly contrasted.

The economist tries to resolve the 'apples against love' comparative problem by way of resort to an attempted common numeraire. Hence, within the 'cost-utility' model varying qualities of outcome are reduced to one 'number'. Originating from nineteenth-century Benthamite utilitarianism, the model assumes that individuals construct 'preferences' (to the economist a technical term) rationally and that, given free choices, they will choose (rationally) on the basis of the varying 'utility' they experience, or predict, from given combinations of 'goods'. A modern day example of a 'health utility' construct is the 'quality adjusted life year' (QALY). Ironically, in the example which compares mental health outcome with civil rights well-being (perhaps definable in terms of 'liberty adjusted life years' or LALYs) the assumption of rationality is often challenged and one of the goods on offer is merely the *retention* of freedom. Also, whilst a cost-utility model *can* be adopted by the state, which values outcomes and makes choices by proxy for its citizens, in this example the individual experiences *disutility* through any imposed loss of liberty. A further irony is that the mental health outcome implied by a health intervention in conjunction with loss of freedom is itself intended to be beneficial to the person. Hence, they are offered the 'choice' of 'take the medicine and get better (whilst retaining your freedom)' *or* 'refuse the medicine, lose your freedom and then get better'. Of course, the clue to the irony is in the words 'get better' by contrast with 'feel better'. The former is objective, and whilst the latter is both subjective and capable of conjoining mental health and civil rights well being outcome, that is, of achieving a holistic measure of outcome. If we link this back to the utilitarian notion of 'preferences', clearly the question which arises is "*whose* preferences?" This relates not only to who is making the choices but for whom they are being made. Clearly, *an* essence of mental health policy choices is that the choices are made, for some, by proxy; however, whether it can ever be justified to choose for someone so that they 'get better' but do not 'feel better' must be open to some ethical debate. A further problem occurs where the (proxy) choice is made for the benefit of someone other than someone to whom the health care is explicitly directed (an unusual phenomenon of some mental health care). Here there is a direct comparison between the advantages to different individuals. Hence, the 'patient' may (a) get better and (b) feel worse, whilst the individual called 'the public' may (a) feel better (for example, because there is a

CTO in place) and either (b) be better off (because of a real increase in public safety arising from a CTO) or merely (b*) feel better off.[6]

The final related tool in the economist's toolbox is 'cost-benefit' analysis. This attempts not merely to compare apples and love (or mental health and justice) in terms of their 'enjoyment' but to put a 'dollar value' upon each, ultimately including putting a dollar value on the quality of life or on life itself. Hence, liberty can have a money value. The theoretical advantage of this 'ultimate' planning or resource allocation tool is that it allows direct comparisons not just between outcomes but between outcomes and costs, measured in the same (money) numeraire. For example, both the direct economic advantage gained through avoidance of homicides by psychiatric patients (for example, the contribution to the economy that the victims would have made had they remained alive) and increased mental health well-being of the patient, as well as of potential secondary victims of the avoided homicide, are expressed in money value. At this level, however, as with cost-utility analysis, the importance of recognising the significance of the underlying assumptions and, in particular, interpersonal weightings is emphasised, as is the need to 'change the assumptions' in order to see how doing so affects the 'choice outcome' (the model otherwise being a route potentially to imposing policy choice on the data rather than the reverse). Similarly, where the choice is between separately spending money on, for example, health outcome and public-safety outcome, it does become necessary to compare the two outcomes in combination with their costs. Interestingly, such economic thinking seems rarely to be undertaken routinely where governments wish to pursue public 'feel-good' policies, taking us back to the distinctions first made within a cost-utility approach.

ETHICS AND LAW

How does current law ethically approach contradictory objectives? There is a tendency for law to be simplistic in its balancing of ethical principles, often to the point of not balancing them at all.[7] Hence, under the 1983 Act if a mentally disordered person does not have a disorder "of a nature or degree" that makes it "appropriate" for them to be detained in hospital for medical treatment then, strictly, they should not be detained, whatever the severity of the consequences either for them or for others. There is no balancing in the 1983 Act of 'appropriateness' against 'consequences' since the criteria for detention (primary and secondary criteria relating to the disorder and its treatment) and criteria relating to consequences (tertiary criteria) should properly be addressed in strict sequence. In practice, however, it seems likely that practitioners do often achieve a balance by conflating the tertiary criteria with the others; thus appro-

---

[6] Thornicroft (personal communication).

[7] See Eastman and Hope (1988) generally and for a description of a 'balance' model of ethical decision-making.

priateness is determined by consequences. That clinicians might do this is not surprising. As we suggested in the first chapter, there is a profound incongruence between the modes of thought of medicine and law, what Bynoe and Holland describe as the law being to clinicians "something out there". Why should clinicians naturally constrain themselves therefore within the ethical thinking which is implicit in the law? Would we not *expect* clinicians ethically to 'balance' rather than to think in a strictly defined logical sequence or hierarchy which implies what seems to them to be an unethical and even 'unjust' result. However, such ethical behaviour seems not to be restricted to clinicians. We know, for example, that MHRTs exhibit similar behaviour,[8] as does the Court of Appeal. For example, in Re A[9] the court held that a psychopath who was deemed to be medically untreatable could still be appropriately detained for medical treatment. This decision seems highly likely to have been driven by an ethical wish to maintain public protection in the face of medical, and even legal, common sense. Thus the law recognises its own deficiencies and contorts itself, structurally or semantically, in order to make up for them. What is really needed, however, is radical law reform which avoids both the contorting and the emphasising of medico-legal incongruence of constructs and thinking.

It is unwise to assume that a high degree of medico-legal incongruence of constructs is unimportant even if both doctor and lawyer wish to achieve the same result. There is danger in ethical collusion, even if the objective is an ethical one. At one level, the danger is that the doctor will join in the contorting, by contorting her own science towards the required objective. For example, in a tribunal hearing of a patient suffering from psychopathic disorder, the doctor may be enticed into describing trivial 'improvements' in the patient as evidence of treatability for the future, and, therefore, appropriateness of current detention; or, as occurred in one tribunal, even describing attending a computer course as *amounting* to 'treatment', again to the same end of continued detention for the public good. Such covert pursuing of effectively preventive detention must undermine both the individual doctor and, ultimately, her science. This surely represents one very strong argument in favour of disintegrating the pursuit of treatment and public protection. A further example of both legal and medical contorting is represented by a case in which, again, the Court of Appeal[10] confirmed that "treatment for mental disorder"[11] (in this case naso-gastric feeding) included treatment of any consequence of that disorder, even though, at first instance, it was determined that the person retained her capacity in common law to refuse that treatment (in the High Court the patient's doctor had even argued, unsuccessfully, that naso-gastric feeding must amount to treatment of the patient's mental disorder, because, without it,

---

[8] Peay (1989).

[9] R. v. *Cannons Park MHRT, ex parte A* [1994]. However, see now also R (*A Patient*) v. *Secretary of State for Scotland and Another* (1998).

[10] B v. *Croydon Health Authority* [1995].

[11] S. 63, Mental Health Act.

there would be no patient alive to treat). Hence, it seems that the patient who recklessly breaks a leg may be operated upon non-consensually under section 63 of the 1983 Act if her mental disorder determined her recklessness. However, the legal means is unjustifying of the ethical end. Only medico-legal confusion will arise which, ultimately, will do little social good. For, even if courts and lawyers can understand the subtle interfaces of statute and common law, clinicians may not. Since most cases are negotiated at the bedside without a legal presence, the law may all too easily not have its intended effect. We must strive, therefore for medico-legal congruence based on medical and legal common sense, not the pursuit of ethical results by way of legal contortions which are ultimately confusing.

Integration of the objectives of mental health and justice requires, therefore, pursuit of an apparently paradoxical approach. That is, there must be pursuit of congruence between the constructs of medicine and law whilst allowing medicine, in particular, to restrict itself to its proper ambit, that of treatment. So, although it is arguable that limitation of self-harm is sometimes properly within the medical role, where the harm arises directly from severe mental disorder, the same cannot be said at all clearly of harm to others. Although there is a phenomenon of 'psychotic drive' which can make a substantial contribution to serious violence in individual cases, the relationship of mental disorder and violence is greatly confused by alcohol, and other substances, and by a range of ordinary criminological factors. Hence, although mental health sciences have a substantial contribution to make in limiting further violence in some cases, their role is necessarily a shared one. Some substantial degree of separation of public protection from mental health care would therefore both be consistent with scientific evidence and allow clinicians to avoid potentially spurious public-protective roles. This might properly extend to avoidance in the criminal law of the direct implication of doctors in the sentencing process, as occurs where doctors give opinions in court under section 2(2)(b) of the Criminal Justice Act 1991 towards 'longer than normal' sentences justified in the interest of public protection.[12] This social function of psychiatry is increasingly perceived by practitioners as required of them, based, for example, on government use of *mandatory* inquiries after homicides by patients,[13] the introduction of supervision registers[14] and ever more protective measures against sexual offenders which are couched in terms of professional 'risk assessment' which increasingly sounds (pseudo-)clinical. The morale-improving effect of clearer separation of treatment and public protection would ripple out far beyond specialist forensic psychiatric services. It would also make explicit any restrictions placed by the law on offenders (some of whom are themselves vulnerable), or on those predicted to offend, pursued in the name of the current communitarian political and social philosophy described by Heginbotham and Elson.

[12] Solomka (1996).
[13] DoH (1994a).
[14] Baker (1997).

MENTAL SCIENCES AND LAW – COULD CAPACITY HELP?

We reviewed in Chapter 1 the extent to which congruence of mental sciences and law constructs was an attainable objective, specifically in relation to the law's tendency towards 'autopoiesis' and its *inability* to be reflective of mental science. However, we further argued that congruence should in any event be *pursued*, since, as we have emphasised repeatedly, the effectiveness of the law is determined very substantially by those who operate it, by comparison with those who adjudicate on its operation, and this is especially so in the case of dis- cretionary law such as mental health care law. As Curran and Harding noted 20 years ago in a comparative international review of mental health law for the World Health Organisation, there should be "pursuit of mental health law which is in harmony with the needs of mental health programme operations, policies and objectives".[15]

At the heart of current debate about mental health law reform is the issue of capacity and the question of whether adoption of an incapacity test for overrid- ing patient refusal of treatment would address both objectives of reform just described. For, whilst we, like others, would argue that new law should be based on principle rather than on pragmatism (as was the 1983 Act), a focus on capac- ity would both encourage proper separation of medical functions from other social functions currently undertaken by doctors, by allowing patients to take responsibility for themselves other than when they lacked capacity, *and* ground the overriding of treatment refusal in a legal concept which naturally translates from medicine, by its association with 'disabilities' of functioning.

One aspect of the law on capacity is itself currently under review[16]; however, a brief rehearsal of how the concept is, and is not used in respect of mental dis- order in various aspects of the law will illustrate why there is a need for broader and simplifying reform, that is, reform which extends legal use of capacity into the law relating to non-consensual treatment of mental disorder. Currently, patients with physical disorders or (non-detained) patients with mental disor- ders can refuse treatment of those disorders if they have the capacity to refuse; (non-detained) patients with physical or mental disorders but without capacity can be treated if the treatment is in their best interests; (detained) patients with not only a mental disorder but also a physical disorder can refuse treatment of their physical disorder if they have the capacity to refuse and the former did not give rise to the latter; (detained) patients with mental disorder can have treat- ment for their mental disorder imposed even if they have the capacity to refuse, where a registered medical practitioner certifies in writing that the treatment should be given "having regard to the likelihood of its alleviating or preventing a deterioration of [the patient's] condition" (section 58(3)(b)) or, where the treatment is for their mental disorder and does not fall within section 57 or 58,

[15] Curran and Harding (1978), at 6.
[16] Lord Chancellor's Department (1997).

where the treatment is given by or under the direction of the responsible medical officer (section 63); and finally, patients without the capacity to consent to admission to hospital may be admitted and treated 'informally' for their mental disorders (under the *Bournewood* principle).

It has been argued that it is simplistic to assume that one concept of capacity will suffice both for those suffering from physical and mental conditions,[17] on the basis that there are added complexities in defining and assessing the capacity of the mentally disordered. However, first, for many people for whom capacity is in question it is a mental disorder which puts it into question, even though the treatment to which it is relevant is for an (unrelated) physical condition. Secondly, the Law Commission's definition of incapacity proposed in relation to the treatment of physical disorder[18] is almost identical to the definition adopted by the High Court in *Re C* (confirmed by the Court of Appeal in *Re MB*), in which the plaintiff suffered from schizophrenia and the definition was relevant to amputation of a gangrenous foot which was unconnected with his schizophrenia. More importantly, Fulford (a philosopher-psychiatrist) has further suggested that, wherever capacity is imported legally, it is its use which should determine to what it is assumed to amount, rather than any attempt being made to define it (beyond the word itself). This raises a profoundly important question. Whilst acknowledging the difficulty of defining many abstract concepts (the author cites "time"), if we were to leave the definition of 'capacity' to those who use it then clinicians (and lawyers) would be ethically highly unconstrained; they could set the nature and threshold for incapacity as they wished. Hence research in the field would investigate, 'what is capacity by how it is used'. The alternative is to define the concept, thereby somewhat ethically restricting it, and then to research both how it is used and whether it is used reliably. The ethical and public policy implications of choosing between the two approaches are great.

It has also been argued that clinicians would have difficulty in switching to a new basis for assessment for detention, or that there would be just as much latitude in the clinical use of a capacity test as there has been with the appropriateness test.[19] However, capacity has the advantage of being both a unitary concept and a concept which is inherently capable of being made operational within mental health sciences; thus, given that most legal effect depends on doctors not lawyers, with fertile soil for clinico-legal discretion, adherence to a 'right' and clinico-legally congruent concept is the course which is at least most likely to deliver justice. By contrast, 'appropriateness' is vague, capable of incorporating numerous (medical and even non-medical) sub-concepts and lacking of

---

[17] Fulford (1998).

[18] Law Commission (1995) recommended that a person should be regarded as without capacity if at the material time (the time of the decision) he or she is "unable by reason of mental disability to make a decision on the matter in question; or unable to communicate a decision on that matter because he or she is unconscious or for any other reason": para. 3.14. See also Lord Chancellor's Department (1997), chap. 3, for a discussion of the Law Commission's proposals.

[19] Thorold, personal communication.

any clearly defined, direct route to clinical translation. Where it is difficult to see how, with any intellectual integrity, public or patient protection could be conflated with capacity, the ease with which it can be done with appropriateness is evident, and evident on research.[20] Capacity also now has a developing track-record of being validly and reliably usable, with established research and clinical tools, most notably the MacArthur Competence Assessment Tool--Treatment (MacCAT–T), an 'easy to use' interview schedule for assessing a patient's decision-making abilities.[21] The Law Society and the BMA have similarly given substantial clinico-legal advice on the assessment of capacity.[22] Capacity will also necessarily be the subject of increasing clinical and research attention if there is implementation of the Government's recent Green Paper[23] relating to consent to treatments for physical disorders and other non-medical decisions, based on the Law Commission's detailed consideration and recommendations.[24]

PRACTITIONERS AND LAW

Whatever form of law we have in the future, what is clear from past deficiencies is that there must be substantial research into its effects and effectiveness, hand in hand with vastly increased training in its use. Training is peculiarly important in this field as law falls outside clinicians' customary 'cognition set'. This does not imply the need for clinicians to become mini-lawyers. Rather, they should have a clear conceptual understanding of both the law itself (statute and common law) and its interfaces with the relevant clinical sciences, as well as a working knowledge of the parts of the law they use frequently and an ability to understand what they read when they look up less frequently used parts of the law. Where the intended effect of the law depends very substantially on those non-lawyers who use it, there should be a particular kind of ethical reciprocity expected, whereby those with the power to override their fellow citizens' liberty should be required to understand the power they wield and its relation to the clinical science they operate. In the absence of a lawyer present at the domiciliary assessment (or the ward round) the clinician is just as much required to be the guardian of the patient's civil rights well-being as of her clinical well being (a kind of *de facto guardian ad litem* role). All such training for this role clearly needs to be multidisciplinary, not in order to blur the distinctions between different clinicians' legal roles but the better to understand and respect them. Training for all clinicians must also be structured so as to encourage them individually to understand the influence on their clinico-legal decision-making of

[20] Peay (1989).
[21] Grisso and Appelbaum (1998).
[22] Law Society/BMA (1995).
[23] Lord Chancellor's Dept. (1997).
[24] Law Commission (1995).

their personal attitudes and ethical positions, in order to increase both the inter-case reliability of individuals and, through corporate training, inter-rater reliability. Finally, quality standards incorporated into NHS service contracts or service agreements should clearly include clinico-legal training and measures of performance. Improved education of clinicians in the law and its interface with clinical sciences and practice must be, given the discretionary nature of mental health law, one of the most important steps towards increasing the effectiveness of such law, in terms of improving both national mental health and justice. It is probably also the easiest to instigate.

RESEARCH AND LAW

Oppenheim makes a number of important basic points about research methodology which can properly be applied to mental health law, especially in such a relatively under-researched field.[25] For example, he asks whether we even know what research is needed? There is certainly, so far, little dissemination of existing knowledge, evidenced by the fact that, when a current major DoH-sponsored research programme was being drawn up,[26] this was done in apparent lack of awareness that a directly relevant study was already under way.[27] Also, whilst research in the field does not start strictly from a vacuum, it does start from a low base and its largely unsystematic nature often makes it difficult to evaluate; albeit it does offer something on which methodologically to chew.

Although there are some existing research data and although the Department of Health has now begun to commission research in the field of mental health law, there is merit in thinking about what presuppositions would arise *were* research to be 'starting from scratch'. Oppenheim addresses, first, the issue of who sets the agenda. Here again, mental health law raises distinctive problems, because there are multiple players with different perspectives. And, unlike medicine generally, the key issues are not solely about curing and caring (where

---

[25] This vol.

[26] This includes studies into the operation of new or 'under-used' provisions (e.g., the use of supervision registers; and after-care under supervision orders and guardianship orders); a study of patients' perceptions of coercion (which will provide some insight into the *Bournewood* dilemma) and of the effects on their subsequent management; reviews of published studies under Parts II, III and IX of the 1983 Act; analysis of data collected by the Mental Health Act Commission for Part IV of the Act; a study of decision-making by MHRTs with follow-up of discharged and detained patients and a major study being co-ordinated by the College Research Unit (CRU) of the Royal College of Psychiatrists in four modules; an analysis of existing data sources on the use of compulsion; a cohort study describing practice, explaining variation and considering alternatives to compulsory admission; an observational study of decisions to admit, and a study of the legal knowledge, attitudes and decision processes of mental health practitioners . The Department has also commissioned programmes of research into mental health services, e.g., into both in-patient and primary care provision for children and adolescents, which invariably touch upon legal issues.

[27] Namely, a study of psychiatric decision-making about compulsory detention undertaken by Oyebode, Barnes and Haque for the South Birmingham Mental Health Trust (personal communication).

patients and doctors may be *ad idem*) but also very substantially about conflict-ing rights, with the Royal College of Psychiatrists and the major mental health organisations (for example, MIND) often historically adopting starkly con-trasting positions. Oppenheim also addresses the supposition that "anyone wants to know the results of any research", making the point that policy and practice changes are often pursued in ignorance of, or ignoring, relevant research. Indeed, it may be true to say that the 'rational activist' cycle may be thought of as applying in a progressively less influential fashion across a research spectrum which stretches from pharmaceutical research at one end, through more experimental and inspirational forms of medical research to research intended to inform law reform, the latter being most clearly driven by politics and policy rather than being research-based.[28] This undermining of law's research base is manifestly detrimental, not only to the conduct of good research but also to the very validity of law. As Harrison[29] has illustrated, the rush to introduce the controversial supervision registers under the auspices of circular HSG(94)5[30] resulted in the government having to concede that the cir-cular did not "have the force of law".[31] Similarly, the introduction of DoH 'guidance on discharge'[32] reflected a clear and apparently unforeseen potential for contradictions of section 72 of the Act *requiring* discharge in certain cir-cumstances.

Hence, the field of mental health legislation is, as Oppenheim suggests, "criss crossed by value constraints", and these constraints can impact both upon the nature of the research conducted and upon its subsequent legislative impact (or lack of it), thus even questioning the ethics of conducting such research if its pos-itive results will not necessarily be incorporated into practice (as would rou-tinely occur in relation to clinical research).

Oppenheim goes on to describe the conducting of mental health law research as "difficult but not impossible". Some such research is clearly *documentary*, in the traditional academic legal tradition, and therefore no more problematic than any other legal research. As regards *factual information studies* however, collecting national data is likely to be very costly; indeed, it was in recognition of the difficulties that the CRU abandoned an original intention, within the recent DoH-funded project, to undertake a national survey of use of the 1983 Act, utilising instead existing databases, even though this had adverse implica-tions for the generalisability of the results. This said, a complementary approach, similarly based on case records, might, for example, track the progress of particular patients through the process of admission, treatment, dis-charge and after-care, enabling a picture of a patient's mental health career to

---

[28] Reform of the 1959 Mental Health Act was most clearly influenced by the work of the legal activist Larry Gostin at MIND; see Gostin (1975) and (1977).

[29] See Harrison (1994) and generally Baker (1997).

[30] Department of Health (1994).

[31] Harrison (1994), at 1017.

[32] DoH (1994a).

be built up[33]; again, data sources would need to go beyond statistics collected routinely on a national basis and descend into the detail of individual patients' case-notes.[34] As regards *evaluation studies*, the ethical and practical problems of such studies are all too evident. Compromise becomes inevitable. One illustration from the arena of drug trials will suffice. Although one might design a double-blind study with a monitoring committee and seek full consent from each patient to being allocated to the experimental treatment or not, what is one to do if the early results show a massive improvement in respect of patients on the new regime; should those in the control group be denied the benefit of the experimental drug even if its long-term consequences might then never be fully established? Alternatively, where patients deteriorate on the new drug, or fail substantially to do as well as those on the standard treatment, should they not be withdrawn from the programme albeit that this may compromise the possibility of establishing a longer-term beneficial effect?[35] And whose assessment of impact is to count – that of doctor or patient? Transposing this model into mental health law research is even more problematic. In a hypothetical study of decisions to use one section or another, or indeed not to section at all, it would be possible to follow up patients once a decision to detain or not had been made (given that the *criteria* for compulsory admission are satisfied in all cases). However, it would be problematic to allocate patients to either legal situation on a random basis, both because of the implied interference with clinical freedom and because it would also clearly be impossible to undertake a double-blind study (for example, of patients admitted on section 2 or section 3). In any event, even if it were not, the benefit of sectioning over (blind) no-sectioning (the equivalent of an active treatment as against a placebo trial) has never been established in mental health.[36] Finally, could it ever be possible ethically to implement any sort of trial of sectioning where, in some cases, there must be obvious face validity in sectioning, for example, in the case of a severely depressed patient who is suicidal? In a drug trial, the solution would be to exclude certain patients from the study; but if one limited the study so as to exclude those for whom sectioning was self-evidently beneficial that would necessarily reduce the likelihood of demonstrating what, in other cases, is likely anyway to be a marginal therapeutic effect of sectioning.

[33] By analogy, criminal careers research, involving follow-up and self-report studies over an extensive period of selected cohorts has proved invaluable in understanding the relationship between human development and criminal careers; see, e.g., Farrington (1997).

[34] This approach has been adopted in the study of aftercare under supervision and guardianship orders (see above); similarly, the method also forms one element of the CRU programme of research.

[35] Breaking the code of double-blind medical trials is well accepted where there is clear evidence of patient disbenefit within the active group, but where there appears to be benefit, the trial will run its course, at least in order sufficiently to establish that the active treatment is better than the established treatment with which it is being compared.

[36] Those studies that are being conducted, comparing the outcomes of sectioned patients as against those of patients where a decision is made not to section, are descriptive only. They do not randomly allocate patients to a section or not, merely following patients about whom decisions have already been made.

HARMONY NOT ANACHRONISM – A NASCENT PRESCRIPTION

Viewed from a distance, Battersea power station has been seen as a monolith. Dominating its surrounds, it has cast a shadow below and carved up the skyline above; it has been a defining feature of London. Yet, viewed up close, it is no monolith. And, with a void at its centre, it is manifestly non-functional and clearly derelict.

It would be foolhardy to draw too close a parallel with the Mental Health Act 1983, for it remains an open question which of "radical refit or honourable retirement"[37] the Act requires. However, its out-datedness, its frequently contradictory objectives, the lack of clarity in some of its central features, its complex and often incoherent relationship with common law and its often adverse impact are uncontested, as is its continued domination of the mental health field.

This book has taken as one of its main themes the notion that it is not its fine detail which governs how the Act is used in practice; accordingly, changing the fine detail, even if it is necessary, is unlikely to be sufficient as a basis for effectively revising practitioners', users' and the public's view of the mental health care field. Equally, there are costs entailed in sustaining the Act in its current form; for its use is both limited and limiting, including by way of potentially alienating from mental health services many who might otherwise benefit from mental health care.

A major feature of current mental health law which emerges from the preceding pages is that it is marked by separations. Some of these separations may be logically unsustainable, for example, that which Matthews identifies in respect of the non-consensual treatment of mental and physical disorders.[38] Some may be socially undesirable and unjustifiable, as Bynoe and Holland suggest again in relation to the separation of mental and physical health care law. By contrast, the twin public policy objectives of improved national mental health and justice are *properly* viewed separately, since they are largely unrelated objectives which are often in conflict with one another and may require different legal approaches. That is most starkly potentially the case in relation to mentally disordered offenders, but it is true also of civilly detained patients; and it is true even though we may properly strive for a 'holistic' approach to mental health and justice, an objective which is emblazoned in the title of this book. However, the integration of mental health and justice as social objectives almost certainly requires substantial disaggregation of the law relating to mental health care, for example, the separation of law relating to those who pose a

---

[37] Fulford (1998).
[38] Research by the MacArthur Foundation has demonstrated both that many of those with serious mental illness have abilities similar to persons without mental illness for making treatment decisions and that, whilst those hospitalised with mental disorders show high levels of impairment for making treatment decisions, these impairments can be temporary and improve with treatment. See generally Appelbaum and Grisso (1995); Grisso *et al.* (1995); Grisso and Appelbaum (1995); Grisso and Appelbaum (1996).

threat to others from those who pose a threat only to themselves, *combined with* the integration of mental health care law into the body (in fact, a further developed body) of general medical law. As Bynoe and Holland suggest, the parts could be redistributed so that there would be an integrated, or unified, body of law for all medical treatment (of both mental and physical disorders), with the public protective effects of mental health law removed from the medico-legal arena and placed in a general legal framework for public protection. There are, then, complex cross-overs of integration and disaggregation required if law is to pursue effectively both mental health and justice. This is particularly the case where the relevant law is characterised by being law without enforcement.

Despite Jacob's timely warning of the impossibility of achieving patient autonomy in practice,[39] we live in an era when medical care generally has seen a shift from medical paternalism to patient autonomy, whilst mental health care, in particular, has emphasised notions of 'users of services' in place of that of 'patients'.[40] In this context, is it not time that we did away with artificial distinctions between the mentally ill and those merely suffering from physical disorders? In any event what are the justifications for special hedging of mental health care with law, when the treatment of physical disorders is not routinely so hedged, unless and until disaster strikes?

We are not alone in suggesting that thought ought to be given to replacing our current structure of mental health law, possibly with generic legislation separately covering incapacity and dangerousness[41], and certainly by legislation which puts on an equal footing the treatment of mental and physical disorders. Whilst it has been cogently argued that the discriminatory locus is in attitudes towards those with mental disorders and not in the law *per se*,[42] we would argue that the special presence of the law underpins these discriminatory attitudes and sustains discriminatory treatment. A further argument is that it would be discriminatory *not* to have specialist legislation, since that would exclude from treatment (and resources) those in need. But is this not true currently of treatment for physical disorders, where access to treatment is, in effect, rationed and prioritised? Why should patients with mental illnesses be any more deserving of treatment than those with physical disorders?[43] The answer which comes most readily to mind, even if it is callously unsettling, is that it is *we* who want them to have treatment in *our* interests. Similarly, why should patients with physical disorders who lack capacity not enjoy a series of safeguards (as do the mentally disordered when they are legally detained) against poor or inappropriate treat-

---

[39] See generally Jacob (1998).

[40] Fulford (1998).

[41] Bynoe and Holland (this vol.); Bingley and Heginbotham (this vol.); Szmukler and Holloway (1998); Rosenman (1994); Campbell (1994); Gordon (1993); Campbell and Heginbotham (1991).

[42] Fulford (1998).

[43] Paternalistic interventions have been justified for patients who demonstrably lack capacity to make reasonable judgements about their health needs where treatment is in the patient's best interests: see Law Commission (1995).

ment, for the "surgeon's knife poses at least as great a threat as the psychiatrist's anti-psychotic medication".[44]

Whilst clearly separating both the paternalistic and protectionist rationales for detention and then applying them to all citizens regardless of mental status[45] has its attractions as a route to combating discrimination against the mentally disordered, two obvious problem categories remain. First, those who inflict self-harm, and secondly, those who offend, but who retain some element of culpability.[46]

It is paradoxical that the public and political debate about the threat posed by the mentally disordered is couched primarily in terms of their potential to cause harm to others. Whilst these concerns should not be dismissed, their emotive power far outweighs the reality of the threat. As broadsheet editors are fond of commenting, one is 20 times more likely to be killed by someone who is sane than by someone who is insane. In fact, the real source of concern to mental health professionals lies in the threat of self-harm, for those suffering from mental disorder are 20 times more likely to kill themselves than kill others.[47] But generic legislation based on a rationale which involved, for example, a need for treatment, the proven efficacy of treatment and the inability of the individual to apprehend the need for treatment, might well capture within its net those currently excluded (for example, a drug abusing individual with learning disability) whilst excluding some of those whom we currently treat and who are at peculiar risk of self harm (for example, the severely personality disordered – satisfying the legal definition of psychopathic disorder). So, whilst rampant paternalism makes us feel uncomfortable, a rigorous approach that permits evident suffering is equally hard for the caring professions (indeed, most citizens) to contemplate. These are not easy issues that can be resolved in this text. However, raising questions in terms of principles and not outcomes at least lays bare the social choice and may even be productive towards *making* a choice.

One illustration of a principled approach to resolution of the problem would centre on the detail of the notion of capacity itself. Starting from the (surely undeniable) axiom that we should allow mentally ordered people to self-harm highlights the central role of disorder in justifying, in *some* way, coercive intervention. What should be the way in which disorder should be translated into incapacity? Accepting that any test will engender its own specific interpretational problems, one solution might be to adopt the Law Commission test but to elaborate its second limb by allowing capacity to be retained if the person (a) can give reasons for their refusal of treatment which do not amount to reasons clearly originating from their disorder (for example, dislike of recognised medication side effects would be an acceptable reason) or (b) where relevant, they can recognise that their attitude to the decision is attributable to their underlying

---

[44] Szmukler and Holloway (1998).
[45] See Campbell (1994), at 557.
[46] See generally Peay (1998).
[47] Sims (1996).

disorder (that is, they have some insight). This would imply that the patient lacking insight, but also able to give other rational reasons for refusal, would retain their capacity, thus placing particular responsibility upon the doctor to search diligently for 'rational' reasons. A much weaker version of the test would require both (a) *and* (b) to be present in order for capacity to be present. This would amount to incapacity being determined either by lack of insight (specifically in relation to making the choice about treatment) or lack of rational reasons, a version of the test surely weak enough to ensure reconciliation between principle and outcome. In applying such an insight test a further important question arises from Barham and Barnes' notion of the "citizen mental patient",[48] namely, in respecting patient autonomy the core question is who gets to define whether or not the patient has insight? Where the patient tells the doctor that they believe her when she says that their refusal is attributable to the illness, is that sufficient to conclude that the patient has capacity? Or does the doctor have to believe the patient? Hence, should the test be objective or subjective?

An illustrative example is offered by the case of Ms B,[49] who had guilty thoughts (not delusions) originating from her 'borderline personality disorder' (itself intermingled with childhood sexual abuse of her). The 'reason' she self-harmed (including by starvation) was that it was, to her, worth the increased risk of dying in order to control the guilty thoughts in this way. For her the 'weighing' of matters towards her refusal was 'rational', even though the discomfort she was trying to achieve itself originated in disorder. Like (normal) others she took a risk rationally. She therefore retained capacity. There is also 'justice' in this conclusion in that, since the thoughts could not be removed therapeutically, it would have been both wrong and even cruel to deny her the reduction of her pain.[50] Suppose, however, that Ms B had become psychotic, her guilty thoughts had become delusions that she should be punished and these beliefs had no connection with the earlier abuse of her? If she had no insight into the (true) origin of her concerns then she would self-starve without 'insight'. She would therefore lack capacity (even though she could give other rational reasons for doing so) depending on whether (a) and (b) are disjunctive (retain capacity) or conjunctive (lose capacity). Similar considerations would apply to the patient with schizophrenia who refuses medication whilst psychotic and 'insightless' about the effect of their illness on their decision.

Although the unpacking of any particular capacity test is necessarily complex, as we have just demonstrated, this does not imply that the test itself needs

---

[48] This vol.

[49] *B* v. *Croydon Health Authority* [1995].

[50] Introducing the notions of justice and treatability adds further nuances which may seem problematic. Capacity (or incapacity) seems then to be defined not just according to current mental phenomena but also according to whether they are amenable to therapeutic alteration. This introduces a different dimension to 'capacity' in that the person's current status is defined according to the possibility of some future status (this is somewhat related to the well-known justification for coercive intervention that the person will 'thank the doctor afterwards'). The problem would be excluded if the 'insight' dilemma discussed in the text gave primacy to the patient not to the doctor.

to be complex. Unpacking is necessary in order to predict the operational practice of any test, however simply defined. In this regard, it is no different from the apparent attractive simplicity of the 'appropriateness' test.

Similar arguments apply to our second problematic category, the 'not fully incompetent' offender. Generic dangerousness legislation with tightly drawn criteria based on established behaviour and a clear and present threat is attractive, if only because it is likely to make us think seriously about the need for protection of the rights of offenders, rather than confusing the advantages of dangerousness legislation with a therapeutic justification. Moreover, since most dangerous people are not mentally ill the balance of any generic legislation would immediately shift the focus of attention away from those suffering from mental disorder. Indeed, the recent deliberations concerning legislation for those deemed dangerous have been aimed at psychopaths (an uncertain and marginal category of the mentally disordered) and pædophiles (excluded from the Act).[51] Where the evidence is that mentally disordered people are in the aggregate little more dangerous – in the sense of having a propensity to cause physical or serious and lasting psychological harm to others – than other citizens and that it is substance abuse that most significantly raises the rate of violence in both patient and comparison groups,[52] it is wrong that the mentally disordered in general should be tainted with an association with these high risk offenders. Equally, where those with mental disorder do engage in the community in acts of violence, such acts are most frequently targeted at family members and friends, and violence most often takes place in the home. This makes their violence substantially comparable with that of the non-mentally disordered.[53] Overall, even though there may be emerging evidence that some people with severe psychosis are more at risk of committing violence than other mentally ill and mentally well people, the contribution of psychosis to social violence is both very small and very poorly predicted.[54] Thus, the notion that the public at large needs to be especially protected from unusual and violent attack by mentally disordered people who are strangers to them is fallacious.

Whilst generic legislation would help to address the issue of inappropriate negative attributions and special legal measures for public protection from mentally disordered people which can often be unjust in their effects, it would also remove some of the advantages from which they have arguably *benefited,*

[51] Any legislation designed specifically to be preventive of violence by psychopaths would suffer either from being invalid and unreliable in 'selecting in' offenders, if the class was defined narrowly, or from being over-inclusive if the class was defined broadly. Justice could only be served by adopting the latter approach and then relying on ordinary criminological predictors of violence, thus properly marginalising any significance of psychiatrists placing offenders, or not, within the broadly defined category of psychopathic or sexual disorder.

[52] Steadman *et al.* (1998).

[53] *Ibid.*

[54] Although there is some evidence that, amongst psychotic patients in the aggregate, 'threat-control override' symptoms may be somewhat predictive of violence, risk assessment relies largely not on generalised psychotic markers but on markers recognised *in the individual* with psychosis as predictive of violence *in them.*

namely, sentencing provisions intended to be overtly therapeutic and not punitive. One such example would be the hospital order. For those few offenders who do fall within the relevant criteria, notions of punishment are foregone in favour of a humanitarian and therapeutic disposal; this fits well with our sense that it is wrong to punish the mentally disordered who may not be wholly responsible for their actions and anathema to place them into a prison system which may be peculiarly damaging to their health. Whilst laudable, these sentiments require some unpacking. First, although perhaps influenced by an overly restricted range of mental condition defences, all but the tiny number of mentally disordered offenders who are found insane or unfit to plead have been found guilty (for which read culpable); indeed, this was one justification offered by the Home Office for recommending that the "hospital and limitation direction" be available not just for psychopaths but for all the four major Mental Health Act categories.[55] Hence, there is indeed justice in hybridising a punitive and welfare disposal.[56] Secondly, the vast majority of mentally disordered offenders do not gain the benefit of a Mental Health Act disposal, albeit that many of the most seriously ill and impaired do. Thirdly, our current prison system is potentially damaging to the health not only of mentally disordered but also seemingly mentally ordered offenders, perhaps testified to by the incidence of suicide in prison. Since currently Mental Health Act disposals do not require a causal relationship to be established between the offence and the offender's disorder, why should not some other classes of offender, for example, drug or alcohol abusers, benefit from therapeutic disposals? So, whilst superficially attractive, our current arrangements are difficult to defend in logic. Indeed, critics have often argued that what needs to be addressed are prior issues of culpability, so that when we seek to impose punishment (however unattractive and damaging that might be) we at least impose punishment on the truly culpable, thereby maintaining our own moral high ground. Regrettably, the poverty and lack of coherence with modern mental health sciences of our current mental condition defences is all too evident.[57] Again, mere tinkering with legislation will have far-reaching ramifications. These issues need to be thought through, including a recognition that separating welfare from justice, with expansion of mental-condition defences, would place an emphatic focus on determining the presence or absence of 'causation' between disorder and offence, itself open to expert variation and abuse.

Whilst the dilemmas set out above are subject to separate practical resolution, their derivation is common; namely, from our inherently ambivalent attitudes towards those suffering from mental disorder. An approach giving pre-emi-

---

[55] Home Office (1996); Eastman and Peay (1998b).

[56] Eastman (1996c).

[57] Mackay (1995). The introduction of the automatic life sentence for conviction on a second serious offence under the Crime (Sentences) Act 1997 is likely to result in added pressure for expansion of mental condition defences since, whereas a defendant has available the low threshold defence of diminished responsibility to a charge of murder, there is only the very high threshold defence of 'insanity' available for a charge of a second 'serious offence'. See also Singleton *et al* (1998).

nence to notions of 'citizenship' and being 'rights respecting and enforcing' does not nest easily with the embodiment of a humanitarian approach which attracts most mental health professionals to their work and which is most readily understood by a community (perhaps one that extends no further than one's immediate family) which strives to care. This may be one reason why Joe Jacob's "The Right of the Mental Patient to his Psychosis" is so unsettling,[58] for his title mirrors this tension.

The tension is not, however, an unexplored terrain. The therapeutic jurisprudence movement,[59] whilst overtly concerned with how the law can function as a therapeutic (or anti-therapeutic) agent, has touched also upon the ways in which a therapeutic approach can be paternalistic (and hence exclusionary and discriminatory) rather than being empowering, rights enhancing and promoting of psychological well-being (which requires an inclusionary approach).[60] Even the founding fathers of the therapeutic jurisprudence movement, David Wexler and Bruce Winick, acknowledge this dilemma, although they resolve it by arguing that, whilst therapeutic interests should never trump other normative values such as autonomy, they are a legitimate part of the balancing process; thus, a hierarchy of the relevant values needs to be established via a democratically valid process (that is embodied in legislation).

One other way in which an exploration of the terrain of tension might assist comes from an explicit recognition that law's impact is neither unidirectional in terms of its own values nor unidirectional in terms of therapeutic values. Some will benefit and some will not. Slobogin argues that the solution may be to do the greatest good for the greatest number[61]; whilst not incompatible with law, this approach rests less easily with clinical norms, where striving to do the best for 'this patient at this time' is pre-eminent. However, the latter is an approach which we have sought to question. Perhaps clinicians would benefit from acknowledging that even medicine, with its lofty moral approach, makes hard choices at the expense of unnamed patients, even if those choices are rarely as explicit as they appear to be in the law's domain, where winners and losers are all too readily identifiable.

We have set our sights high and are inevitably likely to be disappointed. Indeed, the thrust of the government's current review of mental health services may already be somewhat disappointingly clear. As Holloway has noted, policy development in community care has been driven "not by an analysis of the weaknesses of the system, but rather has reflected moral panic on the part of Ministers who have been faced with a series of highly publicised tragic incidents".[62] With the implication that 'community care' has substantially failed, the current government announced recently its new "safety-plus" approach,

---

[58] Jacob (1976).
[59] See, e.g., Wexler and Winick (1996).
[60] Petrila (1996).
[61] Slogobin (1996).
[62] Holloway (1996), at 241.

which will entail a heavily funded package aimed at offering rehabilitation (and, arguably, fundamental re-shaping) of care in the community; this includes round-the-clock services for some patients in the community, combined with outreach teams, more acute care beds and a network of community units; as well as greater powers to visit patients, enter their homes and take them to an appropriate clinical setting for treatment.

This review of services is clearly intended to be accompanied by increased legal powers, specifically aimed at buttressing care in the community. In legal terms, something more than the "power to convey" is envisaged.[63] However, although the government's current review of mental health legislation is based on the policy requirement that "non-compliance with agreed treatment programmes is not an option",[64] the scope of the review is also "root and branch"[65]. In this light, our aspirations for a fundamental review do not look wholly unrealistic. Yet, the eight month review period looks inadequate to the task and seems to reflect a policy driven mainly by immediate and emotive 'feel-good' concerns (to some extent, self-inflicted via the DoH requirement for mandatory inquiries after homicide – an issue which the government is sensibly revisiting) rather than by pursuit of principle. To rush to be seen to be doing something may result in the wrong something being done.

The publication in 1957 of the Royal Commission's report on the law relating to mental illness and mental deficiency reflected four years of effort by the Commission in hearing evidence and compiling recommendations, but it set an agenda for the next 40 years. We would argue that the type of prescription we have advocated would take Percy's recommendations further along their logical route. Whether that is the right route is for all of us to decide. However, surely the enormous cultural and mental health service changes which underpin the need for *some* law reform imply the need for *profound* law reform. Indeed, the complexities and confusions which have developed within the law itself since Percy, in terms of the relationship of treatment for mental and physical disorders, combined with the lacunae in the law for incapacitated patients requiring general medical treatment and the '*de facto*' detained,[66] also greatly reinforce the need for a fundamental and comprehensive legal review. The addition of debating of the proper legal and medical treatment of mentally disordered offenders, particularly psychopathic offenders, would seem finally to drive the point home that there must be a comprehensive review of all law directly affecting those suffering from mental disorder. Should a desire for 'change now' not be tempered by acknowledgement of the need for a reflective time-scale at least equivalent to that enjoyed by the Percy Commission?

[63] See Mental Health (Patients in the Community) Act 1995.
[64] Ministerial Press Release announcing review of mental health legislation 17 Sept. 1998.
[65] *Ibid.*
[64] Eastman and Peay (1998).

Case List

Bibliography

AFRICAN AND CARIBBEAN PEOPLE'S MOVEMENT (1998), *Development of a Pan Birmingham Mental Health Strategy for the African and Caribbean Community* (Birmingham).

AMERICAN PSYCHIATRIC ASSOCIATION (1994), *Diagnostic and Statistical Manual of Mental Disorders* (4th edn., Washington DC: American Psychiatric Association).

—— (1990), *Annual Report for 1988–9* (London: HMSO).

APPELBAUM, P. (1990), "The Parable of the Forensic Psychiatrist: Ethics and the Problem of Doing Harm", 13 *Int. J. of Law and Psychiatry* 249–59.

—— and GRISSO, T. (1995), "The MacArthur Treatment Competence Study: I. Mental Illness and Competence to Consent to Treatment", 19 *Law and Human Behavior*, 105–26.

BAKER, E. (1997), "The Introduction of Supervision Registers in England and Wales: A Risk Communications Analysis", 8 *Journal of Forensic Psychiatry* 15–35.

BARHAM, P. (1984), *Schizophrenia and Human Value: Chronic Schizophrenia, Science and Society* (Oxford: Blackwell).

—— (1997), *Closing the Asylum: The Mental Patient in Modern Society* (2nd edn., London: Penguin).

—— and HAYWARD, R. (1995), *Relocating Madness: From the Mental Patient to the Person* (London: Free Association Books).

—— and —— (1998, forthcoming), "In Sickness and in Health: Dilemmas of the Person with Severe Mental Illness", *Psychiatry*.

BARKER, M. (1984), *A Haunt of Fears: The Strange History of the British Horror Comics Campaign* (London: Pluto).

BARNES, M., and SHARDLOW, P. (1996a), "From Passive Recipient to Active Citizen: Participation in Mental Health User Groups", 6 *Journal of Mental Health* 275–86.

—— and —— (1996b), "Identity Crisis? Mental Health User Groups and the 'Problem' of Identity", in Barnes, C., and Mercer, G. (eds.), *Exploring the Divide: Illness and Disability* (Leeds: The Disability Press).

—— and WISTOW, G. (1994), "Learning to Hear Voices: Listening to Users of Mental Health Services", 3 *Journal of Mental Health* 525–40.

—— BOWL, R., and FISHER, M. (1990), *Sectioned: Social Services and the 1983 Mental Health Act* (London: Routledge).

BARON, J. (1994), *Thinking and Deciding* (2nd edn., Cambridge: Cambridge University Press).

BARTLETT, A., EASTMAN, N., BACKHOUSE, A., and EVANS, C. (1994), *The National Health Service and the Penal and Criminal Justice Systems: Evaluation of the Interfaces* (Unpublished Report to the Department of Health).

BAYLES, M. (1987), *Principles of Law: A Normative Analysis* (Dordrecht: Lancaster; D. Reidel).

—— (1990), *Procedural Justice: Allocating to Individuals* (Dordrecht: Kluwer Academic).

BEACH, A. (1996), *The Labour Party and the Idea of Citizenship, c. 1931–1951* (Unpublished PhD thesis, University of London).

BEAN, P. (1980), *Compulsory Admissions to Mental Hospitals* (Chichester: Wiley).

—— (1986), *Mental Disorder and Legal Control* (Cambridge: Cambridge University Press).

BECK, U. (1992), *Risk Society: Towards a New Modernity* (London: Sage).

—— (1998), "Politics of Risk Society" in Franklin, J. (ed.), *The Politics of Risk Society* (Cambridge: Polity Press), 12–3.

BEVAN, G., HOLLAND, T., and PARTINGTON, M. (1996), "Organising Cost-Effective Access to Justice" in Paterson, A. A., and Goriely, T. (eds.), *Resourcing Civil Justice* (Oxford: Oxford Readings in Socio-Legal Studies, Oxford University Press) 281–303.

BLANKENBERG, E. (1984), "The Poverty of Evolutionism: A Critique of Teubner's Case for Reflexive Law", 18 *Law and Society Review* 273.

BLOM-COOPER, L., *Report of the Committee of Inquiry into Complaints about Ashworth Hospital* (1992, Cm 2028–1, HMSO).

—— HALLY, H., and MURPHY, E. (1995), *The Falling Shadow. One Patient's Mental Health Care 1978– 1993* (London: Duckworth).

BLUMENTHAL, S., and WESSELY, S. (1994), *The Pattern of Delays in Mental Health Review Tribunals Summary* (London: HMSO).

BOSANQUET, N. (1995), "Schizophrenia: Developing New Strategies for Effective Care", 8 *British Journal of Medical Economics* 51–64.

—— (1998), "Managers and Schizophrenia Care: The Missing Dimension of Strategy", 4 *British Journal of Health Care Management* 16–19.

BRADLEY, H. (1996), *Fractured Identities: Changing Patterns of Inequality* (Cambridge: Polity).

BRAITHWAITE, J. (1984), *Corporate Crime in the Pharmaceutical Industry* (London: Routledge and Kegan Paul).

BURNEY, E. (1996), *Crime, Mental Health and the Inner City: The Experience of the Islington Mentally Disordered Offenders Project* (London: Goldsmith's College).

—— and PEARSON, G. (1995), "Mentally Disordered Offenders: Finding a Focus for Diversion", 34 *Howard Journal of Criminal Justice* 291–313.

BURTON, P., and DUNCAN, S. (1996), "Democracy and Accountability in Public Bodies: New Agendas in British Governance", 24 *Policy and Politics* 5–16.

BUSTON, K., PARRY-JONES, W., LIVINGSTON, M., BOGAN, A., and WOOD, S. (1998), "Qualitative Research", 172 *British Journal of Psychiatry* 197–9.

CALDICOTT, F. (1994), "Supervision Registers: The College's Response", 18 *Psychiatric Bulletin* 385–6.

CAMPBELL, P. (1989), "Peter Campbell's Story" in Brackx, A., and Grimshaw, C. (eds.), *Mental Health Care in Crisis* (London: Pluto Press).

CAMPBELL, T. (1994), "Mental Health Law: Institutionalised Discrimination", 28 *Australian and New Zealand Journal of Psychiatry* 554–9.

CAMPBELL, T. D., and HEGINBOTHAM, C. J. (1991), *Mental Illness: Prejudice, Discrimination and the Law* (Aldershot: Gower).

CARSON, D. (1996), "New Approaches to Mental Health Law: Will the UK Follow the US Lead, Again?" in Wexler, D. B., and Winnick, B. J. (eds.) *Law in a Therapeutic Key* (Durham, North Carolina: Carolina Academic Press).

CHIBNALL, S. (1977), *Law-and-Order News: An Analysis of Crime Reporting in the British Press* (London: Tavistock).

CLAUSEN, J. A., and YARROW, M. (eds.) (1955), "The Impact of Mental Illness on the Family", 11 *Journal of Social Issues* 3–7.

COHEN, A., and EASTMAN, N. (1996), "A Survey of the Use of Supervision Registers in South Thames (West) Region", 7 *Journal of Forensic Psychiatry* 653–61.

—— and —— (1999), *Needs Assessment for Mentally Disordered Offenders; Theory, Policy and Research* (London: Gaskell Publications).

COHEN, S. (1972), *Folk Devils and Moral Panics: The Creation of the Mods and Rockers* (London: MacGibbon & Kee).

COONAN, K., BLUGLASS, R., HALLIDAY, G., JENKINS, M., and KELLY, O. (1998), *Report of Inquiry into the Care and Treatment of Christopher Edwards and Richard Linford* (Witham, Essex: North Essex Health Authority).

COTTERRELL, R. (1992), *The Sociology of Law* (2nd edn., London: Butterworths).

COTTINGHAM, J., STOOTHOFF R., and MURDOCH, D. (1985), *The Philosophical Writings of Descartes Volume I* (Cambridge: Cambridge University Press).

COUNCIL ON TRIBUNALS (1983), *Annual Report of the Council on Tribunals 1982–3* (London: HMSO).

—— (1989), *Annual Report for 1987–88* (London: HMSO).

—— (1990), *Annual Report for 1989–90* (London: HMSO).

CRICHTON, J., and SHEPPARD, D. (1996), "Psychiatric Inquiries: Learning the Lessons" in Peay, J. (ed.), *Inquiries After Homicide* (London: Duckworth).

CURRAN, W., and HARDING, T. (1978), *The Law and Mental Health, Harmonizing Objectives: A Comparative Survey of Existing Legislation Together with Guidelines for its Assessment and Alternative Approaches to its Improvement* (Geneva: World Health Organisation).

DAHRENDORF, R. (1988), *The Modern Social Conflict* (London: Weidenfeld and Nicolson).

DAMASKA, M. (1975), "Structures of Authority and Comparative Criminal Procedure", 84 *Yale Law Journal* 480–544.

DAVEY, B. (1998, forthcoming), "Solving Economic, Social and Environmental Problems Together: An Empowerment Strategy for Losers" in Barnes, M., and Warren, L. (eds.), *Alliances and Partnerships in Empowerment* (Bristol: Policy Press).

DAWES, R. (1988), *Rational Choice in an Uncertain World* (San Diego, Cal.: Harcourt Brace Jovanovich).

DAY SCLATER, S., and PIPER, C. (1998), *Undercurrents of Divorce* (London: Dartmouth).

DAY, S., and PAGE, S. (1986), "Portrayal of Mental Illness in Canadian Newspapers", 31 *Canadian Journal of Psychiatry* 813–17.

DELL, S., and ROBERTSON, G. (1988), *Sentenced to Hospital: Offenders in Broadmoor* (Oxford: Oxford University Press).

DEPARTMENT OF THE ENVIRONMENT, TRANSPORT AND THE REGIONS (1998), *Modernising Local Government—Local Democracy and Community Leadership* (London: Stationery Office).

DEPARTMENT OF HEALTH (1983), *NHS Management Enquiry* (London: DoH).

—— (1990), HSC(90)23/LASSL(90), *The Care Programme Approach for People with a Mental Illness Referred to Specialist Psychiatric Services* (London: Stationery Office).

—— (1993), Press Release H93/908, 12 Aug. 1993.

—— (1994a), *Guidance on the Discharge of Mentally Disordered People and their Continuing Care in the Community* (London: NHS Executive, Health Service Guidelines HSG (94) 27, LASSL (94) 4).

—— (1994b), *Introduction of Supervision Registers for Mentally Ill People*, Circular HSG(94)5 (London, NHS Executive, Health Service Guidelines).

DEPARTMENT OF HEALTH (1995a), *Building Bridges—A Guide to Inter-agency Working for the Care and Protection of Severely Mentally Ill People* (London: Stationery Office).

—— (1995b), *The Patient's Charter and You—a Charter for England* (London: DoH).

—— (1996), *Spectrum of Care, Local Services for People with Mental Health Problems* (London: Stationery Office).

—— (1997a), *Mental Health Review Tribunal Annual Report 1996* (London: Appendix 5).

—— (1997b), *The New NHS: Modern, Dependable* (London: Stationery Office).

—— (1998), *Statistical Bulletin. In-patients Formally Detained in Hospitals under the Mental Health Act 1983 and Other Legislation, England: 1991–92 to 1996–97* (London: Government Statistical Service).

DEPARTMENT OF HEALTH AND WELSH OFFICE (1993), *Code of Practice Mental Health Act 1983* (London: HMSO).

DEPARTMENT OF HEALTH AND SOCIAL SECURITY (1976), *Review of the Mental Health Act 1959* (London: HMSO).

—— (1984), Circular No. DDL (84) 4.

DEPARTMENT OF SOCIAL SECURITY (1998), *New Ambitions for our Country: A Contract for Welfare* (London: Stationery Office).

DIXON, D. (1997), *Law in Policing: Legal Regulations and Policing Practices* (New York: Clarendon Press).

DOUGLAS, M. (1985), *Risk Acceptability According to the Social Sciences* (London: Routledge and Kegan Paul).

—— (1992), *Risk and Blame: Essays in Cultural Theory* (London: Routledge).

DYER, C. (1998), "Trust Faces Damages after Forcing Women to have Cæsareans", 316 *British Medical Journal* 1480.

DYER, J. (1998), "Treatment in the Community in the Absence of Consent", 22 *Psychiatric Bulletin* 73–6.

EASTMAN, N. (1987), "Clinical Confidentiality, a Contractual Basis" in Gudjonsson, G., and Drinkwater, J. (eds.), *Psychological Evidence in Court*. Issues in Criminological and Legal Psychology no 11 (Leicester, British Psychological Society).

—— (1992), "Psychiatric, Psychological and Legal Models of Man", 15 *International Journal of Law and Psychiatry* 157–69.

—— (1994), "Mental Health Law: Civil Liberties and the Principle of Reciprocity", 308 *British Medical Journal* 43–5.

—— (1995), "Anti-therapeutic Community Mental Health Law", 310 *British Medical Journal* 1081–82.

—— (1996a), "Inquiry into Homicides by Psychiatric Patients: Systematic Audit Should Replace Mandatory Inquiries", 313 *British Medical Journal* 1069–71.

—— (1996b), "Towards an Audit of Inquiries: Enquiry not Inquiries" in Peay, J. (ed.), *Inquiries After Homicide* (London: Duckworth).

—— (1996c), "Hybrid Orders: An Analysis of their Likely Effects on Sentencing Practice and on Professional Psychiatric Practice and Services", 7 *Journal of Forensic Psychiatry* 481–94.

—— (1997), "The Mental Health (Patients in the Community) Act 1995: A Clinical Analysis", 170 *British Journal of Psychiatry* 492–6.

—— and HOPE, R. (1988), "The Ethics of Enforced Medical Treatment: The Balance Model", 5 *Journal of Applied Philosophy* 49–59.

—— and PEAY, J. (1998a), "*Bournewood*: An Indefensible Gap in Mental Health Law", 317 *British Medical Journal* 94–5.

—— and —— (1998b), "Sentencing Psychopaths: Is the 'Hospital and Limitation Direction' an Ill-Considered Hybrid?", *Criminal Law Review* 93–108.

—— ZIGMOND, A., and McIVER, S. (1998, unpublished), *Report of Royal College of Psychiatrists National Consultation Seminar on Coercion of Treatment in the Community*.

EIGEN, J. P. (1995), *Witnessing Insanity: Madness and Mad-Doctors in the English Court* (New Haven, Conn.: Yale University Press).

ELDERGILL, A. (1997), *Mental Health Review Tribunals* (London: Sweet and Maxwell).

EXWORTHY, T. (1995), "Compulsory Care in the Community: A Review of the Proposals for Compulsory Supervision and Treatment of the Mentally Ill in the Community", 5 *Criminal Behaviour and Mental Health* 218–41.

FADEN, R., and BEAUCHAMP, T. (1986), *A History and Theory of Informed Consent* (New York: Oxford University Press).

FARRINGTON, D. (1997), "Human Development and Criminal Careers" in Maguire, M., Morgan, R., and Reiner, R. (eds.) The Oxford Handbook of Criminology (2nd edn., Oxford: Clarendon Press).

FENNELL, P. (1986), "Law and Psychiatry: The Legal Constitution of the Psychiatric System", 15 *Journal of Law and Society* 35–67.

—— (1996), *Treatment Without Consent: Law, Psychiatry and the Treatment of Mentally Disordered People since 1845* (London: Routledge).

FINCH, J. (1989), *Family Obligations and Social Change* (Oxford: Basil Blackwell).

—— and GROVES, D. (1980), "Community Care and the Family: A Case for Equal Opportunities?", 9 *Journal of Social Policy* 487–512.

FOLKARD, M., SMITH, D. E., and SMITH, D. D. (1976), *IMPACT: Volume 2 The Results of the Experiment*, Home Office Research Study no 36 (London: HMSO).

FOUCAULT, M. (1967), *Madness and Civilisation: A History of Insanity in the Age of Reason* (London: Tavistock).

—— (1972), *Histoire de la Folie à L'âge Classique* (2nd edn., Paris: Gallimard).

—— (1977), *Discipline and Punish: The Birth of the Prison* (London: Allen Lane).

—— (1980), 'Two Lectures', reproduced in Freeman, M. (1994), *Lloyd's Introduction to Jurisprudence* (6th edn., London: Sweet and Maxwell).

FREEMAN, H. F., and SIMMONS, O. G. (1961), "Feelings of Stigma Among Relatives of Former Mental Patients", 8 *Social Problems* 312–21.

FREEMAN, M. (1994), *Lloyd's Introduction to Jurisprudence* (6th edn., London: Sweet and Maxwell).

FULFORD, K. W. (1998), "Replacing the Mental Health Act 1983? How to Change the Game Without Losing the Baby with the Bathwater, or Shooting Ourselves in the Foot?" 22 *Psychiatric Bulletin* 666–668.

GALLIGAN, D. (1986), *Discretionary Powers: A Legal Study of Official Discretion* (Oxford: Clarendon Press).

GENERAL MEDICAL COUNCIL (1993), *Tomorrow's Doctors* (London: GMC).

—— (1995), *Duties of a Doctor: Guidance from the GMC—Confidentiality* (London: GMC).

GERBNER, G., and GROSS, L. (1976), "The Scary World of TV's Heavy Viewer", *Psychology Today*, April, 89–91.

GIDDENS, A. (1994), *Beyond Left and Right* (Cambridge: Polity Press).

GOFFMAN, E. (1959), "The Moral Career of the Mental Patient", 22 *Psychiatry* 123–42.

GOFFMAN, E. (1968), *Asylums* (Harmondsworth: Penguin).

GORDON, R. (1993a), "Out to Pasture: A Case for the Retirement of Canadian Mental Health Legislation", 12 *Canadian Journal of Community Mental Health* 37–55.

—— (1993b), *Community Care Assessments* (London: Longman).

GOSTIN, L. (1975), *A Human Condition: Volume I The Mental Health Act from 1959–1975* London: MIND (National Association for Mental Health) .

—— (1977), *A Human Condition: Volume II The Law Relating to Mentally Abnormal Offenders* (London: MIND (National Association for Mental Health)).

—— (1986), *Mental Health Services—Law and Practice* (London: Shaw & Sons Ltd.).

GRAHAM, H. (1984), *Women, Health and the Family* (Brighton: Wheatsheaf).

GREENHALGH, T., and TAYLOR, R. (1997), "Papers That Go Beyond Numbers", 315 *British Medical Journal* 740–3.

GRISSO, T., AND APPELBAUM, P. (1995), "The MacArthur Treatment Competence Study: III. Abilities of Patients to Consent to Psychiatric and Medical Treatment", 19 *Law and Human Behavior* 149–74.

—— and —— (1996), "Values and Limits of the MacArthur Treatment Competence Study Psychology", 2 *Public Policy and Law* 167–81.

—— and —— (1998), *Assessing Competence to Consent to Treatment: A Guide for Physicians and other Health Professionals* (Oxford: Oxford University Press).

—— —— MULVEY, E., and FLETCHER, K. (1995), "The MacArthur Treatment Competence Study: II Measures of Abilities Related to Competence to Consent to Treatment", 19 *Law and Human Behavior* 127–48.

GUEST, J. F., HART, W. M., COOKSON, R. F., and LINDSTROM, E. (1996), "Pharmacoeconomic Evaluation of Long-term Treatment with Risperidone for Patients with Chronic Schizophrenia", 10 *British Journal of Medical Economics* 59–67.

GUNN, J., MADEN, T., and SWINTON, M. (1991a), "How Many Prisoners Should Be in Hospital?", 31 *Home Office Research Bulletin* 9–15.

—— —— and —— (1991b), "Treatment Needs of Prisoners with Psychiatric Disorders", 151 *British Medical Journal* 674–8.

HALL, S. (1975), "Introduction", in Smith, A. C. H., *Paper Voices: The Popular Press and Social Change* (London: Chatto & Windus).

HARRISON, K. (1994), "Supervision in the Community", 144 *New Law Journal* 1017.

HAUERWAS, S. (1986), *Suffering Presence: Theological Reflections on Medicine, the Mentally Handicapped and the Church* (Notre Dame, Ind.: University of Notre Dame Press).

HAWKINS, K. (1992), "Using Legal Discretion" in Hawkins (ed.) *The Uses of Discretion* (Oxford: Clarendon Press).

HAWKINS, K. (1986), "On Legal Decision-Making", 42 *Washington and Lee Law Review* 1161–242.

—— (ed.) (1992), *The Uses of Discretion* (Oxford: Clarendon Press).

HEALTH COMMITTEE PUBLIC EXPENDITURE ON HEALTH AND PERSONAL SOCIAL SERVICES (1997), NHS Expenditure on Mental Health, House of Commons 297.

HEGINBOTHAM, C. (1998, forthcoming), "The Pyschodynamics of Mental Health Care" *J. Mental Health*.

HENDERSON, L. (1996), "Selling Suffering: Mental Illness and Media Values" in Philo, G. (ed.), *Media and Mental Distress* (London: Longman).

HIMMELFARB, G. (1991), *Poverty and Compassion: The Moral Imagination of the Late Victorians* (New York: Knopf).

HOGE, S., LIDZ, C., EISENBERG, M., MONAHAN, J., BENNETT, N., GARDNER, W., MULVEY, E., and ROTH, L. (1998), "Family, Clinician, and Patient Perceptions of Coercion in Mental Hospital Admission", 21 *International Journal of Law and Psychiatry* 131–46.

HOGGETT, B. (1996), *Mental Health Law* (4th edn., London: Sweet and Maxwell).

HOLLOWAY, F. (1996), "Community Psychiatric Care: From Libertarianism to Coercion. Moral Panic and Mental Health Policy in Britain", *Health Care Law* 235–43.

HOME OFFICE (1996), *Mentally Disordered Offenders: Sentencing and Discharge Arrangements,* Mental Health Unit (Home Office), Mental Health and Community Care Division (London: Department of Health).

HOUGH, M, (1995), *Anxiety About Crime: Findings from the 1994 British Crime Survey,* Home Office Research Study, no. 147 (London: Home Office).

HUNT, A., and WICKHAM, G. (1994), *Foucault and Law: Towards a Sociology of Law as Governance* (London: Pluto).

HURWITZ, B., and RICHARDSON, R. (1997), "Swearing to Care: The Resurgence in Medical Oaths", 315 *British Medical Journal* 1671–4.

HUTTER, B. (1988), *The Reasonable Arm of the Law? The Law Enforcement Procedures of Environmental Health Officers* (Oxford: Clarendon Press).

—— (1997), *Compliance, Regulation and Environment* (Oxford: Clarendon Press).

IGNATIEFF, M. (1978), *A Just Measure of Pain: The Penitentiary in the Industrial Revolution, 1750–1850* (London: Macmillan).

—— (1989), "Citizenship and Moral Narcissism", *Political Quarterly* 63–74.

JACKSON, M., and WILLIAMS, P. (1994), *Unimaginable Storms: A Search for Meaning in Psychosis* (London: Karnac Books).

JACOB, J. (1976), "The Right of the Mental Patient to his Psychosis", 39 *Modern Law Review* 17–42.

—— (1998), *Doctors and Rules—A Sociology of Professional Values* (2nd edn., New Brunswick, NJ: Transaction Publishers).

JANIS, I. (1982), *GroupThink: Psychological Studies of Policy Decisions and Fiascos* (2nd edn., Boston, Mass.: Houghton-Mifflin).

—— and MANN, L. (1977), *Decision-Making: A Psychological Analysis of Conflict, Choice and Commitment* (London: Collier Macmillan).

JANIS, M. W. (1995), *European Human Rights Law: Text and Materials* (Oxford: Oxford University Press).

JEWEL, D. (1952), "A Case of a 'Psychotic' Navaho Indian Male", 11 *Human Organisation* 32–6, reprinted in Apple, D (ed.) (1960), *Sociological Studies of Health and Sickness* (New York, NY, McGraw Hill), 107–17.

JONES, K. (1972), *A History of Mental Health Services* (London: Routledge and Kegan Paul).

—— (1993), *Asylums and After: A Revised History of the Mental Health Services: From the Early 18th Century to the 1990s* (London: Athlone Press).

JONES, R. (1996), *Mental Health Act Manual* (5th edn., London: Sweet and Maxwell).

KIDD-HEWITT, D. (1995), "Crime and the Media: A Criminological Perspective", in Kidd-Hewitt, D., and Osborne, R. (eds.) *Crime and the Media: The Post-Modern Spectacle* (London: Pluto Press).

KING, M., and PIPER, C. (1995), *How the Law Thinks About Children* (2nd edn., Aldershot: Arena).

LAING, R. D. (1967), *The Politics of Experience* (Harmondsworth: Penguin).

—— (1960), *The Divided Self* (London: Tavistock).

LANGAN, M. (ed.) (1998), *Welfare: Needs, Rights and Risks* (New York: Routledge).

LAW COMMISSION (1995), *Mental Incapacity*, Law Commission Report No 231 (London: HMSO).

LAW SOCIETY and BRITISH MEDICAL ASSOCIATION (1995), *Assessment of Mental Capacity: Guidance for Doctors and Lawyers* (London: Law Society/BMA).

LAWS, J. (1996), "The Constitution: Morals and Rights" *Public Law*, 622–35.

LIDZ, C., HOGE, S., GARDNER, W., BENNETT, N., MONAHAN, J., MULVEY, E., and ROTH, L. "Perceived Coercion in Mental Hospital Admission: Pressures and Process", 52 *Archives of General Psychiatry* 1034–9.

—— MEISEL, A., ZERUBAVEL, E., CARTER, M., SESTAK, R., and ROTH, L. (1984), *Informed Consent: A Study in Decision-Making in Psychiatry* (London: Guilford Press).

LISTER, R. (1995), "Dilemmas in Engendering Citizenship", 24 *Economy and Society* 1–36.

LIVINGSTONE, S. (1994), "The Changing Face of Prison Discipline" in Player, E., and Jenkins, M. (eds), *Prisons after Woolf* (London: Routledge).

LORD, J. R. (1927), *Mental Hospitals & The Public: The Need For Closer Co-operation* (London: Adlard & Son).

LORD CHANCELLOR'S DEPARTMENT (1997), *Who Decides: Making Decisions on Behalf of Mentally Incapacitated Adults*, Consultation Paper, Lord Chancellor's Department, Cm 3803 (London: Lord Chancellor's Dept.).

LOUGHLIN, M. (1993), "The Underside of the Law: Judicial Review and the Prison Disciplinary System", 46 *Current Legal Problems* 24–52.

MACDONALD, M. (1981), *Mystical Bedlam: Madness, Anxiety, and Healing in Seventeenth Century England* (Cambridge: Cambridge University Press).

MACKAY, R. (1990), "Dangerous Patients. Third Party Safety and Psychiatrists' Duties— Walking the *Tarasoff* Tightrope", 30 *Medicine, Science and Law* 52–6.

—— (1995), *Mental Condition Defences in the Criminal Law* (Oxford: Clarendon Press).

—— and KEARNS, G. (1994), "The Continued Underuse of Unfitness to Plead and the Insanity Defence", *Criminal Law Review* 576–9.

MARRIOTT, S., AUDINI, B., WEBB, Y., DUFFETT, R., and LELLIOTT, P. (1998), *Research into the Mental Health Act, Phase 1*, Unpublished report submitted to the Department of Health, by the College Research Unit, Royal College of Psychiatrists.

MARSHALL, T. H. (1950), *Citizenship and Social Class* (Cambridge: Cambridge University Press).

MCBARNET, D. (1981), *Conviction: Law, the State and the Construction of Justice* (London: Macmillan).

MCINTYRE, K., FARRELL, M., and DAVID, A. (1989), "What do Psychiatric Inpatients Really Want?", 298 *British Medical Journal* 159–60.

MENTAL HEALTH ACT COMMISSION (1985), *First Biennial Report 1983–5* (London: HMSO).

—— (1991), *Fourth Biennial Report 1989–91* (London: HMSO).

—— (1993), *Fifth Biennial Report 1991–1993* (London: HMSO).

—— (1998), *The Threshold for Admission and the Relapsing Patient*, Discussion Paper Mental Health Act Commission (Maid Marion House, 56 Houndsgate, Nottingham).

——/SAINSBURY CENTRE (1997), *The National Visit* (London: Sainsbury Centre).

MENTAL HEALTH FOUNDATION (1994), *Creating Community Care* (London: Mental Health Foundation).

MENTAL HEALTH REVIEW TRIBUNALS FOR ENGLAND AND WALES (1997) *Annual Report 1996* (London: Department of Health).

MONAHAN, J. (1977), "John Stuart Mill on the Liberty of the Mentally Ill: A Historical Note", 134 *American Journal of Psychiatry* 1428–9.

MONTGOMERY, J. (1992), "Rights to Health and Health Care" in Coote, A. (ed.), *The Welfare of Citizens, Developing New Social Rights* (London: Rivers Oram Press).

NATIONAL SCHIZOPHRENIA FELLOWSHIP (1996), *Is Cost a Factor?* (London: NSF).

NOBLES, R., and SCHIFF, D. (1995), "Miscarriages of Justice: A Systems Approach", 58 *Modern Law Review* 299–320.

—— SCHIFF, D., and SHALDON, N. (1993), "The Inevitability of Crisis in Criminal Appeals", 21 *International Journal of the Sociology of Law* 1–21.

OPCS (1996), *Economic Activity and Social Functioning of Residents with Psychiatric Disorders*, Report No. 6. (London: HMSO).

PATEL, A., and KNAPP, M. (1998), "Costs of Mental Illness in England", *Mental Health Research Review*, May, 4–10.

PATEMAN, C. (1992), "Equality, Difference, Subordination: The Politics of Motherhood and Women's Citizenship" in Bock, G., and James, S. (eds.), *Beyond Equality and Difference: Citizenship, Feminist Politics, Female Subjectivity* (London: Routledge).

PEARSON, G. (1983), *Hooligan: A History of Respectable Fears* (London: Macmillan).

—— (1984), "Falling Standards: A Short, Sharp History of Moral Decline", in Barker, M. (ed.), *Video Nasties: Freedom and Censorship in the Media* (London: Pluto), 88–103.

—— (1995), "Drugs, Crime and Aliens: Re-Writing Cultural History", paper presented to the American Society of Criminology, Boston, Mass., November 1995.

PEAY, J. (1989), *Tribunals on Trial* (Oxford: Clarendon Press).

—— (ed.) (1996), *Inquiries after Homicide* (London: Duckworth).

—— (ed.) (1998), *Criminal Justice and the Mentally Disordered* (Aldershot: Ashgate).

—— (1999), "Thinking Horses not Zebras" in Harris, R., and Webb, D. (eds.), *Managing the Mentally Disordered Offender* (London: Routledge).

PETCH, E., and BRADLEY, C. (1997), "Learning the Lessons from Homicide Inquiries: Adding Insult to Injury?", 8 *Journal of Forensic Psychiatry* 161–84.

PETERSON, A., and LUPTON, D. (1996), *The New Public Health: Health and Self in the Age of Risk* (London: Sage).

PETRILA, J. (1996), "Paternalism and the Unrealised Promise of Essays in Therapeutic Jurisprudence" in Wexley, D. B., and Winick, B. J. (eds.), *Law in a Therapeutic Key: Developments in Therapeutic Jurisprudence* (Durham, NC.: Carolina Academic Press).

PHILO, G. (ed.) (1996), *Media and Mental Distress* (London: Longman).

PICK, D. (1989), *Faces of Degeneration: A European Disorder, c 1848–1918* (Cambridge: Cambridge University Press).

PILGRIM, D., and ROGERS, A. (1993), *A Sociology of Health and Illness* (Buckingham: Open University Press).

PINE, F., and LEVINSON, D. J. (1961), "A Sociopsychological Conception of Patienthood", 7 *International Journal of Social Psychiatry* 106–22.

PLANT, R. (1992), "Citizenship, Rights and Welfare" in Coote, A. (ed.), *The Welfare of Citizens: Developing New Social Rights* (London: Institute for Public Policy Research, Rivers Oram).

POLICY STUDIES INSTITUTE (1983), *Police and People in London* (London: PSI).

PORTER, C. (1917), "Citizenship and Health Questions in War-Time", 25 *Journal of State Medicine* 300.

PRIOR, D., STEWART, J., and WALSH, K. (1995), *Citizenship: Rights, Community and Participation* (London: Pitman).

RANSON, S., MARTIN, J., McKEOWN, P., NIXON, J., and MITCHELL, R. (1995), "Citizenship for the Civil Society", paper presented to the ESRC Local Governance Workshop, "Participation, Citizenship and New Management", University of Birmingham, 4/5 Oct. 1995.

READ, J., and BAKER, S. (1996), *Not Just Sticks and Stones: A Survey of Stigma, Taboos and Discrimination Experienced by People with Mental Health Problems* (London: MIND).

REINER, R. (1992), *The Politics of the Police* (2nd edn., London: Harvester Wheatsheaf).

RICHARDSON, G (1993), *Law, Process and Custody: Prisoners and Patients* (London: Butterworths).

—— (1994), "From Rights to Expectations" in Player, E., and Jenkins, M. (eds.), *Prisons After Woolf* (London: Routledge).

—— CHISWICK, D., and NUTTING, I. (1997), *Report of an Inquiry into the Treatment and Care of Darren Carr* (Reading: Berkshire Health Authority, Berkshire County Council, Oxfordshire Health Authority and Oxfordshire County Council).

RITCHIE, J. H., Q.C., DICK, D., and LINGHAM, R. (1994), *The Report of the Inquiry into the Care and Treatment of Christopher Clunis* (London: HMSO).

ROCHE, M. (1992), *Rethinking Citizenship: Welfare, Ideology and Change in Modern Society* (Cambridge: Polity Press).

ROGERS, A., PILGRIM, D., and LACEY, R. (1993), *Experiencing Psychiatry* (Basingstoke: Macmillan and MIND).

ROSE, N. (1996), *Inventing Our Selves: Psychology, Power, and Personhood* (Cambridge: Cambridge University Press).

ROSENMAN, S. (1994), "Mental Health Law: An Idea whose Time has Passed", 28 *Australian and New Zealand Journal of Psychiatry* 560–5.

ROSS, N., and COOK, S. (1987), *Crimewatch UK* (London: Hodder & Stoughton).

ROTHMAN, D. J. (1971), *The Discovery of the Asylum* (Boston, Mass.: Little, Brown).

ROWNTREE FOUNDATION (1995), *The Inquiry into Income and Wealth Volumes I and II*, chaired by Sir Peter Barclay (York: Joseph Rowntree Foundation).

ROYAL COMMISSION (1957), *Report of the Royal Commission on the Law Relating to Mental Illness and Mental Deficiency 1954–1957* (The Percy Commission), Cmnd 169 (London: HMSO).

RUSSO, J., and SCHOEMAKER, P. (1989), *Decision Traps: Ten Barriers to Brilliant Decision-Making and How to Overcome Them* (New York: Simon and Schuster).

SAINSBURY CENTRE (1997), *Pulling Together* (London: Sainsbury Centre).

SAMPSON, H., MESSINGER, S. L., and TOWNE, R. D. (1962), "Family Processes and Becoming a Mental Patient", 68 *American Journal of Sociology* 88–96.

SAYCE, L. (1998), "Distress and Disability", 89 *Open Mind* 8–9.

SCHEFF, T. J. (1966), *Being Mentally Ill: A Sociological Theory* (London: Weidenfeld & Nicolson).

—— (ed.) (1967), *Mental Illness and Social Processes* (New York: Harper & Row).

SCHIFF, D., and NOBLES, R. (1996), "Criminal Appeal Act 1995: The Semantics of Jurisdiction", 59 *Modern Law Review* 573–81.

SCHNEIDER, C. (1992), "Discretion and Rules: A Lawyer's View" in Hawkins, K. (ed.), *The Uses of Discretion* (Oxford: Clarendon Press).

SCHUM, D. (1994), *The Evidential Foundations of Probabilisitic Reasoning* (New York: John Wiley and Sons).

SCHWARTZ, C. G. (1957), "Perspectives on Deviance: Wives' Definitions of their Husbands' Mental Illness", 20 *Psychiatry* 275–91.

SCOTTISH OFFICE (1991), *The Tenant's Charter* (Scotland)

SCULL, A. (1989), *Social Order/Mental Disorder: Anglo-American Psychiatry and Historical Perspective* (London: Routledge).

—— (ed.) (1981), *Madhouses, Mad-Doctors and Madmen* (London: Athlone Press).

SEDGWICK, P. (1982), *Psycho-politics: Laing, Foucault, Goffman, Szasz, and the Future of Mass Psychiatry* (London: Harpers & Rowe).

SHOWALTER, E. (1987), *The Female Malady: Women, Madness and English Culture, 1830–1980* (London: Virago).

SIMS, A. (Chairman) (1996), *Report of the Confidential Inquiry into Homicides and Suicides by Mentally Ill People* (London: Royal College of Psychiatrists)

SINGLETON, N., MELTZER, H. and GATWARD, R. (1998) *Psychiatric Morbidity Among Prisoners in England and Wales* Office for National Statistics (London: Stationery Office).

SKOLNICK, J. (1966), *Justice without Trial* (London: Wiley).

SLOBOGIN, C. (1996), "Therapeutic Jurisprudence: Five Dilemmas to Ponder" in Wexler, D. B., and Winick, B. J. (eds.), *Law in a Therapeutic Key: Developments in Therapeutic Jurisprudence* (Durham, NC: Carolina Academic Press).

SOLOMKA, B. (1996), "The Role of Psychiatric Evidence in Passing 'Longer than Normal' Sentences", 7 *Journal of Forensic Psychiatry* 239–55.

SPARKS, R. (1992), *Television and the Drama of Crime: Moral Tales and the Place of Crime in Public Life* (Buckingham: Open University Press).

SPITZER, S. P., and DENZIN, N. K. (eds.) (1968), *The Mental Patient: Studies in the Sociology of Deviance* (New York: McGraw-Hill).

STEADMAN, H., and COCOZZA, J. (1974), *Careers of the Criminally Insane.* (Lexington, Mass.: Lexington Books).

—— MULVEY, E., MONAHAN, J., ROBBINS, P., APPELBAUM, P., GRISSO, T., ROTH, L., and SILVER, E. (1998), "Violence by People Discharged from Acute Psychiatric Inpatient Facilities and by Others in the Same Neighbourhoods", 55 *Archives of General Psychiatry* 393–401.

STILL, A., and VELODY, I. (eds.) (1992), *Re-Writing the History of Madness. Studies in Foucault's Histoire de la Folie* (London: Routledge).

SZASZ, T. (1973), *Ideology and Insanity: Essays of the Psychiatric Dehumanisation of Man* (London: Calder and Boyars).

—— (1974), *The Myth of Mental Illness: Foundations of a Theory of Personal Conduct* (London: Harpers & Rowe).

SZMUKLER, G., and HOLLOWAY, F. (1998), "Mental Health Law is Now a Harmful Anachronism", 22 *Psychiatric Bulletin* 662–665.

TEUBNER, G. (1993), *Law as an Autopoietic System* (Oxford: Blackwell).

THOMPSON, C. (1995), "New Powers for Care of the Mentally Ill", *The Times*, 23 March.

THOMSON, M. (1998), *The Problem of Mental Deficiency: Eugenics, Democracy and Social Policy in Britain, c. 1870–1959* (Oxford: Clarendon Press).

THOROLD, O. (1996), "The ECHR and UK Mental Health Legislation" *EHRLR* 619.

TITMUSS, R.M. (1959), "Health" in Ginsberg, M. (ed.), *Law and Opinion in Britain* (London: Stevens) 299–318.

Tuck, M. (1989), *Drinking and Disorder: A Study of Non-Metropolitan Violence*, Home Office Research Study 108 (London: HMSO).

Ungerson, C. (1987), *Policy is Personal: Sex, Gender and Informal Care* (London: Tavistock).

Unsworth, C. (1987), *The Politics of Mental Health Legislation* (Oxford: Oxford University Press).

Warner, M. (1985), *Recovery From Schizophrenia* (London: Routledge and Kegan Paul).

Weiner, D.B. (1993), *The Citizen-Patient in Revolutionary and Imperial Paris* (Baltimore, Mld.: John Hopkins University Press).

West, A. (1997), "Regeneration, Community and the Social Economy" in *Community Economic Development. Linking Grassroots to Regional Economic Development*, Conference Papers from the Regional Studies Association Annual Conference, Regional Studies Association.

Wexler, D., and Winick, B. (1996), *Law in a Therapeutic Key* (Durham, NC: Carolina Academic Press).

Wilkinson, R. (1996), *Unhealthy Societies: The Afflictions of Inequality* (London: Routledge).

Wing, J. (1962), "Institutionalism in Mental Hospitals", 1 *British Journal of Social and Clinical Psychology* 38–51.

Wintenfeldt, D. von, and Edwards, W. (1986), *Decision Analysis and Behavioural Research* (Cambridge: Cambridge University Press).

Wittgenstein, L. (1958), *Philosophical Investigations* (trans. Anscombe, G. E. M., Oxford: Basil Blackwell).

Wolff, G. (1997), "Attitudes of the Media and the Public" in Leff, J. (ed.), *Care in the Community: Illusion or Reality?* (Chichester: John Wiley).

World Health Organisation (1992), *ICD-10, Classification of Mental and Behavioural Disorders: Clinical Descriptions and Diagnostic Guidelines* (Geneva: WHO).

Yarrow, M. R., Schwartz, C. G., Murphy, H. S., and Deasy, L. C. (1955), "The Psychological Meaning of Mental Illness in the Family", 11(4) *Journal of Social Issues* 12–24.

Zigmond, A. (1995), "Special Care Wards: Are They Special?", *Psychiatric Bulletin* 310–12.

Index